Dedication

To God and my mom, dad, brother, wife, sons, relatives, and all
those who helped make me who I am.

Table of Contents

SECTION 4: PURDUE UNIVERSITY

Introduction

PEOPLE ASKED ME, "WHY DID YOU WRITE THIS book?" Good question! I certainly was not a scholar, inventor, entrepreneur, or athletic star. I do not feel my life was exceptional or out of the ordinary in most ways, considering the times in which we were raised. You will read hundreds of stories and meet family and friends from my birth through college years who fashioned me into who I became; therefore, these are my five reasons for writing this adventure:

1. For the Lord—it is to magnify our Lord and Savior. While my salvation did not occur until *after* the events depicted in the main body of this book, I saw hints all along my life that pointed me toward Him. When I was twenty-four and a half years old, He entered my life and changed it! Thank you, guardian angel, for guiding me in this direction!

2. For my family—especially for my two sons, their wives and six grandchildren. You will read stories that happened to my grandparents, parents, brother, and me. A time will come when my brother, Roger, and I will pass. When that happens, most of these stories will be lost forever, except for this book. I wanted my children and grandchildren to know about their family's background, how simple (or complicated) life was back in the '40s, '50s, and '60s, and to have a written record about some of their ancestors. I guess it is called *a legacy*.

3. For those in the book—all of you helped to make me who I am today—I want to say, "Thank you" for being there, providing help, and the many great memories.

4. To the general public—here is hope you may have enjoyment as it may bring back fond memories of your own youth. You might even relate to similar events, and you are encouraged to share your stories with your children and grandchildren in some permanent fashion. Also, if you do not know Him, may you seek our Lord Jesus Christ now!

5. Personal Pleasure—it was quite enjoyable and pleasant to remember individuals and events. Over my life, I talked about my childhood with many people, and they, likewise, told me about their childhood; however, I have yet to find anyone with whom I would trade places!

While this book has truly been *a labor of love*, there have been hindrances during its creation. All three hindrances are directly attributed to me; they were:

1. Procrastination: I started thinking about this book in 2004/2005. I would think about this story, or that event, and how I wanted to express my feelings, understandings, and the ways to talk about them. I bet I have written this book a dozen times in my mind.

2. Typing: I do not type, period! I hunt, murmur, and peck (HMP) a keyboard, but I do not type. I only employ three fingers in this activity. When email started at work in earnest, I became petrified. I knew I could not survive, so I used one of my wife's old typing books during lunch hour to learn how to type properly; however, it seemed whenever I had to answer an email in a hurry, I went back to HMP. The typing book helped me learn where the letters were on the QWERTY keyboard, but my brain is not wired to coordinate ten fingers at a time. Heck, I have problems

just maneuvering the three I use in reasonable fashion. My three fingers can now fly along at almost twenty words per minute, if the words are short!

3. Snuggles: For Christmas 2003, I broke down and got my wife a unique present, a cat. We had four previous cats; the last died, being twenty years old in 1998. We swore we would never get another one, but I weakened, went to the local shelter, and picked out a nine-week-old white-and-black female. Like me, Sue instantly fell in love with her, and the rest is now history. My problem is, whenever I sit down at the computer, she jumps onto my desk, stands in front of the screen (like she is right now), or lays down on the keyboard. You would not believe the number of weird "blue screens of death" I have encountered thanks to her. (Note: The above was written in 2014. Snuggles passed away December 2017. We adopted an almost all-black kitten in November 2018, Cuddles, and in March 2020 Covid-19 hit. In mid-March I had nothing to do, and Cuddles was not interested in computers, so over the next two and a half months I composed the last half of this book after having been stranded in the middle of my junior year of high school for six years! *Whew!*)

My biggest regret about this book is I did not do it sooner. Why? Because by delaying, many of the people mentioned throughout have now passed away. I would have loved to pay tribute to and honor them for their lives and impact they had on me while they were still with us. Sorry for the delay!

Please sit back, turn on your visual imagination, and enjoy!

Section 1
The Early Years

Chapter 1

The Beginning

To put everything in perspective, World War II was going very hot and heavily in March 1944 when I was *brought forth*. There were all kinds of products being rationed like sugar, gasoline, rubber, and so on. Most of the country's young men were off to war, and many women were working in factories to support the war effort. Mom was a little scrawny woman, five-foot, one-inch tall, weighing between 98 to 110 pounds, depending on if she was soaking wet or not. Dad was a short man like me: five-foot, seven-inches tall but built like a fireplug. He worked in Chicago as a customer support representatative for Continental Can Company. We, along with my older brother, Roger, lived in a small house in Elmwood Park, Illinois. Our front lawn was no bigger than twenty-two feet wide by fifteen feet deep.

I was trouble from the time I was born! I was in the hospital ten days, and even before I left, I caused problems. Mom talked the doctor into providing me with formula, which was easy to fix. After all, with a new baby, another three-year old child, and a husband who was always on the road making sure foods were canned properly, she wanted something to make life a little simpler. Who can blame her for that!? Right before I was discharged, Grandpa Hunziker, who was a renowned dairy scientist,[1] entered

---

[1]   *The Ten Masterminds of Dairying*, Meredith Publishing Company, Des Moines, IA, 1930, p 72–78.

the hospital and announced to the nursing staff, "I am Doctor Hunziker, and I would like to change this baby's formula to whole milk!" The nursing staff complied and threw out the original prescription. As Mom was leaving, she was extremely surprised and *very* perturbed it had been changed. She asked who made the change and they said, "Dr. Hunziker!" Mom said she did not know if she was more upset at her father-in-law for changing my formula or at the hospital nurses for not knowing who was on their staff! She said she *shot daggers* at Grandpa as we left the hospital and added he had a *sheepish look* on his face!

The biggest disappointment in my homecoming was reserved for my brother, Rog. His birthday was the day after mine, so he was only two years and 364 days older than me, not *three* years older! Had Mom been able to wait three hours and twelve minutes, we would have had the same birthday. Rog always said, "Our parents were creatures of habit!" Having birthdays close meant we always celebrated them together and shared the same cake and party favors. He was extremely excited about me coming home because it meant he now had a little brother for a playmate. Yeah, right! Little did he realize all I did was eat, sleep, poop, pee, and cry! What kind of a playmate was that!?

As the war continued, a woman working for the government came to our front door and arrogantly asked Mom, "What are *you* doing for the war effort!" This was not a good question to ask my mom! She was having a bad day with us; the usual situation with a new baby, a three-year old, and husband who was out of town *again*. Mom squinted a little and looked the woman right in the eye and announced, "I am raising two boys to fight in the next war!" The woman almost dropped her clipboard, put her tail between her legs, and slinked off our front porch never to be seen near our house again. Mom may have been small, but she had fire in her furnace as Rog and I later found out many times. Now, think how prophetic her answer was since Rog and I would be prime draft bait during a little scrimmage in Vietnam!

Life did not start out great for me since I went to the hospital three times before I was three and a half years old. The first time, I fell in the bathroom and split my lip open on the toilet. It needed several stitches, so off to the hospital's emergency room I went. Another time, I was being babysat by our neighbor's son, Davy Shibley, who was a young teenager. He took me to a neighborhood playground, and *somehow* I got hit in the face with a baseball bat! This was quite severe and required reconstruction surgery fifty years later!

I remember the last incident to this day even though I was only three and half years old. Grandma Alexander was out of town, so Aunt Peggy was staying with us because she was only ten years older than me. I went outside thinking I would show off and did a cartwheel; however, the grass was wet from dew. My hands slipped on the wet grass and my left arm went under my body as I fell on it. I remember lying there in a very *uncomfortable* position; my left forearm was broken! A neighbor took us to the hospital, and Mom called Dad to tell him what I did, *again*!

I can still vividly remember a mask being placed over my mouth and nose while someone, wearing a mask, was shaking ether onto my mask to put me under. The first thing I said when I came out from under the anesthetic was, "Where are my pants?" I guess I was a shy one! I made out like a bandit with the broken arm in a cast. People gave me candy or small toys just to be able to take my picture. I found the cast also had another purpose; it served very well as a club against the other kids in the neighborhood. It made me a worthy opponent, at least until it came off. When the doctor cut it off, I asked him to put it back on since my arm felt so weak. I never showed off for my aunt again! Oh yes, I also received lots of retribution from neighborhood kids for the punishment I earlier doled out!

Since Dad was gone a lot, many times for three weeks and several times for six weeks,[2] Mom had to take care of us as well as stoke the old coal furnace, do the lawn with a non-powered hand-pushed lawnmower, walk to the local market, carry the groceries home, wash clothes, hang them on the line, and so on. You know, the things women *love* to do! Things always seemed to happen when Dad was out of town. Once, Rog chased after me to get a rubber ball from me. I ran into the bathroom, slammed the door, and before Rog could open it, I threw it into the toilet and flushed it! Well, guess what? The ball did not go all the way down, and it got stuck! Imagine that! The water would not flush, and since we only had *one* toilet in the house, Mom called a plumber. He came during dinner and extracted the ball. While we were at the kitchen table eating, he came to the kitchen and announced his triumphal deed by saying, "Here's your little ball, sonny!" He rolled the wet ball to me across mom's newly washed-and-waxed kitchen floor! I can still see the water spraying into the air from the backside of the ball as it was coming to me. Again, more *daggers* emanated from mom at the plumber *and* me, but these *daggers* were the size of *swords!* And yes, it cost Mom $5! You have to understand something; my brother and I were mischievous "Calvin" from Bill Watterson's "Calvin and Hobbes" and "Dennis" from Hank Ketcham's "Dennis the Menace" cartoons. The problem was we often switched as to who we were and who was the worst!

During the summer, Mom and Dad had a thing about us going to bed at 9 p.m. If you ever lived in the Chicago area, you know the sun does not set until well after 9 p.m. in early summer. Since it was still light and probably warm, we had our bedroom window open to cool our room, which meant we could hear other kids playing outside. Our bedroom window faced the Shibley's house, and there were times when Mrs. Shibley or Davy came over and

---

2   Otto F. Hunziker, *Continental Can Project*, Oral History Research Office, Columbia University, 1975, p 22.

talked to us. Eventually, our talking, whether to someone outside or just between of us, got too loud, and Mom or Dad heard us. When this happened, the *giant*, better known as Dad, came in. He gave us one warning; the second time we got spanked! He just used his hand, but that was enough. You must understand Dad was a powerful and fit man even though he was not extremely big. He was quarterback and captain of his undefeated high school football team, led his fraternity at Purdue to two all-campus football championships, and he regularly played pick-up football games at a local park. With a menacing smile, he often bragged that he broke his fraternity paddle on his big brother's butt during initiation— *the paddle battle!* So now you see why we were not happy to see the *giant* come into our room a second time! He never spanked us in anger, but knowing how *Calvin* and *Dennis* behaved all of the time, we probably deserved every one we got!

There is an adage, "Divide and Conquer!" Mom and Dad did it every summer. Dad was an avid, I mean *avid* fisherman! He only had two weeks of vacation, and one week was always for fishing. Sometime in the 1930s, Mom's dad, Grandpa Alexander, came across a fishing resort, Pine Ridge Resort,[3] in northwestern Wisconsin. It was located on the north shore of Big Sissabagama Lake ("lake with many bays"). We called it Big Siss. It had twelve rentable log cabins, which had two bedrooms, a small sitting room, and a bathroom. There was also a dining hall and an office building. The dining hall made the trip worthwhile for Mom because she did not have to cook! They rang a big bell, which could be heard anywhere on the lake, and guests had one hour to get their meal. This area of Wisconsin is Muskellunge or Musky territory. The prize catch was a *keeper* musky, one longer than thirty inches. Every summer when they went to Big Siss, they used *divide and*

---

[3] Pine Ridge Resort no longer owns the cabins; however, the main lodge has been transformed into the Pine Ridge Restaurant; see www.pineridgewi.com.

conquer by sending me to one grandparent's house and Rog to the other's! As Rog got older, he could go with them, but while living in Elmwood Park, I never got to go! This was not all bad! Why? Grandma Alexander always had a big cookie jar filled with raisin oatmeal cookies! Her backyard had a gazebo which Grandpa built and a bunch of apple trees, which always allowed for *entertainment!* She lived in Glen Ellen, Illinois, and in the summer, fireflies were in abundance, so every night after dark (notice I got to stay up later), I filled a glass canning jar with them; this was my night light.

When at Grandma and Grandpa Hunziker's home, Grandma tended to find a neighborhood boy about my age, introduced us, and we played together for the time I was there. Grandma and Grandpa Hunziker lived in LaGrange, Illinois, and had a big, three-story, spooky house with a basement. The basement ceiling was low, and it did not have much lighting. There were a lot of things stored down there, so the dangling light bulbs cast many scary shadows. This was not the place for a little boy with an imagination! Grandpa had his office on the third floor, and he was still researching and writing his dairy books, so he was not around much during the day. They had a unique intercom system; about ten minutes before a meal, Grandma opened the cabinet under the kitchen sink, grabbed an old pipe wrench, and banged on the pipes. Grandpa's third-floor office was next to the bathroom, so he could hear the banging. He washed and came into the kitchen whistling as the meal was being served.

For breakfast, he always had the same thing, two slices of toast which were broken into a bowl with whole milk and sugar. According to Mom when I was five or six, I had an epiphany! Grandpa related to her that he and I had a rather *serious conversation* about life. Grandpa was about seventy-five, and he was lamenting his life was passing very quickly. He said to me, "Life is like a boat floating on a river; you just keep going down stream with the current and there is nothing you can do about it!" After a few seconds, I turned to him and with the innocence and the wide-eyed look only a small child could have, I said, "Grandpa, why don't you just throw out the anchor?" Only a small child can explain life in such terms! Mom said he was in tears as he laughed so hard!

The last time they went to Pine Ridge without me, Rog promised to bring me a present, a frog. I thought about it all week while I stayed with Grandma Alexander. When they got home, Rog gave me a cigar box. We carefully opened it so the frog would not jump out, looked inside, and there was nothing but brown spots and a little skin. He kept it in the back window on the drive home and the sun cooked it! No frog, but I must give Rog credit for trying to fulfill his promise. Next year I would be allowed to go. *Yes!*

When I stayed at home with Mom, I sometimes got to go the local bakery. Oh, how good it smelled! I told Mom when I grew up, I would work in a bakery! Even today, that unique and wonderful smell of freshly baked goods reminds me of that small shop. On the way home one day, we met a police officer. Mom apparently knew him because she introduced me to him. She then said something to me I still remember today, "If you ever get in trouble or need help, look for a policeman, and he will help you." What wise advice she gave me then, and someday in the not-too-distant future, I would need it.

Occasionally, our phone rang, Mom picked it up and talked to the person on the other end. Again, here is how my weird mind worked. I had the concept that when she moved the phone around, the person on the other end was moved around in the same fashion. If she was walking back and forth, then the person on the other end was moved back and forth. If she shook the phone, then the person on the other end was shaken. How I came up with this notion, only the Lord Himself knows. It never dawned on me that we would have had earthquakes if the person on the other end of the line shook the phone!

The people who lived on the other side of the Shibley's were the Heicks, who had a daughter named Laurie. We went trick and treating together, played board and card games together, and just hung out together because we were best friends. One time I was invited to a birthday party for Laurie; we were the only two there. We sat at a small table in their living room and music was coming from their TV. They were the only ones on the block who had a TV, and I saw it occasionally. When TVs were turned on, it took a long time for the tubes to heat up before the picture appeared. All night I kept looking at the TV waiting to see the picture. I bet I looked at it fifty times to see something on it. My weird mind said the TV was turned on and the picture would appear shortly, *and* I did not want to miss it. I never did see a picture; the Heicks had a record player in the cabinet above it!

Here is another *major* weirdness my mind generated. As I prepared for kindergarten, Mom, Dad and even Rog helped me with my ABCs and numbers. By the time it started, I could count to 100 and easily say my ABCs! During the months leading up to it, we often met relatives and acquaintances who asked if I was in school, and Mom said, "He'll be going to kindergarten this fall." These people then said to me, "Boy that's exciting because you'll learn to read!" I bet I heard this fifteen times! I was excited when Mom walked me to kindergarten the first day. That night when I came home, I was depressed! Why? Because I could *not* read! Everyone said I would be able to read when I went to kindergarten, so what happened to me? I went to kindergarten, but I could *not* read! Again, my mind played weird tricks on me!

Dad was also an *avid* Purdue football fan. Whenever their game was on the radio, he listened to them. One day Dad was invited to watch a Purdue football game on the Heick's TV. Purdue must have won because he came home and said, "I've got to get me one of those TVs!" The problem was, they were very expensive. Later, he arranged to get a TV on a one-week trial loan. Every night that week we watched whatever was on, Milton Berle, Sid Caesar, Imogene Coca, Texaco ads, professional wrestling, and so on. We intently stared at that twelve-inch, black-and-white screen.

The last night all four of us moped around the house and were sad we had to give it up. While watching our last programs, the phone rang, and Dad answered it. When he hung up, he said, "The TV dealer said they didn't need the TV back for another week, and we could keep it until then!" It was *victory* time in the Hunziker household! I think this was planned all along by the dealer to sucker us in; Dad bought that twelve-inch Stromberg Carlson TV!

Since Dad did customer service for Continental Can and traveled a lot, they gave him a company car. In the spring of 1949 while in Michigan, he called and told Mom he had a surprise for her. The town he was visiting was known for tables, and Mom was desiring a dinette set, so she thought he was bringing her a dining room table. Mom was in the kitchen cooking dinner and I was sitting on the couch looking out the front window when he pulled in front of the house. I yelled to Mom, "He has a car!" She replied, "Of course he has a car; he drove to Michigan." As she was coming into the living room, I said, "No, he is pulling a car!"

Mom rushed to the window and saw Dad's company car with a second one behind it. She just stood there for a while before she reacted and then said, "Oh no, now I'll have to learn to drive!" As he got out of his car, he had a *big* smile on his face! We opened the front door and ran out. Mom held back since she was not sure what to think. We asked whose car it was, and he said, "It's ours!" Mom had never driven a car before, so learning to drive was a major task for her to achieve. She put it off as long as she could.

It was a 1948 Chevrolet, and it had manual shift on the column, which made it more difficult to coordinate shifting while steering, watching oncoming traffic, sticking her arm out the window to signal a turn, and so forth. Of course, having *Calvin* and *Dennis* in the back seat laughing every time gears were grinding did not help! The laughing did not last long, and Dad made sure we quieted down, but he realized having us in the car while she was learning was not going to work. They dropped us off at his football-playing park; it became our babysitter for Mom's hour of driving lessons. Over a couple of months, we survived our times alone at the park, thanks to our guardian angel, *and* Mom learned how to drive!

Shortly after getting our car, Dad had to go to northern Michigan, so he thought we could make a vacation out of it. Instead of driving all the way around Lake Michigan, he decided to use a ferry and cross it. We drove to Milwaukee and caught an overnight ferry to northern Michigan. I had never been on a ship before, and while waiting to board, we had a few moments to look over the fine ship that would transport us. I clearly noticed it had a *round* bottom! Wait a minute, if it had a *round* bottom, would it not tip over!? My mind did not let go of this concept. Dad drove us on, we took our bags, and found our berth. It consisted of bunk cots attached to walls, and we had one small port hole. We were tired, so we went to bed; Dad did his snoring and Mom and Rog made their *sleeping noises*, but I was wide awake! Hmmm! When was the ship going to roll over!? Would water come through the port hole? Would we be able to get out of the ship and into a life raft? I spent hours thinking about these and similar questions before I finally succumbed to the sandman.

Since the ship did not roll over, we drove off it the next morning in Michigan. We stayed near the lake and the water was ice cold! After a few days, we left, and Dad visited several packing plants. He stopped at one plant and said, "I'll only be a few minutes." Hours later he reappeared and gave us a candy bar for lunch! *Daggers!?* At another plant we waited at a little city park. *Calvin* and *Dennis* climbed all over their parking meters, so a policeman asked Mom, "Could you keep your kids off government property?" More *daggers!* At one plant we hit gold! A man came out with Dad and gave us two kites and balls of string—something useful! Now, seventy-one years later, I still remember my hero's name: Butch Fox!

When I look back on the timing when Dad bought our car, I wondered if he had a premonition he was going to be transferred to Milwaukee. He started working there in early summer of 1950, so on weekends, Rog and I were farmed off on the grandparents so they could look at homes. By the middle of the summer, they sold our house and bought one in Wisconsin and we moved north. Mom and Rog were in our car, and I rode with Dad in the company car. Mom was in the lead as we approached an intersection close to the Illinois/Wisconsin border; Dad started to slow since we had to stop. This was a "Y" intersection, a three-way stop. We watched in horror as Mom never slowed down and drove right through the stop sign! It was a scary situation; however, we were on country roads, and thanks to our guardian angel, no other traffic was present. When we got to our new house, Dad told her what she did, and she was a little shaken. She swore there was no stop sign there. Over the next few years, we often drove through that same intersection, and Rog or I always reminded Mom to stop! It became one of our many family jokes!

(Note: While I often talked about Mom *shooting daggers*, she really was a kind, loving, and caring mother, but I picked *my holy-terror* times to show examples of our lives. The rest of the time, we were not an *interesting* family!)

Chapter 2
Ancestry

"MOMMY, WHERE DID I COME FROM?" THIS IS A daunting question when a five-year-old asks it. Like any mother, Mom could choose many answers: She could have told me about the birds and bees, "And then the bee with its antenna heavy with pollen ..." Or, she could have elaborated on the sexual encounter that starts the process. Or, she could have given a more biological answer about how a sperm cell fertilizes an ovum cell. Or, she could have said, "In a hospital," after all, that was where Mom *brought forth* her second-born son! Or, she could have said I came from an engineer and homemaker! The choices were many, but what she said was, "Well, you know where you came from!" Okay, so where did I come from? I will dispense with the bird and the bees, the sexual description, fertilization, and skip right to my heritage. Let me start by going back and talking about my grandparents. First, I will talk about Mom's side.

Grandma Alexander was born in Brighton, Iowa, in 1888. According to her wedding announcement, Grandma was described as:

> The bride is well known in North St. Paul and very popular among the young people, having made her home here with her sister, Mrs. Andrew, for two years, leaving here to go to Iowa three years ago.[4]

---

[4] *Alexander–Israel Wedding Announcement,* No Date.

Grandma Alexander was a *debutant* and *society* type in St. Paul, so I guess Grandma was a mover and shaker! Grandpa Alexander was born in Frankfort, Indiana, and graduated from Purdue University in 1906. According to his memoirs,[5] he spent two years building railroad bridges in the Philippines, returned to the US, and was employed for five years with the Northern Pacific Railroad Company. He and grandma married in December 1911, and went to Centralia, Washington, but returned to Illinois and joined the Illinois Central Railroad Company. In 1918 he joined Massey Concrete Products Corporation in Chicago, was made their chief engineer in 1940, and died of a heart attack in February 1942. I never knew him! Mom often told how she flew back from New Jersey in a DC-3 with Rog when he was less than a year old to attend his funeral. Between a bumpy ride, air pressure changes, and Mom feeding Rog mashed bananas, many of the passengers were air sick!

Grandpa Alexander was a prankster. I was often told the story when one day he wanted an especially tasty meal, so he called Grandma and told her he was bringing his boss home for dinner. Grandma went into high gear, cleaned the house, walked downtown to buy groceries, and then prepared a scrumptious meal, which she was very capable of doing. Grandpa came home alone, so she asked where his boss was, and Grandpa said, "April Fool!" Hmmm, I wonder how many *daggers* Grandma put into him? He did have a scrumptious meal, although I suspect it was *very* quiet!

I also asked Aunt Peggy about her folks, and here is partly what she wrote back:

> I was very fortunate to have two very loving and caring parents and was very close to them, since my sister was eighteen years older and my brother twenty years older than I. It was almost like being an only child; however, my relationship with my father was a brief one as he passed away when I was seven years old.

---

[5] *American Society of Civil Engineers Memoirs Earl Cutis Alexander, Assoc. M. ASCE*, Memoir No (1614), Died February 9, 1942.

What I do remember about him was that he was a hard worker, and his three main interests were musky fishing, working in his garden, and attending as many Purdue football games in the fall as he could. Each year we would go to Pine Ridge Resort in Stone Lake, Wisconsin, which was not too far from Hayward. Though none of us could swim, my father, mother, and I would be in a boat. My mother and I fished for perch, sunfish, and crappies while my dad went for bass or the elusive musky. His love of fishing was almost his undoing when he went out alone one day to fish (he usually went with us or a guide). A violent storm came up very quickly, and his boat was blown clear across the lake. When the storm subsided, they sent out a search crew and were making preparations to drag the lake when my father showed up at our cabin door, wet and exhausted. He had walked halfway around the lake. Mother said she was never going back there, and we didn't since the following winter he died.

My dad was a practical joker. I remember on one occasion he made a plaster cake for my sister on her twenty-third birthday, put the number 23 on the top of the cake with nuts and bolts, and shipped it to her in New Jersey where she was living at the time. It cost him quite a bit since it was so heavy. Another time he gave her a small jewelry box with a June bug (an insect she absolutely hated) inside.

My mother was an exceptional lady. She not only was a very loving mother to her family but well-liked by her many friends. She was very outgoing and had a great sense of humor. She loved to read and was a great cook. I think her favorite holiday was Christmas, and she enjoyed making homemade fudge and divinity to give to friends.

After my dad died, my mom was on a very fixed income, consisting mostly of a small amount of insurance and Social Security. To supplement her income, she rented out one of the bedrooms upstairs to roomers. Several of these people became life-long friends.

Grandma and Grandpa Alexander had three children. The oldest was my uncle Bill. My mother, Mary F. Alexander, was born in Sheridan, Iowa, in 1916. Grandma Alexander always said, "The day she was born was the longest day!" Yep, June 21, the longest day of the year, was her birthday! Aunt Peggy blessed their mid-life years. Uncle Bill must have been very much like his dad, being jovial, always ready for a laugh, and full of practical jokes. I got to see Aunt Peg and Uncle Bill on a regular basis. As a result, they were my favorite aunt and uncle because of their stories and how much fun they were.

On the Hunziker side, we have a book entitled, *Dei Hunziker Von Aarau, Familiengescichte Eines Alten Aarauer Geschlechts.*[6] Yep, you guessed it, it is in German. The translation is: *The Hunzikers from Aarau: The Family History of an Old Aarau Lineage.* The book is lengthy, but the first relative at the top of our family tree is Hans Hunziker, whose birth date is anticipated to be about 1480. He had two sons, Niklaus and Hans Hunziker. Included with the book, are two, two-foot by four-foot fold-out sheets, one for each son, containing the entire Hunziker family, as of 1962. We are from the Hans (1512–1579) side of the family. Mrs. Erika Gautschi, who used to teach German at Purdue, provided me with a raw translation of those in my lineage. Many were vicars, ministers, or educators; none were bank robbers, murderers, or horse thieves! *Whew!*

---

[6] *Dei Hunziker Von Aarau, Familiengescichte Eines Alten Aarauer Geschlechts,* Aarau, 1962.

Like with Mom, let me start with Grandma and Grandpa Hunziker and forget about the Renaissance period! I do not have much on Grandma Hunziker. She was Florence Belle Burne of Endicott, New York. She was born in 1880, married Grandpa in 1905 and passed away in 1965.

Now, when it comes to Grandpa Hunziker, he was the famous one in our family! Below is a short summary from the chapter on him in *The Ten Master Minds of Dairying*.[7] First, Grandpa started out right at the top; he was born on *Christmas Day*, 1873, in Zurich, Switzerland! He graduated from a local agriculture college and in 1893 immigrated to a job paying $5/month plus room and board at a dairy farm in Attleboro, Massachusetts. He went to college in Providence, Rhode Island, graduating in 1896. After college he went home but returned to the US in 1898 and went to Cornell University. After graduating he worked a year, then took a job at a condensed milk plant in Ellicottville, New York.

He became a US citizen on December 20, 1903. Besides loving his dairy work, he also fell in love with something else—Grandma! They were married in early1905, and he became an instructor and two years later was named Chief of the Dairy Department, Purdue University. During their time at Purdue, he and Grandma must have gotten along very well since they produced six children: three boys and three girls: Thelma Belle (1905), Florence Louise (1906), Karl Otto (1908), Walter Burne (1910), Isabelle Mary (1912), and Otto Frederick (my Dad, in 1915). I guess they thought Dad was going to be the last child, so Grandpa made him *Junior!*

While at Purdue, Grandpa was a founding member of the American Dairy Science Association and its third president. In 1917, he moved to LaGrange and took charge of the manufacturing department of the Blue Valley Creamery Company. "His love for practical dairy work would not let him stay in the laboratory. This time it was an ambition to translate science into actual dairy manufacturing."[8] He received an Honorary PhD from Purdue in 1932.

---

[7] *The Ten Master Minds of Dairying*, Meredith Publishing Company, Des Moines Iowa, 1930.

[8] Ibid, p7

In 1939, he became an independent consultant. He was involved in many national and international activities with the US, the World Dairy Federation, and consulted for over a half dozen countries. *The Ten Master Minds of Dairying* states:

> Of all the official recognition that has come to him he treasures most highly the Distinguished Service Medal presented to him by the Swiss Dairy Federation at the time of his visit to his native Switzerland in 1928. This medal is for 'distinguished service to the dairy industry as a whole' and is the fourth of its kind to be awarded since 1886.[9]

Dad often talked about that trip to Switzerland in 1928. They spent the whole summer there, and Dad got to climb the Matterhorn mountain with his brothers and father.

To put the honor in perspective for being one of *The Ten Master Minds of Dairying*, let me quote from the book's introduction:

> We asked the secretaries and presidents of our five national dairy cattle breed associations ... officers of all of the national dairy organizations including both the production and dairy products groups ... editors of national dairy and trade papers ... heads of the various divisions of Dairy Bureaus and heads of dairy departments in colleges in the 20 leading dairy states ... These 10 men, Babcock, Hoard, Eckles, De Laval, McCollum, Pasteur, Haecker, Borden, Henry and Hunziker, represent the combined opinion of the present-day dairy industry as the greatest in our dairy history.[10]

In 1986 my family visited Purdue's Agriculture/Food Science Department which absorbed the Dairy Department. We met

---

[9] Ibid, p78

[10] Ibid, p7

professor emeritus Dr. Jack Albright, who knew Grandpa back in the 1930s. He showed us a 1915 medal and plaque when Purdue won a national dairy competition with a score of 97 while Grandpa headed their Dairy Department. He said the Hunziker name was still very well regarded, and to prove his point, he told us years earlier the American Dairy Science Association took a revote at a national convention, and Grandpa was now Number 3! Also, in a recently written book about The Purdue Creamery, entitled, *Ice Cream Cones as Casualties*, author John M. Cleland stated, "In 1964, nearly 300 leaders of the American dairy industry voted Otto Hunziker as the third most influential person in American dairy history, even ahead of Gail Borden."[11] I met with Mr. Cleland in July 2018, and showed him Grandpa's memorabilia. He said, "I consider your grandfather to be the Babe Ruth or Lou Gehrig of dairying!" *Wow!* Way to go, Grandpa!

Grandpa's real claim to fame was the industrialization of the dairy industry; how do you make butter for the masses! The first books he authored were *Condensed Milk and Milk Products*[12] in 1914 and *The Butter Industry*[13] in 1920. Grandpa summarized his own life in a quote found in *Die Hunziker Von Aarau*:

> I believe that at the university, where one may freely choose a major, a field of study, there exists the danger of examining non-essential matters that perhaps are of scientific interest, but are not helpful in practice. I therefore consider it necessary that each scientist must also feel responsible for the solution of certain problems in practical application.[14]

[11] John M. Cleland, *Ice Cream Cones as Casualties*, Published by the author in association with IBJ Book Publishing, Indianapolis, IN, 2018, p. 16.

[12] Otto F. Hunziker, *Condensed Milk and Milk Powder*, Published by the author, LaGrange IL, 1914.

[13] Otto F. Hunziker, *The Butter Industry*, Otto Frederick Hunziker, Published by the author, LaGrange IL, 1920.

[14] Erica Gautschi, *Die Hunziker Von Aarau Translation*, 2006, p. 18.

Basically, Grandpa wanted to *apply* his work to better mankind, not just study things for studying's sake! How practical is that!? For all these wonderful and great things said about grandpa, in my earlier years they did not matter one bit; he was just plain Grandpa to me. He loved me, and I loved him, too. I had the great privilege as a little kid to know and admire him, although most of my admiration for who and what he accomplished was not really appreciated until much later in my life. *Thank you so much*, Grandpa! Incidentally, you can still buy his books! Hmmm, I wonder who is getting the royalties?

As for my dad, it was obvious Rog and I were certainly his sons since he was a *pill* as a kid. Being the youngest of six children, they dubbed him "Babe!" Do you have any idea how hard it is to look at your dad, whom you consider to be a *giant* and hear him called "Babe?" One time he thought he could defy gravity and *float* to the ground; basically, it was the old *crash-and-burn* scenario! They had a three-story garage, he climbed onto the roof, opened an umbrella, jumped, the umbrella immediately collapsed, and he hit the ground hard. He was lucky he had no broken bones, just a broken ego and umbrella!

Dad's oldest brother, Karl, started college, dropped out, but went back to Purdue in dairying! This truly thrilled Grandpa to no end! At the same time, Uncle Burne (Walter Burne) was attending Purdue. Because of the market crash of 1929, finances were tight. Dad only wanted to go to Purdue but was told they could not afford having three Purdue students! Dad told how he became a disrespectable idiot and nasty with his folks the fall of his high school senior year! Then on November 3, 1932, the unthinkable happened. Karl and one of his friends were in a car accident and Karl was instantly killed. Grandpa's dreams were killed along with his son! Dad said Grandpa was never the same after Karl's death. His passion for his work even waned, though most would have never noticed the change, but his family definitely saw it! As a result, Dad got to go to Purdue after all. He felt remorse for how he acted that fall and often wondered if he was part of the cause of Karl's death!

Dad lived in East Cary Hall his freshman year and pledged Kappa Delta Rho (KDR—remember his *paddle battle*). Oh yes, one more point Dad always made about KDR, it was known as the "Brewery on the Hill!" Hmmm, I wonder what the school administration thought about that?

Dad was the adventurous type. He never stayed home during the summers between his college years. After his freshman year, he and three of his high school friends bought a used Model T and went to Oregon. When they got to the coast, they pitched their tents, had their evening meal, and went to sleep listening to the sound of breakers. They awoke sleeping in salt water! The tide came in and flooded their campsite! Dad learned he could get free transportation by driving new cars, so he took a driving test to prove he could handle a car while towing a second one behind it. For the next two summers, he joined convoys of cars towing a second one to the West Coast. The second summer, he jumped on a banana boat and went to Central America. He had not contacted his folks all summer, so when he showed up the day before he was to leave for Purdue, Dad told me, "Dad was so mad at me, he almost killed me! It was the maddest I ever saw him get at me!"

"So, how did your Mom and Dad meet?" Thanks for asking! In the fall of 1934, Grandma and Grandpa Alexander and their two daughters came to Purdue to visit their son, Bill. Peggy was less than a year old, and Mom was working the first year after high school. When they arrived at KDR, Bill was in class, so his roommate, Otto, offered to show them around until Bill returned. While touring, Mom said her mother kept whispering to her, "Isn't he such a pleasant lad!" Later that year, they almost met again.

Dad visited Bill at his Glen Ellen home, which had a circular floor pattern. Mom did not know he was coming, and she was in the kitchen ironing, but only wearing her panties and brassiere!

When Bill invited Dad in, they sat in the living room, and Mom was trapped in the kitchen; there was no way she could get upstairs to her bedroom without being seen! She said it seemed like forever before he left. She could have killed Bill for not telling her ahead of time and always thought he prolonged her agony by keeping Dad in the house so long! She did say, however, she was thankful Bill did not invite him into the kitchen for a bite to eat! Oh my, that would have been an interesting story!

Mom started at Purdue the fall of 1935 and pledged Alpha Chi Omega, which was about a half mile walk from KDR. Dad said she dated a lot, and he was too shy to ask her out because she was so popular. They eventually did date and it turned serious.

Dad graduated in the spring of 1937 and got a job at Continental Can; this employment marriage lasted for thirty-five years, and he started working in Chicago. Mom quit school and worked at places near Glen Ellen. On April 15, 1939, they married in Grandma Alexander's living room and had a quick honeymoon in Gatlinburg, Tennessee. Shortly afterwards, Dad was transferred to New York, and they moved to East Orange, New Jersey. It was here Mom became pregnant in mid-1940. Their doctor said he would deliver their child, but it would cost them one month's salary! In early March 1941, Roger Hunziker came into the world. Shortly after Mom's dad died, Dad was transferred back to Chicago. With the help of Grandma and Grandpa Hunziker, my folks bought their Elmwood Park house in 1942. Mom always said the first check they wrote each month was to his folks. Two years later, yours truly was *brought forth*, and the world has never been the same!

Section 2

Brookfield

Chapter 3
First Years, 1950–1952

FOLLOWING THE NEAR DISASTEROUS DRIVE TO Wisconsin, we arrived safely at our new home. The yard was a *tiny bit* larger than the one in Elmwood Park—almost twenty-five times bigger—since we now had one full acre! What a playground! All the lots were an acre, so it was like being in the wide-open *wild west*, but with no mountains! The town we moved to was Brookfield, which was fifteen miles west of Milwaukee. The town sign read, "Brookfield, Pop. 250," but someone wrote just below the population, "Dogs 450!"

We were located on south side of Lothmoor Drive Upper, just south of town and west off N. Brookfield Road; the west end of our road had a big hill which was used for snow activities. Three lots west of us were the Kampschroers. Catty-corner to the northwest was the Draeger's grandparents. To go to town, we took N. Brookfield Road down a big hill and across railroad tracks before reaching the "megatropolis" of Brookfield. In 1950, there were a gas station, two grocery stores, a hardware store, post office, and train, fire, and police stations.

Our home was a long ranch house with a basement. Our two-car garage led to an enclosed breezeway, followed by a kitchen, dining room, living room, two bedrooms, and our only bathroom separating them. Rog and I shared the back one on the SE corner of our house. Dad built an L-shaped desk; along the south side was Rog's desk and on the east side was mine and we both had windows.

Dad had a very daunting task, making a lawn from nothing but stone and gravel. His six- and nine-year-old sons were a real big help, or should I say, *hindrance*. Many loads of good fill dirt were dumped in the front yard; it looked like a miniature model of the Rocky Mountains, but without snow on the tops. Eventually, he was able to plant seed and, voila, a month later we had the start of a grass front lawn. Later that summer when the grass grew, Dad took pity on us and replaced the manual push mower with a powered, self-propelled reel lawnmower. Dad paid Rog $1 for mowing the backyard because it was bigger, and I got $0.75 for the smaller front yard. I guess I finally became an entrepreneur! Remember my weird mind? One time I ran out of gas, fetched the gas can, and filled the tank. In the process I got gas on my hands, and a bug flew into my mouth. I fished it out of my mouth, but I could taste the gasoline from my fingers. I thought I was going to die! As I mowed, I wondered when I would just drop dead! I survived that mowing, and much to my chagrin, another seventy-plus years of mowing!

One night at a restaurant, which had dog pictures on the wall, I remembered a promise Dad made about a year before; he said, "If we moved out of the city, we could get a dog!" I asked, "When are we going to get a dog?" He hemmed and hawed a little, but said, "Soon." As always, Dad was good for his word. They bought a German Shepherd named Thunder. He was only eight-weeks old, and he played fifteen minutes and then slept for two hours. I really liked him, but he was always partial to Mom, Dad, and Rog. Dad put up two big six-foot tall poles about thirty feet apart in the backyard, strung a thick cable between them and attached a chain leash from the cable to Thunder's collar. This gave him a controlled run.

Our house was on top of a hill and our front window offered a spectacular view. On a clear day, we could see thirty miles! Dad put up a tower that was thirty-feet tall and installed a big TV antenna with a rotor for better reception. In addition, we saw amazing lightning displays that made most Fourth of July celebrations pale in comparison; however, when we were the highest point in the area and lightning was bouncing around us, we were bound to be a target. One time, the lightning and the thunder occurred simultaneously, along with a big spark from behind the TV. It was impressive and we jumped well off the floor when it hit!

The first kids we met were Jim and Tom Kampschroer. Jim was slightly younger than Rog, and Tom was a year older than me. A few days later we met another boy, Russ Draeger, who was Tom's age. He lived in Milwaukee, but on weekends and during the summer he stayed with his grandparents. That winter, a house was built right across the street from us; this is where Russ, his folks, and younger sister, Linda, moved to in the spring of 1951. The Brookfield five became a hardened group of friends. Our life in the summers was simple: eat breakfast, play outside, eat lunch, play outside, eat supper, play outside until dark, and come in to go to bed! There certainly were days when we stayed inside, but during the summer, we had woods and a river to play near, around, and in.

The Milwaukee County Fair started, and one day, Mom and Mrs. Draeger took us. It was crowded, and we were told to stay close. We walked down the midway where there were food stands, rides, games, and oddities like bearded ladies, and so on. As we passed one of the hawkers touting a show, I stopped to listen. Finally, I looked around for Mom, Rog, or the others, but they were nowhere in sight. I was terrified! I saw a policeman, and I remembered the great advice Mom gave me. By the time I got to him, I was crying. He suggested we start looking for them, but I told him Mom told me if I got separated to stay where I was, and they would come looking for me. He agreed. A few minutes later, Mom, Rog, and the others came down the midway, and I spotted them. I believe I pretty much held onto Mom's hand tightly the rest of the day, but her advice was solid!

I stated in my first autobiography, *Brother Rick*, written in eighth grade, "When it was starting to be fun, school started."[15] How true! It was now time to go to the drudgery of school. Brookfield Elementary School was located a quarter of a mile from our house. In 1950, the school was a two-story building with a basement. There were only five classrooms: one for kindergarten, and each of the other four classrooms held two grades. What caught me off guard was I did not know anyone at this school, except Rog, because Russ lived in Milwaukee, and Jim and Tom went to the Catholic school. Mom took us the first day as Rog started fourth grade and I headed to first grade.

The first- and second-grade classroom was in the basement, which also served as the school's cafeteria, so there were distractions, smells, and noises I had to get used to. Mrs. Hiack, an elderly and kindly woman, served as my first- and second-grade teacher. Most of my classmates already knew each other because they went to kindergarten the previous year, so I was the new guy, the *outcast!* It took me no time to get back into my groove; on the third day, I fell off the ten-foot-high slide and got a serious bloody nose. I was taken to the nurse's office; Mom was called and came to check the damage, but I survived and went back to class. However, I was always wary of that slide!

Being in the basement did have its advantages. As the cooks prepared lunch, we were surrounded by the wonderful food smells, or not-so-good smells when we had sauerkraut! The one smell

---

[15] Rick Hunziker, *Brother Rick*, Crystal Lake Junior High School, 1958, p20

I liked the most was when we had rice. Once a week we had white rice, but they put bowls of cinnamon-sugar out so we could sprinkle it on the rice. That cinnamon smell oozed to every corner of the basement and was truly delightful. To this day, I still put it on my rice! I did meet several boys who I palled around with for the next four years, but they did not live near us, so summers were with the Brookfield five!

Remember how I wanted to learn to read? Well, this year was my chance to really start! We used a reader called, *Fun with Dick and Jane*.[16] It was exciting reading: "See Dick. See Jane. See Dick run. See Jane run. See their dog Spot. See Spot run. See Dick and Jane run and catch Spot and tie him up!" OK, so the last part did not happen, but you get the idea. This was the classic first-grade reader then. I immediately found out reading was not simple. The book had about 160 pages, and we had to read all of it before moving onto the second-grade reader. As a result, I did not finish my first-grade reader until partway through second grade.

(Flashforward: Years later when talking about my reading skills, or lack of them, with my sister-in-law, Sybil, who did special education teaching, she suggested I may be slightly dyslexic. I was never tested, but I suspect this had been part of my problem in reading and other things as you will see. At least that is now my story and I am sticking to it!)

Basic English and writing skills were also emphasized. Mrs. Hiack wrote block letters and words on a blackboard that we were to copy. I was horrible at penmanship and all through grade school got poor penmanship grades. Spelling would be notorious for me too! *Ugh!* I flunked third-grade spelling and have never recovered! Teachers told me, "If we didn't know how to spell a word, sound it out, and look it up in the dictionary." Yeah, like that is going to help! I once spent almost half an hour trying to spell the word *sure*. Try finding *shure* in a dictionary! How about the word *know* or *pneumonia*! Unless you know all the special 50,000 rules of English, good luck finding them! To this child, it was all Greek!

---

[16] Pearson Scott Foresman, *Fun with Dick and Jane,* Internet: https://www. goodreads.com/book/show/487599

Mom had a problem with English too. Well, not *real* English, but the English the *Brookfieldites* used. Many came from different heritages like Poland and Germany, so there was a little bit of a problem saying proper English. As an example: most said, "I am going to town today" or "Today, I am going to town." In the early 1950s, the *Brookfieldites* said, "To town I am going today." This used to drive Mom nuts! Even today as I write, this tends to creep into my writing; you might even have noticed it in this book on several, OK, many occasions!

Since the Korean and Cold Wars were raging, there was a big push for more math and science. Math was picked for the big push at Brookfield. Fortunately for me, I understood it. We spent hours per day learning our addition, subtraction, multiplication, and division tables all the way up to twelve! We had blackboard contests to see who was the fastest and most accurate, did written pages with thousands of problems to solve, and used flashcard games. Math was pounded into us! By the time I entered third grade, we started on fractions, and we went through *two* math books each year! Math was Brookfield's thing!

Every year the school put on a Christmas play, using all nine grades. The younger kids sang well-known Christ-centered Christmas carols, the middle kids did small skits, and the oldest ones were the main actors/actresses. Since I was one of the shorter kids, I was in the front row. I was proud I knew all the words to the songs and was singing away with gusto, but I noticed Mom making some kind of motion, but I could not figure out what she was doing. She kept repeating it, but it made no difference to me as I blissfully kept singing along. When the entire program was over, and I saw Mom, she said, "Rick, would you please zip up your pants!" *Oops!* So that was what she was mimicking! I always had problems with my clothes; in half of my Brookfield school pictures, I had my knit shirt on backwards, and you can see the label stitching just below my chin!

Thunder was getting bigger and stronger. Another dog came into our yard, Thunder took off after him, and the cable/chain rig Dad made did not even slow him down. To Dad's chagrin, he had another major job; build a five-foot-high fence round ninety percent of the back yard. The good news was to let the dog out, all we had to do was open the back door.

Dad believed if we had a dog, we should train it. They joined the German Shepherd Dog Club of Wisconsin.[17] The dog training took place on Sunday mornings, so they first dropped Rog and me off at the United Methodist Church. There were three main levels of obedience training. The lowest level had the dog heel (walk along with the owner), sit, stay, lay down, and so on. The next level involved both high and broad jumps as well as long sits and downs. The last involved finding and retrieving something based only on the dog owner's scent. Thunder was a fast learner, and by the time he was one and a half years old, he entered the last stage of training; however, his personality was changing. I was becoming afraid of him because he had bitten me three times on my right hand!

Once I was sick and Mom went to get groceries. I wanted to make friends with Thunder, so I gave him a dog biscuit. When he was done, I scattered the remaining crumbs with my right foot so Mom or Dad would not know I gave him a treat. I was only wearing a slipper as my foot swiped across the area when Thunder grabbed my foot and bit down, hard! I limped into our bathroom, took off my slipper, saw a large amount of blood coming from my foot and ran water over it; I figured I would bleed to death (you know my weird mind). Finally, Mom came home and asked what happened. Because I really did love Thunder and did not want to get him into trouble, I told her I rocked onto his tail, and he

---

[17] German Shepherd Dog Club of Wisconsin, https://www.facebook.com/gsdcw.

yelped and bit me. I must have not been too convincing because they asked me 1,000 times!

Several weeks later I came home from school and Thunder did not greet me. I asked Mom where Thunder was and she said, "Gone!" Finally, she explained they had to put him down. I was devastated; I caused Thunder's death! I went into my room and cried my eyes out. What had I done!? Later Mom told me their vet suggested this because Thunder was big and powerful; if he was ever in a bad mood and she turned her back on him, he could easily attack and kill her! The vet said it was in his disposition. As Dad put him into the car, Mom was crying and saying "Goodbye" to him, but Thunder snarled and growled at her! She said she could not believe it, but the vet was right; he had to be removed! That night before dinner, Dad went behind our fence and built a bonfire to thaw the ground. It was one of the quietest dinners the Hunziker clan ever had. Rog and I sat at our desks and could see Dad's shadow as he dug Thunder's grave, lowered a bag, and covered it. As I went to bed, my weird mind thought the way they put an animal asleep was by putting two shotgun-shell like devices in the dog's nostrils (Hey, I told you I was weird!) I kept thinking if I dug Thunder up and pulled those plugs from his nose, he would awaken. It is probably a good thing I did not do this; Dad would not have been happy! Goodbye, Thunder!

There were dangerous activities. Many of the trees were oak trees, so in the fall it meant acorns were in abundance. These *bullets* were used for throwing or with home-made sling shots. What was the target? Usually, each other! Being the youngest of the five, I seemed to take the most hits, literally! Rog and I got the bright idea to store ammo when no one else did. We each collected a shoebox full of acorns and put them in the bottom of our closet. Sometime near spring, we remembered our acorn ammo boxes and got them. The boxes seemed a little damp and when we opened them, the insides were pulsating! Small white worms came out of the acorns and were swarming all over the box. We screamed, and when Mom came into the room, she was not happy! We dumped the acorns out back and threw the boxes in the garbage. When we came back in, *daggers* were emanating from Mom's eyes. For some reason we never saved acorns again!

When we moved to Brookfield, I had a bike with only fifteen-inch wheels. The real problem was the pedals and back wheel were connected directly so I could not coast! Using this bike to go up the big hill from downtown was a real struggle. I asked for a new bike, and the *Birthday Fairy* came through. Since I was still short, they got me a twenty-four-inch bike, but there was one problem! I could not get on it! Until I learned how to really handle it, I had to find a step, ledge, or rock to stand on so I could swing my right leg over the seat and sit before pushing off. At home, this was no problem since Dad placed several big rocks along the top of our driveway.

On my inaugural ride after pushing off, I was on my way! I did mention earlier we lived on a hill, right? As I started down the driveway, the bike accelerated! Everyone yelled at me, "Hit my brakes!" What brakes!? No one told me I had brakes—or how to use them! No cars were coming as I swiftly crossed the road and entered the elderly Draeger's driveway. I was still going fast as I steered into their back lawn. The bike decelerated and when it got to a reasonably slow speed, I laid it down on its side, tumbled off, and broke no bones. When everyone got to me and saw I was OK, we just laughed. I was then taught how to use the brakes! This bike improved my transportation problems greatly, but when I initially took it to school, I had to go to the flagpole and step on its base to get started for home!

We missed Thunder, and about six months later, we got another puppy. He was known as Pronto, was mostly black, and was so tiny that he fit sideway in a shoebox! Like Thunder, he played a few minutes and slept for hours! He also had another trait like Thunder; he always went to someone else but not me! Once, everyone quickly left so just Pronto and I remained. Pronto did not really come to me, but I did have a small victory; he used my shadow to get out of the heat of the sun! Pronto really did become a family dog, and he had a great disposition! On Sundays, Mom and Dad resumed their routine of dropping us off at church while they went to the dog club.

Pronto was not as fast a learner, but he did progress much further than Thunder. Many weekends, we repeated the dog show circuit. Pronto really became a Mommy's boy! If she was sitting near the arena, he went over to see her; if she left during his performance, he went and stood near her empty seat! Eventually, Mom had to be well away from the arena, and he performed well. When it came to picking out the article Dad handled, he excelled and easily passed the third level.

Every time we left Pronto alone at home, he grabbed a piece of Mom's clothing, brought it to the front door, and slept there until we returned. Mom had an old sweater and it finally got to the point where she left it where he could easily get it; this way he did not ruin any of her good clothes. This sweater had all kinds of rips and tears because he stepped on it while he carried it. He also had another weird habit. Our dining room had knickknack shelves, and Rog and I often bought Mom small knickknacks for birthdays. One was a little two-inch green elf; it probably cost the massive sum of a quarter, and it always sat on the lowest shelf. OK, it was not *always* on the shelf because, like with Mom's sweater, Pronto carried it to the door! We tried black pepper, red-hot pepper, and anti-dog spray on it to keep him from doing this. After a while we gave up, and I think we were glad he did not take something more expensive. Today, that little green elf is one of my prized possessions!

After Pronto finished his training where he could find things by smell, we realized we could use him to find arrows! Dad bought bales of hay and stacked them in the backyard as a backstop for archery practice. For us, shooting at a plain old bull's eye target was not too exciting! We would rather shoot the arrows straight up into the air and see how close to us we could get them to land! Sometimes, with five guys shooting into the air, this could get hairy, but we had guardian angels and no one ever got impaled!

When we did do target practice, sometimes we missed the entire stack of hay. Hey, I did not say we were good shots! The arrows that went beyond the hay landed at a very shallow angle, which caused them to slither under the grass, and it was difficult to find them. The answer? Pronto! We could give him our scent, and he jumped at the chance to find our hidden arrows; we never lost another one! There was one problem using him for these recovery missions; the first time we sent him hunting, he found the arrow, grabbed it in the middle of the shaft, pulled upward, and broke it in two. We had to be close to him when he found it so we could retrieve it and praise him. He was an expensive arrow finder, but he enjoyed every minute of it!

Chapter 4
Last Years, 1953–1954

ONE OF OUR HIGHLIGHTS THE LAST TWO SUM-
mers at Brookfield was listening to Milwaukee Braves
baseball games! They moved here in 1953. Whenever we had
money, we bought baseball cards and bubble gum. One summer
I bought so much I got sick on the bubble gum! Dad took us to
a game between the Braves and the Chicago Cubs, which was
Rog's favorite team. I was sure I would get a homerun or foul ball,
so I took my baseball glove. When we got to our seats, we were a
million rows back of home plate and well under the upper deck.
For a ball to get to me, it would have to be hand carried by one of
the hotdog salesmen! We saw one home run by Del Crandall, and
the Braves won 3–2! Where we sat did not matter; just seeing our
hometown heroes play and take in the excitement of my first-ever
major-league baseball game was just awesome! Rog and I did not
even fight; Dad sat between us!

One of the Braves' best hitters and always in the hunt for the
lead in home runs in the National League was Eddie Mathews.
Russ, Linda, and their folks moved to a new house a few lots west,
and the Schmidts moved in across the street from us. They had a
son, John, and Eddie Mathews was a cousin! On several occasions
Eddie visited them and one time, Mom got the bright idea that
I should go over, meet him, and get his autograph for Rog, Russ,
Tom, Jim, and myself. This sounded like a plan to me, so she gave
me five blank index cards, and off I went. My heart was pounding

as I hesitantly rang their doorbell. When Mrs. Schmidt answered, I got so shook, I said, "I would like to *leave* these five cards for Mr. Mathews to sign and I can pick them up later." So much for *meeting* my hero! She said that would not do, and I should come right in! *Pound! Pound! Pound!* Be still, my heart!

Sitting at their dining room table was my *hero!* When he stood up to meet me, it seemed like he was ten-feet tall! At about three and a half feet tall, everyone seemed like a giant to me! My eyes probably bugged out when he shook my hand and asked me my name. I think I said what it was! He asked what I wanted, I gave him the five index cards, and explained what I was doing. He had a big grin and asked me to come over to the table. I followed him, he sat down, and wrote his name five times! You get that? He wrote his name *five* times! *Wow!* I thanked him as he walked me to the door and shook my hand again.

On the way home, my smile was all the way around my head, and my feet never touched the ground! What a *great* few minutes! I also figured I would become the neighborhood hero when I gave out his autographs. The real world brought me back to earth because when I went over to Jim, Tom, and Russ's homes to give them a fresh Eddie Mathews autograph, they were mad at me because they wanted to meet him and get their *own* autograph! They did not take their autographs, so after giving Rog one, I still had four!!!

A short time later, Eddie bought, built, and lived in a home right behind the elder Draeger's home. Russ's new home had a baseball diamond in the side yard. Several times during the summer of 1954, Eddie hit fly balls to us. Are you kidding! One of the greatest homerun hitters of all times hitting us fly balls, how great can that be!? Unfortunately, what we did not realize was when he hit a pop up, it was not like when we hit them to each other; his fly balls went into orbit! From the time the ball came off his bat until we had a chance to catch it, notice I said "chance" because I do not think I ever actually caught one, the lapsed time was five minutes! OK, probably only forty seconds! And, oh yes, the ball did not go into orbit, but it was hot from re-entering the atmosphere! These were truly *great* moments!

I mentioned previously our folks dropped us off at the local United Methodist Church on their way to the dog club. Since we were three years apart, we went to different Sunday School classes. After our classes, we went to the church service and then walked home. The Bible was part of our culture, and every school day was begun when we all stood, faced the American flag, put our hands over our hearts, and said the Pledge of Allegiance. Next, we had a minute of silence to say our own prayers followed by our classes. In 1954, "Under God" was added to the Pledge! I believe because of these activities, school violence was almost unknown then. This is the way it was back in the 1950s!

The winters in Wisconsin were rough and cold. One time it got down to −34 degrees F, not wind chill, but real temperature! Most winters, we had snow drifts above the windowsills. Dad and Rog loved being outside, even in winter, but winter was not my forte. Dad thought we should give Mom a rest by going ice fishing! *Ugh!* He put our post hole digger, a crowbar, blankets, rods, and so on into our car, and took off for Pewaukee Lake, about seven miles west of us. It was a cold and *very* windy day, and he picked a spot near the center of the lake and proceeded to chop a hole in the ice. It was thick and it took him quite a while before he *hit water*. I was already frozen before I put my bait into the water; I do not remember how long we stayed or if we ever got a bite, all I wanted to do was get out of the wind. Finally, Dad gave up, and we headed back. Just to let you know, even outdoorsman Rog thought it was unbearable, and neither of us ever ice fished again!

The "hot" spot for us in the winter was the hill on the western end of our street. It was our community hill, but it did not have a ski lift to get us back to the top. There were woods, so we had to make sure we steered appropriately. My sled tended to dig into the snow; however, one time I was going fast when I hit a hidden rock, the sled stopped dead, and I kept going being flung up onto my feet and ran about ten feet before stopping. I suspect had I been laying on the sled, it would have been another hospital visit for me—another guardian angel's job well done! When I was nine, Dad bought me a pair of skis, but they were very awkward for me to handle. When I, by luck, got them pointed in the same direction and started downhill, I was afraid to go fast, so whenever I picked up speed, I purposely fell. *Chicken!*

One day at school, Rog and I got into it during recess. Most of the time because of our age differences, this was not a problem; however, this day it was different. It was the only time I can remember this happening; I somehow sat straddling him and was washing his face with snow! This was strictly against school policy, so Mr. Haift came over and told us to stop. He knew Rog from Boy Scouts, but he did not know me. I turned to him and said, "He's my brother!" He must have understood I did not get opportunities like this often, said, "OK" and walked away! I know I paid for it later, but it felt good to have a small victory that day. About a week later, the scout troop was meeting in our basement. I was in my bedroom and Mr. Haift was upstairs and relaying this story to Mom, and Dad; they all laughed. I smiled!

I had a new experience after moving to Brookfield; I was *finally* allowed to go to Pine Ridge to catch my own frog! It was a long trip, and I probably asked a million times, "Are we there yet!?" In the early 1950s, there were no superhighways or Interstates, so 99 percent of the driving was done on narrow, curvy two-lane highways. Going up, we had a break near the Dells. This was a neat area because of the many sandstone formations and pillars. Our folks were happy to have us run off our energy so maybe we might sleep for a while. One of these roadside areas had stuffed animals and for a fee, we could get our picture taken while sitting on one. Dad finally gave in, and Rog got to sit on a buffalo! Instead of it, they wanted my picture on a donkey! *Ugh!* I wanted to sit on something wilder than a domestic donkey! Oh well.

Pine Ridge was true to its name. There were countless numbers of tall pine trees, and the air really had that clean pine scent. Whenever I smell pine trees, my mind goes back to Pine Ridge! There was a downside to the pine trees: ticks! They were small, about the diameter of a ladybug, but very thin. They dropped on us and got some place nice and cozy, buried their heads into our skin, and had dinner on our blood! Every night before going to bed, we were checked for blood suckers! When we found one with its head buried in our skin, Dad lit a match, blew it out, and while it was still hot, applied it to the tick's butt! When he did this, the tick backed its head out.

I liked the cabins, and the food at the dining hall was great. Every morning I had a stack of pancakes! Every cabin had a boat; these were fourteen-foot wooden rowboats. It was not long before I learned how to row. Later Dad bought a seven and a half horse-power Elgin outboard engine so he could get across the lake in a reasonable amount of time. Sometimes the resort was not sold out, and other boats were available. Our family rule was when Mom and Dad were out fishing, we were not allowed in another boat.

If they were on shore, we could take a boat out, but we always had to wear a life preserver. Rog's life jacket was solid color, but mine was light blue with little naked kids *skinny* dipping! I hated it, but wearing it gave me privileges I loved. We often swam in the heat of the day, and the water was fairly clear, not too cold, and the sandy lake bottom sloped very gently so we could walk out far. The first time I came out of the water, I thought I had an old dead leaf caught between two toes. I reached down to pick it off, but realized it was attached to my foot! I screamed! Dad took his fingernail and scrapped it off, but blood oozed out from where it was attached! I was not enamored with leaches! Thunder and Pronto enjoyed the water too but had to be daily and carefully checked for ticks and leaches.

In front of the dining hall was the main pier. This pier had an earthen walkway about fifteen feet long to a twenty-foot circular island. On the outermost side of this island was one of the narrow piers with several boats docked along its sides. It was from this pier Rog and I did a lot of our fishing while Mom and Dad were on the lake because to the west was a big patch of weeds, and fish were always there. Also, since this pier was out in the open, this is where Dad taught me how to fly-fish. Lots of room for a beginner was needed, and this pier fit the bill. It was *great* catching bluegills, perch, crappy, and bass out there with a small fly rod. The action made it exciting!

It seemed when we got presents, either for birthdays or Christmas, they were mostly items to make things. Rog already had an older erector set, but one Christmas I got my own. This was different because Rog's set only had a small wind-up motor; mine had a big electrical motor with a gear box attached! That Christmas, as soon as we finished opening all our presents, Dad invoked the old adage, "You don't know how to do it, so let me build it!" All Christmas Day, he and Rog worked on a big crane using *my* new erector set and its electric motor. When Dad went to work the next day, I finally got to play with *my* erector set! I connected and operated many things because of the different gear ratios available. *Cool!*

One Christmas, we got the ultimate present, an electric train set. It was a *joint* present; probably not the smartest thing to give two boys who fought over everything, but we were very happy to get it. Before Christmas, we snooped in the closets, so we knew we were getting it. On Christmas Eve after we went to bed, Mom and Dad set it up in the living room. Little did they know, we watched them do the set up! Rog positioned a couple of small mirrors so we could watch them work on it! Our tradition was to eat breakfast before we opened any presents, so Dad came to our bedroom, blindfolded me, and led me through the living and dining rooms into the kitchen. He then got Rog. We smiled at each other as we ate. When we went into the living room, were we surprised? *Yep!* It was even better than expected! Unfortunately,

Dad again invoked the old adage, "Let me do it!" As a result, we had to wait for him to go to work so we could play with *our* train! After the newness wore off, we moved it to the ping pong table in the basement. There were many hours of train operation in the Hunziker household and it probably helped me drive and operate a big locomotive later!

Once my best friend, Russ, and I watched Mr. Wizard on TV. He placed a small amount of corn starch on a piece of paper, rolled it so it was like a drinking straw, lit a candle, and then blew the corn starch through the flame. This resulted in a mini flamethrower! We thought we should try it, but we did it over his kitchen sink in case burning pieces survived. It worked just like on TV! (WARNING: Do NOT do this inside!) A window was directly above the Draeger's kitchen sink and it had thin lacy curtains. *Oops!* Only one small corner got burned; it was almost unnoticeable!

When we had company, we often placed a plastic pile of dog poop where they would see it, and they would *tell* on Pronto. One of us would go over and say, "Well, it looks hard," and, to our guest's astonishment, grab it with our bare hands!!! I took the plastic poop to Russ' house, placed it so Mrs. Draeger saw it, and she got upset with their cocker spaniel. I said, "It looks hard," but as I approached to pick it up, she kept saying, "Don't do that! Stop! No…,"but it was too late! I held it for about twenty seconds before I told her it was plastic!!!

Danger always lurked around the corner, whether it was trying to ride a bike, sledding, or whatever. One of the real dangers in our area was trains; not model ones, but *real* ones! For young kids, trains were like magnets; they just pulled us into them. One time after we bought popsicles, Russ and Tom were ahead of me. A train was coming, and they easily crossed the tracks, but I was well behind them. I did not want to wait for a long train to pass, so I started running. I heard the horn blowing full blast as I crossed the track just in front of it. The train was probably going about fifteen miles per hour, and I doubt I made it by more than ten feet because I felt the air wake of the engine as it went past me! A guardian angel saved me!

Electricity fascinated me. Why does a radio play? Why does a light come on? I was curious enough to find out, so one day I took a night light, plugged it in just far enough so the light lit and placed a finger across the two prongs! *Zap!* I got bit! I was not sure what I experienced, but I did not wish to repeat it and put the light away! This would not be the last time I got bit, and electricity played a role later in my life!

Water was also a danger for us. Mom took us swimming to Pewaukee Lake. I was on an old inner tube, but this time instead of sitting with my butt in the hole with arms and legs dangling over the sides, I straddled the tube with one leg in the hole and the other leg on the outside. I got into a water fight, and my opponent pushed the tube over, so I was on the underside as it lay on top of me. One leg was still caught in the tube, and it was too deep for me to stand up on my free leg. I thrashed around under the tube and tried to get my head above water, but I could not force myself upward. Every once in a while, I got a little air, but I was taking in more water than air. I was panicking! I do not remember the guardian angel who grabbed my arm and righted me, but I immediately vomited from all the water I took in. I stayed *very* close to shore the rest of this visit, and never straddled an inner tube again!

Tied to water was one of the best playgrounds ever: The Fox River. It started about five miles north of Brookfield and went to central Illinois where it dumped into the Illinois River. It was about a mile from us and fifteen-feet wide where we played. Nearby was a small bridge on River Road and the railroad bridge over it. We were never exactly *forbidden* to go to the river, but it was close! None of us knew how to swim, and we were never sure how deep it was, so we did not know what true danger we faced.

By the summer of 1954, and because of the amount of time we spent there, our parents decided it was time for us to learn to swim, so we were signed up for swimming lessons. Right before they started, Grandma Alexander got sick, and Mom took Rog and me to Glen Ellen. We ended up staying almost two weeks before she got better. I was disappointed because now all my friends knew how to swim, but I did not. When we got home, all were sick! The pool had bacteria that caused ear infections, so they only had a few lessons! Grandma's sickness had been a blessing in disguise! Another guardian angel!

We desired to drift down the river like Tom Sawyer or Huckleberry Finn. The railroad company did work on their track bedding and bridge, and several old, treated, eight-inch-square railroad ties were thrown into the grass near the river. The five of us realized the *river god* just supplied the means to raft! We lashed logs together and added the back seat from a nearby old junk car; the platform was about ten feet long and five feet wide. It was time to take the first excursion on *our* river. This was one of the few times in early childhood where my older brother was my guardian angel! We piled on and pushed off. The raft immediately started to sink because there was too much weight on it. Russ, Jim, and Tom jumped back toward shore but went into the river's edge. Rog grabbed me and said, "Wait!" Sure enough, with them off the raft, it slowly started to rise and float again! The three of them were soaked, but Rog and I only had wet shoes! I think we got scared since none of us ever tried rafting again!

Our life near the river was truly magical, albeit a dangerous playground. There are memories Rog and I still talk about and usually are in tears from laughing so hard. I will turn to my book, *Brother Rick*, for my last river story because I cannot improve upon how I told it, if you ignore spelling and punctuation:

> That fall we thought of an idea or rather Roger did,
> so we went to work on another *failior*. We found a
> bottle, bought a cork and a candle and Roger put
> a note in the bottle. The note had our address on it
> and offered anyone twenty-five cents for returning

it to us. There were five of us, so we each gave Roger five cents. The purpose *im* it was to see how far down river it would go. About four days later four kids came to our house, and they had the bottle. Roger *ask* them where they found it and they said, "We found it down by the railroad bridge." That was where we put it into the river. It *didnot* get far because it had *frozzen* that night after we had put the bottle into the river.[18]

Yep, another failed adventure, but what a memory! And it was not dangerous!

In early summer 1954, Dad got a major promotion to head quality control in Continental Can's largest division and was transferred back to Chicago. In July, we spent every weekend looking at homes in Chicago's northwestern suburbs. I remembered Dad once saying, "If I move again, I want to move to a lake!" That sounded great to me, but most of the homes we were looking at were not near water! They decided to look during the week too, so *divide and conquer* was invoked. Dad and I stayed at the Hunziker's, and Rog and Mom stayed at the Alexander's. Dad left work early, picked up Mom, looked at a couple of homes, dropped her off, and stayed overnight in LaGrange. One morning two weeks later, I heard Dad putting stuff in his car, so I stuck my head out the window and sleepily asked, "Any luck?" He said they bought one, so I asked, "Is it on a lake?" He said "No," and my heart sank, but then he added, "It's only about a block from one!"

In the meantime, they put our house up for sale, but so far, we had no takers. In mid-August, they hosted a farewell party for all the adult neighbors. The party was right before several showings

_____

[18] Rick Hunziker, *Brother Rick*, Crystal Lake Junior High School, 1958, pp. 29–30.

48

of the house. While they were partying, Rog and I needed entertainment and, again, Rog had a brilliant idea. We already had our windows opened since we had no air conditioning, so we pushed our screens out, Rog gave me a flashlight, and we quickly attracted moths. Rog caught one and released it into the area where our neighbors were partying. We repeated this about a dozen times, but then Mom squealed, "Where are all of these moths coming from?" At that point *Calvin* and *Dennis* decided we had pushed our luck to the limit, shut our screens, and went to bed. I wonder if these moths were the reason we did not sell the house for another year and a half!

Very early on Wednesday, September 1, 1954, a moving van backed up our driveway and our move to Crystal Lake, Illinois, started. All the neighborhood kids watched as they loaded boxes and our furniture; our beds were the last things loaded. About 8 p.m., we said goodbye and headed for a new adventure! As I looked out our back window at my friends waving, I had tears running down my cheeks. My weird mind asked, "Would I ever find new friends like Russ, Tom, and Jim?" Only time would tell!

Section 3

Crystal Lake

Chapter 5

Our New Digs

A FTER NAVIGATING THE INFAMOUS "Y" INTER-change when crossing the state line, we arrived safely at our destination: 1410 Broadway Street, Crystal Lake, IL. This town of about 6,000 in 1954 was a *bedroom community* fifty-five miles northwest of Chicago. It is on US Route 14 that goes from Chicago to Madison, Wisconsin, and it was on a Chicago and Northwestern Railroad line. About 10 p.m., the movers parked their truck in front of our house, and a police car pulled up behind it. The officer asked what was happening, and Dad explained we were moving in. He said his name was Ed O'Neil and welcomed us to the neighborhood. We moved to the Village of Lakewood, and this night before anything was moved into our home, we met the *entire* Lakewood police force!

Lakewood had four east–west roads: from the lake and working southward were South Shore Drive, Lake Avenue (the main drag), Broadway, and Country Club Road. South Shore Drive was one lot from the shoreline, so homes could be built directly on the water. The north–south roads were called Gates; those north of Lake Avenue were odd numbered, and those south were even numbered. Broadway was a divided gravel road, and our house faced it, so we were on the northwest corner of Broadway and Gate 14.

This was Rog's and my first time in our new home. It was a tri-level built in 1950, and it looked a like a two-story fort block house with an *extension* on the west end. On the main floor was a dining room, living room, and kitchen. When I entered the kitchen, I saw why Mom liked this house! It was large and had lots of cabinets and counter space!

The upper level had four bedrooms and the main bathroom. The bathroom was between the master bedroom and the other big bedroom, which Rog claimed. Figures! I could choose either the front bedroom, which was the largest of the two but had the smallest closet, or the back bedroom, which was smallest room but had a biggest closet. I took the back bedroom! *Home sweet home!*

The lower level had a bathroom/shower, a back *working* half with sinks, washer, dryer, furnace, and so on, and a front half was for recreation; Dad later built sliding doors to separate the halves. As soon as Rog and I picked our rooms, the movers brought in and set up our beds and left. It was after midnight when I lay down on my bed in *my room*, and I quickly went to sleep with a smile on my face, but I still wondered if I would ever have friends like the ones I left!

When I woke up, I looked out my north-facing window. Right behind us was a field and then a red brick ranch home. In Wisconsin, we only had two trees Dad had planted, but the trees I saw here were *huge*; most had trunks more than two feet in diameter! When I stood at Broadway and looked north up Gate 14, I had an awesome sight. About twenty feet on both sides of Gate 14 and about every thirty feet along it, a giant elm tree existed. They were so large the top limbs arched and touched over the road! It was like being in a great cathedral, truly inspiring! The whole area was like this! What a great plan—at least until the Dutch elm disease came along in the 1960s and killed all them!

True to their word, the movers came back. Thursday and Friday were unpacking and organizing days! I was outside for a few minutes when the boy who lived catty-cornered to us came over and introduced himself. His name was Dick Beber; he was a year younger than me. Mom called for me, so I said goodbye for now.

Lakewood had three private beaches at Gates 7, 13, and 21, and each had the same equipment: a fifty-foot T-shaped pier, a twelve-foot square raft in deep water, a string of buoys marking the swimming area, and one green bench! At the Gate 13 beach, the land was ten feet higher than the lake, so we had concrete steps down to the pier and beach. Lakewood owned the property for 100 yards to its west, and many boats were moored just offshore.

When we got to the Gate 13 beach on Saturday, Dick was there along with another kid his age, John Woodman, who lived about fifty yards southeast of the beach. There was a five-foot square raft next to shore, and the three of us played on it. They wanted to take it to deeper waters, but when I, embarrassingly, said I did not know how to swim, they kept it in shallow water. The next day, I met another neighbor, Jim Harwood, who lived in the red brick ranch home two lots from us. We became lifetime friends. That weekend, the great stone-throwing pastime started at the lakeshore. Three kinds were involved: the farthest throw, who could hit the outer buoys, and skipping stones on the water. Dad canceled the second contest after hearing us ping a buoy a few times. I won none of the contests! I slept well those nights, having been tired by the sun and water, and now having met a couple of new kids.

One project Dad started instantly was fencing the back yard for Pronto. He used the same structural design as Brookfield's, except he painted it white to match the house. The post holes were much easier to dig since they only hit dirt and sand, and *no* flagstones! What a difference 150 miles made! I even dug a few! Since we had very nice grass, Dad trained Pronto use the extreme northwest corner of the field behind us, so we did not have copious quantities of dog poop in the yard. We mowed three-fourths of the field and left the rest grow naturally; this was the section Pronto used. On the lot just west of us was where Chet and Florence Battles lived; we had not met them yet, but they had a German Shepherd, Bruno, who had a small, fenced area with a doghouse in the center. While building the fence, Pronto was loose and Bruno ran around his house barking viciously. As time passed, they became friends. When we let Pronto out to use the field, Bruno barked at him. When Pronto was done, he looked at us and whined. If we said, "OK," he took off, ran to Bruno's pen, and they sniffed noses and gently barked at each other. Now even Pronto had a friend!

There were ten lots on each side of Gate 14, and on our side were the Harwoods, four other homes and four empty lots. Jim's folks, Leroy and Lynn, were a neat couple and were always very gracious toward me. Living in the next-to-last house on the north end of Gate 14, were Bill and Winnie Albertz. They had a daughter, Bonnie, who was two years older than me, and a Heintz-57 variety, dark brown dog named Ginger, who Mr. Albertz walked every night. There were nights when he had ten kids following him; we affectionately called him *the Piped Piper!* He, along with Mr. Chet Battles, became two of my most unforgettable characters, and they played major roles in our lives as well as being lifelong friends to my folks. On the east side of the street were the Bebers and four other homes, which were built on multiple lots each. Oral and Margret Beber had two kids, Carol, who was Rog's age, and Dick. This initially completed our little community until other homes were built.

Chapter 6

South Elementary, Fifth Grade

O K, NOW THAT IT WAS FUN PLAYING IN THE LAKE, school restarted and ruined everything, *again!* Rog went into eighth grade at Central Junior High School, and I went into fifth grade at South Elementary School. Crystal Lake had three elementary grade schools, South, North, and Central; all three fed into Central Junior High School. There was one high school, and it served kids from several surrounding towns besides Crystal Lake; hence, its name Crystal Lake *Community* High School (CLCHS).

Mom took me to school the first morning. Mr. Husmann, South's principal, met us, and Mom filled out paperwork. When he saw our address, he said, "Sorry." Sorry? Sorry for what? He informed us the boundary line for using the bus to South was the lot line between us and the Battles; therefore, I had to walk, ride my bike, or catch a ride to school! The winters were nasty in Chicagoland, and this meant I had to trudge one mile (minus 100 feet) to school, going uphill both ways, in blizzard-like conditions! OK, so it was flat! After Mom completed the paperwork, he took me to my classroom and introduced me to my teacher, Miss McWilliams.

What stuck out most while walking into my classroom, everyone stared at me and I knew *no one!* My mind thought, "Didn't I do this before!?" Class was OK, but our recesses and lunch hours were staggered, and our time was with the sixth graders, so I knew no one at recess or lunch! About the third day, a big kid asked me my name, where I moved from, and so forth. He was a great kid, and his name was Frank Sibr. Frank was a Patrol Boy which also made for support. He lived on Gate 20, so he was not too far from our home. We became good friends. Frank introduced me to Len Zitnik; he lived on Gate 18. He and I did scouts together.

They served hot meals at both schools, so Mom told us she would provide the money to buy lunch or we could *make* our own. It took too long to go through the line, so we both decided to make our lunches. Rog was partial toward baloney sandwiches, so for the next five years that is what he made. I liked peanut butter and jelly. For the next eight years Mom bought jars after jars of Peter Pan Peanut Butter and Welch's Concord Grape Jelly. Every day, I made my sandwich, cleaned an apple, stuffed them along with a couple of Oreo cookies into a brown paper bag and put it with my books. If she had carrots or celery, I included those. Milk was three cents/pint for regular milk or five cents for chocolate; I always bought chocolate milk. One thing I never learned to correct (I guess I was a slow learner) was to place the apple on the side of the sandwich which had the peanut butter. It was always on the jelly side which meant I ended up with a big purple dent in my sandwich! Several times a year, Mom made her awesome ham salad! When she did, Rog and I fought over it. If we were careful, we could get two days each!

When I walked or rode my bike, I went straight down Broadway until it ended at Country Club Road; South was one and a half blocks east of there. One day as I was walking, a kid, who I had never seen before, stopped me. He acted tough and he was slightly bigger than me. He asked me questions and then sucker punched me in my stomach and ran off. Before I could do anything, Don Harrington, a big sixth grader and brother of George in my class, rode up on his bike. That kid must have seen Don coming and decided to do his thing and beat a hasty retreat. I asked Don who that kid was, and he told me his name was Powers McGuire. It was next summer before I saw him again. Dick and I were coming home when we met him. He pulled the same stunt and hit Dick in the stomach! What gives with this bully anyway!?

Shortly after school started, a new kid came into our class, Jim Eby. Jim lived on Gate 18, so Frank, Jim, and I started to hang out quite a bit. We had an interest in electric trains, a big surprise! Frank had a subscription to *Modern Railroader* magazine. We still had the O gauge outfit Mom and Dad gave us, but the smaller HO gauge trains were starting to catch on. They had two benefits: (1) The engines, cars and track were smaller which meant smaller display area requirements; a ping pong table could make for a pretty sophisticated set up; and (2) The engines and cars had realistic details. The three of us sat on Frank's porch and drooled over his current and past issues, dreaming what our sets might look like. The more I saw Frank's magazines, the more I wanted to build my own set. Eventually, I asked for track, a transformer, and a switching engine called, "Little Joe," for Christmas. When I got them, I was on my way, but it took years to develop it.

The Holidays in Crystal Lake were different than those in Brookfield because both sets of grandparents lived fairly close. Initially, we tried to go both places the same day, but that became too much, especially when having *Calvin*, *Dennis*, and Pronto along. They agreed to alternate and only go one place each Thanksgiving and Christmas, and reverse the visits the following year. Thanksgiving did not bother me, but on Christmas morning, things were not to my liking. We still ate breakfast and then opened our presents, but now instead of fighting Dad to play with my new toys, I had to change clothes and leave them for the whole day while we went to a grandparent's home!

The visits to our grandparents were completely different. When we went to Grandma Alexander's home, we spent the whole time there. She cooked the entire meal whether it was the Thanksgiving turkey with all its trimmings or a roast for Christmas; her meals were mouthwatering. One Christmas we did have *an event!* Dad carved the roast and placed it on the dining table while the rest of the food was organized. Pronto just reached up, pulled a slab of roast off the plate, and had his own Christmas dinner! Aunt Peggy, a master storyteller, was always there, and everyone ended the meals in tears with our stomachs hurting from laughing so hard. These were times when it was a downer to have to get up from the table and end the meal!

When we went to Grandma and Grandpa Hunziker's, the atmosphere was more sedate, dignified, or formal. Most of the time Uncle Burne, his wife, Mary, and their daughter, Ann, were there. Grandma, while being a great cook, did not cook on Thanksgiving or Christmas. Instead, Grandpa made reservations at The Old Spinning Wheel in Hinsdale. We sat at a long table for nine or more and a very distinguished Grandpa sat at the head of the table. The food was good, and when we were done, Grandpa picked up the check and we went back to their home. Grandpa brought out a bottle of wine to share with the adults, but as he came into the room, he tossed it up into the air from behind his back and caught it. Grandma told him to stop before he dropped it and had wine all over the carpet. He never dropped it, and Grandma's carpets stayed clean. By now Ann, Rog, and I warmed up to each other, and we played Hide and Seek because there were many places to hide on just this floor. One of the favorites was the closet between the front entrance and Grandma's office. One side of the closet went under the main stairwell, and Rog and Ann always told me there was a hole in the floor back there. I never hid there because I did not want to fall through the floor into their creepy basement, which probably was in *total* darkness! Not me!

We saw several different sides of Grandpa. First, he was mostly happy and a little devilish. They had a chandelier in their living room that had five lights around a pewter-colored shallow metal bowl about eighteen inches in diameter. When Grandma was out of the room, he gave us wads of paper to see if we could *make a basket!* Of course, they stayed in it if we did our job right, so he got a chair, stood on it in his stocking feet, and retrieved the wads. We took more shots, but the fun ended when Grandma caught Grandpa standing on the chair! He got that same *sheepish* look and little smile as he did when he tossed the wine bottle and caught it.

A completely different side of him once showed through: his temper. He shipped his dairy books all over the world, including the Soviet Union. "Look what those guys did!" he proclaimed as he handed Dad what looked like an old book. The pages were made from old cheap yellow paper, the edges were not cleanly cut, and the printing was in a foreign language. He was hopping mad because they took the book he sent them, reproduced it exactly, and published it under their own author's name! They completely ignored copyright laws and willfully stole his life's work; he never sent another book to a communist country! Finally, we also saw another change starting to happen. In the mid-1950s, he stopped writing. When we visited, he was confused about why we were there. We thought it was senility, but as we looked back on it later and knew people who had Alzheimer's disease, we believed this brilliant dairy mind fell victim to it. What a shame and a waste! In his last six months, he reverted to his native language and never spoke English again. In November 1959, we lost him. Auf Wiedersehen, Grandpa!

Winter was a rich time in Crystal Lake, but how rich depended on the ice texture on the lake. We always hoped for a very still night so the ice was smooth. The lake was pretty small, about 1.3 miles long and 0.2 to 0.3 miles wide, depending on where you measured it. Once the ice froze and we had a snow fall, we shoveled an area to make a hockey rink. This was a regular meeting place, and the players were over a wide range of ages; the two oldest boys picked sides. Since I was new at ice skating, I was the last one picked. When we played, there was no body checking, but occasionally someone was tripped or fell. My hockey skates became too small, so I bought a pair of figure skates to help my ability to play and perform *graceful* moves. *Wrong!* On the front of figure skates were several little spikes to help stop quickly and plant the skate before doing a jump. They did just that for me and did it very well! The first time I bent forward, they stopped me instantly! Every time I leaned forward, my face said, "Hello!" to the ice. When I got home after this disastrous session, I made my figure skates into hockey skates by grinding off those wonderful, *useful* toe spikes!

The most dangerous thing we did was at the end of that first winter. Remember, Rog and I did not know how to swim, although in this situation, it probably would not have mattered! Spring was coming, the ice was breaking up, and there were several large *icebergs* along the shoreline. Rog and I took ten-foot-long tree branches and got out on the ice. We were on separate slabs and poled our little *ice rafts* all over the place. I was about 200 feet offshore and had to use all my branch to reach the lake's bottom to push myself along. I was lucky the wind did not push me further out into the lake, or the *ice raft* broke up. My guardian angel allowed me to safely get back to shore, and Mom and Dad never found out—or would they? One of Rog's friends, Jim Petrillo, was at the lake, took pictures of us on the *ice rafts*, later gave Rog the pictures, and Mom happened to find and see them! *Ugh!* We never did this again, even when we knew how to swim! Dumb kids!

Over the years, Rog and I developed a great game, but it was played only when Mom and Dad were not home! Hmmm! The objective was to shoot each other! I went to one end of the house and Rog went to the other, and once we started, we had to evade the other's bullets and shoot our brother! The first one hit lost; we then switched starting places and started again. You might ask, "How did we shoot each other?" With a gun, of course! These were the old dart guns that shot a six-inch plastic dart with a suction cup on the front end. Oh, I forgot, as dumb as we sometimes were, we always wore Dad's eye protection goggles. Dumb, but not *stupid*! That Christmas I got a new dart gun that allowed me to load *and* shoot three darts! It fired as fast as I pulled the trigger and put a lot of *lead* out quickly, which gave me an advantage until Rog started using two pistols. We never broke anything, and we both walked away with two *good* eyes!

Chapter 7

Summer 1955

REMEMBER, DAD OWNED AN OUTBOARD MOTOR? This summer he decided to buy something to use it on; a StarCraft 12-foot aluminum rowboat. He did splurge and buy wood seats, so we did not get our butts singed in the summer. This 100-pound *yacht* had three seats with float materials under them, so it did not sink. I always had to wear my trusty blue life jacket with all the naked kids (I hoped no girls were around!). The first time alone in it, I got the motor started and pulled away from the new boat dock at the Gate 13 beach. I went very slowly, and Dad told me, "Open it up!"

Unfortunately, when I applied power, the motor was at a very sharp angle, so the back of the boat dipped and went around in a *very* tight circle. The water was *above* the back and side panels, and I thought I was going to capsize—and in fact almost did. Dad yelled to cut the power which I did right away. I suspect my face was as white as the foam I caused while doing my *wheelies*. Dad learned three lessons from this little episode: (1) Do not trust your youngest son in the boat alone; (2) Better balance the weight; and (3) Make a better control system. He assembled a steering wheel in front of the middle seat and installed a remote throttle control. He also said I could not take the boat out alone until I could swim across the lake; this way I could always swim to shore no matter where I sank it!

When the main beach opened, Mom signed us up for swimming lessons. I was the oldest kid in the beginner's class; most were five or six years old, but dear old Rick was eleven! I hated those classes! We spent hours, OK, maybe minutes, each day holding onto the pier with our legs behind us kicking. The instructor stood on the pier and keep yelling, "Kick harder! Faster!" My class was at 9 a.m., and many mornings the temperature was in the low sixties! In the afternoon, I had to show Mom what I learned; it seemed like nothing! After about two weeks of lessons, I tried a swim stroke, and it worked. It was like a light bulb going on! I could swim! Voila! The eleven-year-old got it! I did finish the lessons but never went back for more instructions. I was now free to swim anywhere I wanted to *and* take the boat out by myself!

In the mid-1950s, water sports on the lake were a very big deal. There were always fishermen trying to catch their dinner at their favorite fishing spot. Every Sunday, the sailboats lined up between two buoys in the west end, and when a cannon fired, the sailors took off to the east, raced to a buoy near the main beach, circled it, and returned to the start. At the end of the season, champions were crowned. Unfortunately for the sail boaters, our lake also sported large numbers of *stink pots* (motorboats). Did I mention the motorboats usually had a seventy-five-foot tow line trailing them with someone hanging on for their dear life as they skied past the sailboats? So, on a given day, boats active on the water could range from a dozen fishermen anchored, as many as forty sailboats doing 3–6 mph, and sixty motorboats going from 15–50 mph, most towing skiers! All fought for their little piece of quiet water. It was a busy mishmash, mass confusion, and a recipe for a disaster, but amazingly, everyone was reasonably courteous to others. Our motorized twelve-foot aluminum boat started Dad thinking about buying a *real* boat with a *real* engine. He was *smelling* the bait!

We still owned the house in Brookfield. Buyers wanted three bedrooms, not two. Several Saturdays we visited, mowed, weeded, and trimmed to give it curb appeal. I also had a chance to see Russ, Jim, and Tom. They were into different hobbies while my expertise was shown in stone throwing. All those hours pitching stones and denting the beach buoys when Dad was not around was about to pay off. When we were about 100 feet away from Tom's mailbox; they had thrown many stones but never scored. I picked up a stone and nailed it. They stopped and just looked at me and said, *"Wow!"* I did not pick-up others because I figured I could never top my feat, and why should I give up the *awe* they showed for me!

Chapter 8

South Elementary, Sixth Grade

R OG ENTERED HIGH SCHOOL, AND I WENT TO
sixth grade, which was a very interesting year for me. First, when I walked into the classroom, I knew all of the other kids; a welcome situation! Second, we were the top dogs at South! Finally, it was the year of joining!

We had Mrs. Bond in the morning for English and social studies; in the afternoon Mr. Husmann taught us math and science. Mrs. Bond was one of the nicest persons I ever met or had for class. English, and especially spelling, were my major problems, and she exhibited great patience toward me. My only objection about her was she thought spelling bees were good instruction tools! For me they were the perfect embarrassment tool! We stood along the edge of the classroom as she gave us words to spell. When we missed, we had to sit at our desk and watch the others continue; for me this meant I was sitting at my desk *alone* for a *very* long time, usually being the first to sit down! She even tried to help by giving me simpler words; I could often hear kids whisper, "That's easy!" Unfortunately, when I misspelled it, the embarrassment was even greater! I only made it through the first round once!

All the sixth-grade boys made up most of South's flag-football team. I was getting *chunky*, so I was slated as a defensive lineman but was seldom used because of my lack of aggressiveness; I was afraid! Steve Halsted was probably our best athlete and the most adept in playing football. Wayne Markee, Corky Iverson, George Harrington, Forest Hare, Walt Isaacson, and Frank were major contributors. We beat Central, but had to play our archrivals, North! The game was at South, so the crowd of ten gave us home field advantage! We heard they had a big lineman, Jim Maclure, who weighed over 210 pounds. When they arrived, I had this feeling all their kids looked alike. My weird mind was playing tricks on me again, and I concluded those that lived on the north side of Crystal Lake all had similar facial features! This was the first time I ever saw identical siblings. The Fanter twins, Bill and Bob, went to North and were my age. I thought I saw five or six of them and was later surprised when there were only two!

During the game, I made one of my few great plays; OK, just a lucky one! I grabbed the flag out of the belt of North's runner as he came through the line but was pushed backward by their linemen. Steve yelled at me, "Fall forward when you grab the flag, so they don't get more yardage!" Hey, Steve, I was proud I even got the flag! With the help of the Fanter twins, they beat us, and I had to *rethink* football because it involved more than just playing catch with Dad in the backyard.

Safety patrol was a lot safer, and Frank was named captain, and one of the lieutenants was Linda Petrillo. We were assigned different stations, and I always got the morning shift. Halfway through the year, the other lieutenant moved away, and Frank had to pick someone new. I begged him to pick me and he did. I got a special lieutenant's badge and could wear the safety patrol belt to all classes; I had *status!* I also had extra work and made out monthly schedules; it was the first time I had a place of responsibility! In late May, all the kids from our area went to a Chicago Cub's baseball game as a *thank you* for serving. It also meant I could spend a little more time with Frank, and, of course, Linda, who I liked and thought was cute!

I was interested in playing an instrument; the trumpet or cornet appealed to me. I promised to practice *every* day, so Mom and Dad bought me a cornet. When I started to practice in my bedroom, I was told to shut the door. When they could still hear me, they moved me to the lower-level bathroom, shut the doors, but guess what? They could still hear me, so I got to practice in my bedroom. The good news was most of the time the house was quiet because I did *not* practice! Mr. Trumpke was our band teacher and about fifteen South kids were in band.

About this time a new house was built next to the Bebers, and the woman who moved in was a concert pianist. She offered to do half-hour music lessons for $5.00. Mom signed me up and for the next two years I had lessons on Saturday morning. Jim Harwood played the clarinet and took lessons from her. A couple times a year, she hosted a recital to show our progress. The problem was, to progress, I had to practice, which I faithfully did *not* do! I do remember playing, "Danny Boy" and "When Johnny Comes Marching Home Again" at one of the recitals. She had six students, so we and our parents had to suffer as each student played two to three songs! *Toot! Toot!*

Mom thought I needed more *culture* than just music lessons, so she signed me up for dance lessons. *Say what!?* Fortunately, several other guys I knew also participated, including Jim Harwood. There were about twenty of us in the class, and it was evenly split between boys and girls. There were kids from all the local schools. One of the first kids I met from Central was a tall, skinny kid with glasses, Ken Kies. We learned, or should I say *tried* to learn, the waltz, foxtrot, jitterbug, tango, and other dances. Half the time was spent reviewing past steps. It was hard to practice between lessons unless I danced with Mom!

The last thing I joined was the Boy Scouts. Jim Eby, Len Zitnik, and I were interested in scouting; however, we did not have a troop in Lakewood. We joined a troop sponsored by the local American Legion Post. They had their own club house, which had limited heat in the winter, but it was ideal because we disturbed no one. There were about a dozen other kids and one scoutmaster whose name was Gene. I also met a kid named Tom Peterson, who went to Central. Gene often missed meetings due to his job, so we were not well organized. I did progress slowly and eventually after about six months, I passed my Tenderfoot rank. Since I could play the cornet (well, almost play), I was named the troop's bugler. It meant another patch, so it was worth it! Scouting would become a large part of my life for nearly four years.

After-school TV was not new to us, and initially, we used to watch *Elmer the Elephant*. What we liked the most, and argued heatedly over, were their turtle races. They had four box turtles named: Eeney, Meaney, Miney, and Moe. We bet which one would win, but most of the times, one of the other two won! A new TV show started called "The Mickey Mouse Clubhouse;" it pulverized the competition! Everyone, including us, watched it! Besides their great Disney cartoons, they had a special series called, *The Adventures of Spin and Marty*, which was about two kids working on a Western horse ranch. They also had the Mouseketeers! All the boys fell in love with the one and only Annette Funicello! Every day at school, the boys talked about her, "Did you see Annette yesterday? She was sssooo cute!" We, including me, were overwhelmed by her! However, living in Illinois, I had *no chance* to be with her!

At the end of the school year, two interesting things happened. First, construction was finishing on a new junior high behind South. Mr. Husmann asked the sixth-grade boys if they wanted to help unpack and distribute the students' desks; we eagerly helped so we could get out of class for a week! Second, our class treasury had money left over. The class decided to buy a record player to leave behind for future generations; *how noble!* After purchasing it, we still had enough for two 45-rpm records. Debates erupted, but we quickly agreed: The boys wanted "Sixteen Tons," and the girls wanted "The Yellow Rose of Texas." They were played every recess and lunch hour. My guess is the needle almost wore its way through the records! I wonder if they still have the player and those records?

Chapter 9

Summer 1956

D AD GAVE UP HIS PINE RIDGE TRIP SO WE COULD enjoy Florida! We loaded our Chevrolet station wagon and took Dinah Shore's advice to "see the USA in our Chevrolet." It took us two days to get to Florida's capital, Tallahassee. At our first Florida breakfast, we ordered orange juice but were promptly told, "We are out of orange juice!" We just stared at our waitress and said, "Let's get this straight; we're in Florida's capital, and we cannot get orange juice! Is that right!?" Yep, no orange juice! This was added to the Hunzikers' most memorable list.

Our Treasure Island motel had shuffleboard and sat on that beautiful white sandy beach on the Gulf of Mexico. Dad taught us how to play shuffleboard, but what was most interesting was watching two preteens from Georgia play. When they started, one asked the other, "Dddooo yyyaaa'lllll want the rrreeeddd or the bbblllaaaccckkk?" Being from the Chicago area, we had never heard southern drawls this pronounced and drawn out!

Dad hired a thirty-five-foot fishing charter to take us out to the Gulf. When the captain spotted tarpon, he maneuvered the boat ahead of them, baited our hooks with live bait, and we fished as they approached the boat. Unfortunately, my bait was on the leeward side of the boat, so the wind pushed the boat toward my bobber which meant the line was never taut! My bobber disappeared and then a giant tarpon, probably four-feet long, jumped straight up into the air ten feet from the boat, shook his head, flung the bait and my hook into the boat, and fell back into the water. That was it; in two seconds everything was over. Later, he set us up again, and this time I tried to keep the line taut. I slowly got mesmerized and complacent. As I stared at my bobber, it vanished, and I said so, which was a mistake! Dad turned and immediately took his open hand, put it under my pole, snapped it upwards to set the hook; he did not want me to lose another tarpon! Instead of the pole being quickly pushed way up, it suddenly stopped; my face was in the way! I think I had a dent in my forehead! After four hours of fishing, those two encounters were the extent of our action. The youngest, who was the ineptest in the boat, had the only two strikes! I am still waiting for that trophy fish!

Mom loved the beach and was content to sit in a lounge chair by the water and read a book. We loved to walk and hunt seashells. The most coveted was a sand dollar. Dad limited each of us to one shoebox of seashells, but we did learn one thing the hard way: When keeping a shell, make sure nothing was living in it! After a day or two in the heat of the car, a dead animal begins to stink, *big time!*

Next, we headed to the East Coast by cutting across Florida on Alligator Alley. Dad thought it might be a nice place to stop, but this was not a good idea! When we got out of the car, every mosquito within a billion miles descended on us! *Oh my gosh,* I had never seen so many mosquitoes in all my life! We jumped into the car and quickly sped off. For days we found those little blood suckers in the car! We stayed in a high-rise hotel in Hollywood by the Sea, which was situated right on the Atlantic Ocean! Our next stop was Daytona Beach where we saw cars on the beach, but Dad stayed on the roads. We visited Marineland and saw a great show featuring seals and dolphins. The bottle-nosed dolphins were the neatest, especially the way they *walked* on the water using their tails. At St. Augustine we visited a wax museum. They had the likenesses of the presidents, sports figures, and other famous people, but they did not have one of me! I just did not understand that!

Mom and Dad were interested in seeing what Gatlinburg looked like since they honeymooned there seventeen years earlier. There were many more shops, stores, and restaurants than they remembered. The next day in the Smokey Mountains, we stopped at an overlook. While parked, two black bears showed up. Dad always opened the window of our tailgate to get air through the car, but they must have smelled food and headed for that open window; however, he was able to quickly get away from the bears. I had a hand-me-down camera and was still learning how to use it on this trip. After the scare was over, I said, "I suppose if they got into the car, I would have had to use my flash to take a picture of them!" We all had a good laugh.

Our last stop was for dinner in Champaign, Illinois. My favorite pie is lemon meringue. I asked for it every lunch and dinner and not once did anyone have it! You would think Florida would have had lemons, but I guess they went the same way as oranges! This last night I hit gold, and it was *good*! We got home about midnight; thus, our first real traveling, sight-seeing vacation came to an end, and it was a smashing success, even without the oranges!

Another great adventure for me was going to my first week-long Boy Scout camp. Camp Lowden was on the Rock River near Oregon/Dixon IL. There were an endless number of things to do: rowing, canoeing, swimming, rifle shooting, horseback riding, crafts, and so forth. The bad part was we did not go as a troop, so the eight of us were put in a communal campsite with other kids in the same situation as us. The days were structured so we had to be at a certain place at a specific time to participate in each activity, but we did have free time; shooting a 22-caliber rifle was my main free time activity. The bad part was shooting was not free; we paid fifty cents for ten shots, so I had to limit my shooting time.

They had big campfires each night, but on Wednesday night, our parents were invited to participate. With Dad's schedule, I knew they would not attend. That night I was the only one of the eight who did not have his folks there. This did not bother me too much because I knew their situation. Mrs. Peterson talked to me for a minute and then gave me an envelope from Mom. I did not think too much about it, but when I opened it and read her note, my eyes welled up. To soften the blow because they were not there for my first, or any, Boy Scout camp, she included $10. The rest of the week I did as much shooting as I wanted and probably spent $9.50 of the $10 at the shooting range!

About sixty percent of our pool time was spent on swimming lessons. The rest of the time was free time, but we had to pass certain tests to go to different sections of the pool. The shallow end was for nonswimmers or beginners. The middle third was for those who could do basic swimming but could not pass their test for all strokes. The deep end, where they had two diving boards, was reserved only for the accomplished swimmers. Getting to use the diving boards was a real incentive for me to learn all my strokes. At the beginning of the week, I was in the mid-section, but by Wednesday, I had passed all my swimming skill tests, so I could now use the diving boards during my free time!

Chapter 10

Junior High, Seventh Grade

ROG ENTERED HIS SOPHOMORE YEAR, AND I attended seventh grade at Central Junior High School. I finally got to ride a bus to school! Something new was the teachers stayed with the room, and the students moved from one classroom to another! I noticed my favorite class, recess, no longer existed! Finally, like first and fifth grade, I did not know most of the kids in homeroom! *Ugh! Not again!* In homeroom, I only knew Ken Kies (dancing class); Peter Hellman, John Stephani and Val Sir (South); and Tom Peterson (scouts).

There was one other thing that became obvious to me right away: We were divided by *ability*, how well we performed in sixth and earlier grades. None of the *accelerated* kids from South were in any of my classes. At South, since we only had one class of fifth or sixth graders, all of us were in the same class no matter what our *abilities* were. This was no longer the case, and it also became obvious to me, I was not in the *accelerated* group. We were told the reason for putting us together by similar *abilities* was so the whole class could progress at similar rates and not fall behind or be bored.

(Disclaimer: In my weird mind, I considered some fellow students as *accelerated*. The *accelerated* students just *applied* themselves at an earlier age. As an example, the *accelerated* person, who I considered to be my best friend in high school (you have not met him yet), told me during our junior year how many hours per night he studied. When he said this, I thought to myself, "I do not study that much all *week!*" This did not relate to *intelligence* but to *application!* For *nonaccelerated* ones like myself, we had other priorities like watching that new gadget called TV and Annette Funicello, or our *light bulb* had not yet lit that we *should* study, or we lacked *interest* in the subject material, or a combination of each! You will see when I had a desire, liked what I was studying, and applied myself, I matched or even exceed my fellow *accelerated* students. Unfortunately for me, these periods of *desire* and *application* were far and few between as a student! Please remember above all else, *I do not wish* to imply that if you were in my classes, you were *unintelligent!* That is definitely *not* my intention!)

During lunch hours, I did meet and make new good friends: Richard Hruby, Bill Coss, Maurice Kennedy, and Tom Peterson pretty much became my core group at school. My homeroom and English teacher was Mrs. Kempf. She had a tremendous amount of patience and perseverance with us, especially with me! She always tried to get us to read to improve our reading skills, which for me were very lacking. At the end of seventh grade, she wrote a note saying, "Perhaps Richard could do some reading this summer to help him increase his rate of reading. It could be reading for enjoyment. Best wishes for an enjoyable summer. Maxine Kempf." I guess reading at three words a minute was not fast enough! Interestingly, both my fifth- and sixth-grade teachers had written similar notes, but the *call of the lake* seemed to always win out! Obviously, reading was not my best subject, along with spelling and writing! The good news was she held *no spelling bees!*

I became interested in books about World War II, which did help my reading. I know reading about war is probably not the best thing to engage in, but all I ever read outside of school was *Mad Magazine.* Their cartoon "Spy vs Spy" was my favorite cartoon because it had no words! The school offered a discount book club, and the ones that interested me were about airplanes, ships, and World War II. Mom and Dad gave me whatever money I needed to buy books since any reading I did was a 1,000 percent improvement. Some of the first ones I read were about General Chuck Yeager breaking the sound barrier, General Jimmy Doolittle's raid on Japan shortly after Pearl Harbor, and the sinking of the

German battleship *Bismarck*. Many times, I joined others like Christine Hurley, Gloria Stewart, Maurice Kennedy, Bill Coss, or Ralph Stoerp on a library pass so we could visit too; this cut into my reading time! By the end of eighth grade, I had a box of books, all of which I read in the next four years. But for me, unfortunately, reading, along with spelling and writing, would always be my nemesis as you will later learn.

Looking over my seventh-grade report card, it showed I got all As on the cornet. I find this very hard to believe since it stayed nice and cozy in its case and was never exposed to my hot air at home! I had Mr. Porterfield for math, who was willing to kid around with us during class. I had Mr. Bird (gym) and Mr. Kolze (shop). Both had Rog when he was in eighth grade, and they always asked about him, which I thought was neat. I especially enjoyed the mechanical drawing part of Mr. Kolze's class.

Our social studies/history class focused on the history of Illinois. One of the biggest projects ever conceived by our school's history department culminated at the school's parent night. Teachers and students covered the entire gymnasium floor with a map of Illinois; however, it was to come alive. "How?" We had to make items having to do with our state's history and place them at the appropriate spot on the map.

Tom Peterson and I signed up to make a fort for an Indian battle at Starved Rock. This was a disaster! Every time we got together, we went off and played. The day before it was due, we had accomplished nothing, so when I got home from school, I painted a two-foot square sheet of plywood green. Next, I lined up strings of toothpicks side by side until I had rows of various lengths. I glued thin pieces of balsam wood to the center of the toothpicks and mounted them onto the plywood board. About 10 p.m., I had a fort that even had block houses in its four corners. When I turned it in, the teacher thought it was great, and Tom and I got a B+ for it. Tom was very happy at how well it turned out and with his B+!

Ninth period was an activity class which was unique. We had a wide variety to choose from, but Tom Peterson and I joined an automobile shop class because we thought it would be interesting to see what made a car run. Mr. Bob Seaver was our instructor and taught us the basics of how an internal combustion engine worked. Through Mr. Seaver's efforts, I learned things about cars, and he and I had several laughs about this class years later.

We still had our twelve-inch TV, and Dad put up a high antenna with a rotor on our roof. Sunday night was saved for *The Ed Sullivan Show*. It was unique because he brought acts from all over the world, and each show was different. Rog told us about a new guitar-playing singer some of his friends saw and he was going to be on his show. That September night, a guy named Elvis Presley, who sported a duck-tail haircut, sang two songs. When he finished, none of us were impressed, but the girls in the studio were sure screaming a lot! Our bet was he would never make it *big*!

Dad still listened to Purdue football games. This year promised to be a good one since they had an experienced senior quarterback in Len Dawson. He was one of the best Big Ten passers his first two years, and there was no reason to expect anything different this year. Mom called him Purdue's "Golden Boy." Dad thought this year was a good year to take Rog and me to a Purdue football game. They were playing at Northwestern in Evanston, so it would be a short trip. The game itself was a disappointment because two weeks before, Dawson separated his throwing shoulder, and he only played the last two minutes, so we lost.

The most notable thing I saw was a locomotive the Purdue students operated. I asked Dad about it, and he said it was the mascot of Purdue, the Boilermaker Special. I asked him how they got to the stadium, and he said students drove it. He told me there was a group of men at Purdue called Reamers who were responsible for it. I looked again, but closer this time. Nowhere could I see any tracks, so my weird mind was wondering how it got here without tracks. This bothered me, but I never pursued it further.

Rog had wrestling in gym class. We went to our lower level where we had a rug, and he explained the rules and showed me general moves. After a few *lessons*, we wrestled. I was one-hundred pounds and was five-feet, four-inches tall while Rog weighed 150 pounds and was five-feet, ten-inches tall, so it was a major mismatch! All I can remember about our match was spending my time counting tiles on the basement ceiling! This was just like the old days at Brookfield when we used to fight; I always lost, except for that one time in the snow! Would this ever be reversed!?

Dad loved to go for walks, especially if it was cold out. We took Pronto and walked all around the Crystal Lake Country Club but we were careful not to go on the greens or tees. Along our walk, Dad purposely dropped an old glove of his. When we were about to exit the course, Dad called Pronto, let him smell his hand and sent him galloping off looking for his glove. He absolutely loved this as he flew through the snow while sniffing. He backtracked our trail, found the glove and came running back to us at a blistering pace. Dad never lost a glove, and Pronto was in seventh heaven looking for it, especially in the snow.

Chapter 11
Summer 1957

S INCE WE WENT TO FLORIDA THE YEAR BEFORE,
we returned to Pine Ridge. After twenty-plus years of
Alexanders' and Hunzikers' visits here, this would be the last
one! The cabin next to ours was empty, so we used their boat too.
Mom and Dad used our aluminum boat, but Rog and I now had
our own boats, and we could use them while they fished. We
rowed all over the northern end of Big Siss, honed our rowing
skills by racing, conducted water fights, and fished! Mom struck
gold; she caught a *keeper* musky. Dad was frustrated because he
could not hook one. We experienced an unusual situation; the
walleyes were biting from 9:00 to 9:15 every evening, so we took
our boats out about 100 yards and cast towards shore. If we cast
before 9:00 or after 9:15 p.m., we were wasting our time; we got
zero strikes. However, during that time, we had a strike on nearly
every cast! Catching a dozen walleyes during those fifteen minutes was common! What a phenomenon!

On Friday nights, they gave out prizes to those who caught
the largest fish of each species. The Hunzikers cleaned up: Mom
won for her musky, Rog won for bass, and I won for crappies.
Dad was not there because he was fishing for a musky, but just
before the end of the meeting, he came through the door with
a huge fish, a walleye; he ended up getting the prize for the
largest walleye. The prizes were nothing great; mine was a dozen
minnows. Actually, my prize was useless since we were leaving

first thing in the morning to drive home. It was great to have the Hunzikers go out on top for our last-ever family visit to Pine Ridge!

Since Dad had no more vacation and Mr. Albertz knew Rog and I liked to fish, he asked Dad if he could take us fishing. He told Dad he just had his brakes relined on his car, and he was ready to catch fish. As it turned out, our guardian angel must have whispered in his ear to redo the brakes! He picked Escanaba Lake about twenty miles southeast of Boulder Junction, Wisconsin, and we used our car-top carrier to take our aluminum boat. While driving through rolling hills on a two-lane road, we got behind a pickup truck towing a trailer holding a black box about a four-foot cube. We were going down a hill and gaining a little speed when suddenly the box came off the trailer! Mr. Albertz hit his brakes hard and, fortunately for us, the box rolled the same direction we were going. When we and the box came to a halt, we were about twenty feet from it and could now see it was a smokehouse made of three-quarter-inch steel plate! We *almost* hit a moving smokehouse! Our guardian angel came through yet again!

We made it safely, and he showed us how to set up his ten-foot square tent as well as other camping equipment. The campground was right on the lake, and we did reasonably well fishing, but we had two days of rain, which brought out the mosquitoes! We put our boat in another lake, Lost Canoe Lake. Mr. Albertz decided we were at the *perfect place* so we dropped anchor. I used my old fly rod without a bobber because the tip would go down if I had a strike. I started catching perch and blue gills; lots of them! They asked me to raise my rod so they could see exactly how deep I was and put their rod tips right next to mine, but did not catch much! That day I was the *champ*! I caught 102 fish, the most I ever caught in one day, before or since! They did catch a lot too by *inventing* their own bait. They used a pike lure and added a worm to it. These made a tasty morsel for the fish and worked. Even with the rain and the smokehouse, it was a successful fishing trip!

Rog wanted his own pets. First, he bought tropical fish, but after a year of hearing gurgling air bubbles, his eyes eventually rested on a green parakeet, Rocky. Mom said she was having problems keeping track of Roger, Ricky, and Rocky! Initially, Rog kept him in his bedroom and bought a record which repeated the same word over and over to get Rocky to repeat it. His first month, he was a nonspeaking, nonchirping, defective bird! We even moved him to the living room behind Dad's reclining chair, so he had more interaction with us.

One day we heard a horribly loud screech and ran to see what was wrong; he was just sitting on his perch in the cage as usual, but now he was talking, not human *words*, but bird *words!* Once he started chirping, we could not shut him up! During our evening TV viewing, we had to shroud his cage with its overnight cover to shut him up so we could hear the TV! One day when Mom was home alone, she heard a loud squawk and found Rocky lying motionless on the bottom of the cage, dead! Rocky was a full-fledged member of our family for almost five years. The house was quieter when he departed!

Dad took us to a waterskiing show at Navy Pier in Chicago; it was Tommy Bartlett's Water Ski Show. The star was the ski-boat driver because they mentioned his name 12,586 times that day, "Watch as Scotty Scott so carefully and precisely adjusts the dual throttles of his powerful twin Mercury motors as Scotty Scott sets the boat in its perfect attitude before this next jump by ..." A lot of energy was put forth by the performers, even Scotty Scott!

The other great thing about it was, it got Dad thinking again about getting a *real* boat, one we could ski behind. He also took us again to Chicago's Boat Show where the three of us *thought big*. The good news was Dad *took the bait* and was now *hooked*. If he was reeled in, a power boat was certainly in our future!

Chapter 12

Junior High, Eighth grade

BEING EIGHTH GRADERS, WE WERE *THE TOP DOGS*! My homeroom/science teacher was Mr. Hal Wajrowski. At the end of summer, a new family moved into the Woodman's home near the Gate 13 beach. They had a son my age, and he was in my homeroom; his name was Ross Annable. It was obvious he must have been *accelerated* since I had no classes with him except for homeroom. We started to see each other at the bus stop and got to know each other better, like lifelong friends!

In eighth grade, Rog did not have the best relationship with his English teacher, so guess who I got, the same guy—Mr. Smale. In seventh grade I had him for study hall, and I tried to be friendly with him. One day I created a maze, which only had one pathway from the outer edge to the center. I entitled it, "*Witch* side was up?" and showed it to him as I was leaving; he just smiled and said, "It was nice." I showed it to Mom; she commented, "You used the wrong *which!* Did you show this to anyone else?" I said, "No," and felt very embarrassed! Now Mr. Smale knew how bright, or not, the second Hunziker was going to be! *Ugh!* It was in Mr. Smale's class when Rog wrote his autobiography, *Climbing Through the Years*, and this year I wrote mine, *Brother Rick*. This book has been a good source for people and events when writing *Heartland Raising*. When writing *Brother Rick*, I wrote a draft chapter, Mom proofread it, marked it up, and then I copied it onto the pages in my book. Unfortunately, many times I copied things wrong and misspelled sssooo many words. It was not Mom's fault; it was *all* mine!

Mr. Roy Willis was my history teacher. I liked his class, and he made American History interesting. We had to memorize the entire Preamble of the US Constitution and all four verses of "The Star Spangled Banner." The words had to be right, spelled correctly, and the punctuation had to be accurate. The latter two items were not simple for me!

I was still *playing* my cornet, and we also had regular math, music, art, industrial arts, health, and physical education. This rounded out my curriculum except for our ninth period activity class. This year I picked chess club. I played a reasonable amount of chess with Dad and Rog, but I usually got *my clock cleaned*! I was paired with a seventh grader, so I thought this would be a snap—*wrong*! The first game he beat me in four moves; it is called *Fools Mate!* The next game he beat me in eight moves! I could not wait for this hour to be over! We continued to play over the year, and I improved, but I never beat him! In March, I came down with the measles, and Rog asked if I wanted to play chess. We set the board up on the living room floor, and I pulled the old *Fool's Mate* on Rog and beat him in four moves! Dad howled; he thought that was cool. The next game I beat Rog in six moves, and Dad howled again! Little bro had improved, and it was again one of my very few victories over my older brother!

This year I thought I would try football again! When the meeting of seventh and eighth graders started, we were divided by weight; 105 pounds was the split! Mr. Seaver and Mr. Johnson were the light-weight coaches. After a short talk, we tried on equipment. The next day we turned in our permission slips and had physicals. One of my coaches suggested I play tackle since I was one of the biggest kids on the team. Bill Coss, who was shorter than me, became a guard, and we initially partnered for practice. The difference was, Bill was good, and I was not! Out of five tackles, guess who was the fifth? Yep, yours truly! Blocking and tackling were not my thing, so it was an easy decision for the coaches.

In September Aunt Peggy and Jim Abbott were getting married, and since Mom was Peggy's matron of honor, we had to be in Glen Ellen for the Friday night's rehearsal. I told the coaches I would miss a Friday night's practice and why. Some of the other players started to kid me and ask, "Why, are you the flower girl?" After turning forty-eight shades of red, practice continued, and I was excused Friday night. Jim Kempf, a seventh grader, was our quarterback, Paul Koch was our fullback, and the Fanter twins played halfback and receiver. We played four games; our first was a home game against Woodstock, and we got to play on the high school's football field! Mom showed up and helped cheer the team and me onto victory. I was involved in a dozen plays, which was cool.

The second game was an away game at Belvedere, which we won and I played about the same amount of time. Dundee was next, but their offense used a single-wing formation instead of a T-formation like all other teams. Mr. Johnson wanted to take advantage of the fact the center had to hike the ball two yards to the quarterback. He put me over the center and wanted me to crash into him as soon as he hiked, hoping after a while he would start making bad hikes. For five days I practiced this. On game day, I was sidelined, and I never did play over center. I was never told why, but I probably could guess. For once I thought I might make a real contribution to the team, but all I played was a few downs at defensive tackle, which was not what I wanted to do. We lost!

Our last game was at Sycamore, and we were behind when our coaches called time out with only time for one play! They diagrammed a play where Jim pitched the ball to Bill, Paul blocked to protect him while Bob ran down the field, and Bill was to pass it to Bob. Believe it or not, it worked just like it was diagrammed and went for a touchdown; we won! The Fanters were swarmed by all. It was the most exciting game I *almost* participated in. Yep, I never got in the game because it was too close to take a chance on me playing at tackle. My football career, other than sandlot football and playing catch in the backyard with Rog and Dad, was over!

Scouts changed as school started. Gene was replaced by a robust guy, Mike Arakelyan, who always had a smile. He loved to kid around and always wanted us to call him Mike, not Mr. Arakelyan. His assistant was Mr. Hal Price, a tall skinny guy, and I always called him Mr. Price. Our new leaders brought a lot of "new blood" from their area—about twenty new kids. Right from the start we could tell things were going to be different because they had a plan and were organized; something we desperately needed! There were only a few of us left in Troop 165 at this time: Tom Peterson, Jim Eby, Len Zitnik, a couple of others, and me. I had been in the troop for over a year and a half and was still a Tenderfoot! Mike said he wanted me to finish all the requirements for Second Class because in a month, we were going to have parents' night. *Wow!* No one ever pressed me to do much or set goals before!

When parents' night arrived, I made Second Class and was also made a Patrol Leader. Of course, since I semi-played a cornet, I was still the troop's official bugler. Once I obtained Second Class, I was able to also start working on merit badges, which I need for Star, Life, and Eagle Scout. By the time eighth grade ended, I made First Class and was earning merit badges. I even got a merit badge for bookbinding. After all, I had to write *Brother Rick* in a home-made book for Mr. Smale's class. Luckily, Mike did not have to read it, but just had to make sure the bookbinding was OK. *Whew!*

On October 4, the Union of Soviet Socialist Republics (USSR) successfully launched man's first satellite into orbit around Earth and the world changed! Newspapers and TV news showed photos, movies, and drawings of Sputnik I and how it was orbiting the world. I cut out many stories and still have them. The US had been trying, but our rockets exploded on the launch pad or just went awry. Finally, in January 1958, the US succeeded in launching our first satellite, Explorer I. It was a fascinating time, and it captured my interest!

One day in November, Pronto was not feeling well. He was always peppy, but he laid by the back door and wanted to go out. When I opened the door, he did not bolt out, but slowly walked through it. He appeared to have a stomachache and tried to heave. Dad took him to the vet, and he told us the vet was going keep him overnight to do tests. The next morning as I was putting on my jacket, the phone rang. I could hear Mom's side of the call, and it sounded strange. When she hung up, she was crying. I asked what was wrong and all she said was, "It was the vet, and he didn't think Pronto would live!" I could not believe my ears!

She handed me my lunch and ushered me out the door. All I could think of as I walked to the bus stop was Mom saying, "he didn't think Pronto would live!" It was the same way in each of my classes, "he didn't think Pronto would live!" When I got off the bus, I ran home and burst through the back door, looking for Mom. When I saw her red eyes, I knew the answer before I even asked the question. She said, "The vet called back about 8:30 and told me there was nothing he could do, and he had just passed away!" Oh my! I lost my four-legged friend! I completely broke down bawling and went to my room! I finally got up, went through all my photos and scotch taped all my pictures of Pronto to my wall.

When Dad got home, his eyes were red also. It was the quietest dinner our family ever had. All four of us were deeply affected by this; it was probably a week before any of us laughed again. They did an autopsy; he died of rat poison. There were German Shepherds that ran loose, and someone probably threw food into our yard laced with poison, thinking he was one of them. We had Pronto five-plus years, and Mom said she could not go through this ever again, so we never had another dog. Rest in peace, Pronto! You were *really* loved and missed!

I mentioned earlier, our holidays were much different. When eating breakfast, opening presents, cleaning up, and traveling to either Mom's or Dad's folks, Christmas morning and day were hectic. This year they decided we would start a new tradition; after dinner on Christmas Eve, we would open our presents and go to the candlelight service at the Congregational Church. This Christmas Eve, Mom cooked a great meal. We ate and all helped clean up the kitchen. The Christmas tree was glowing, but as we sat down to open our presents, the doorbell rang. Ginny, the Battles' oldest daughter, was there and crying. She told us Bruno got out, was running when one of his back legs went into a gopher hole, and he probably broke it.

Dad put on his coat, took our station wagon keys, and said he would be back as soon as possible. It was after 10:30 p.m. before he got home and told us Bruno did break his leg. He and Mr. Battles slid him onto a blanket and lifted him into the back of our station wagon. As they started to lift, Bruno grabbed Dad's hand with his mouth and relatively gently bit on him, like telling Dad he was hurt, but he understood Dad was trying to help him. They drove to a veterinarian who set the leg, and when they knew Bruno would be all right, they came home. What a way to start our new tradition! We did open our presents but did not make it to the candlelight service and went to bed about midnight. The good news was: we did not have to get up early in the morning, Bruno did recover and, in the future, we attended the Christmas Eve candlelight services!

I played around with crystal radios in the past, but I saw an ad in a magazine for a three-tube shortwave/AM radio kit. I never built a real radio before, and this one was priced right—cheap! About ten days later, I received my kit and started laying out the parts. Dad told me to take my time and "double and triple check all things" before I mounted and soldered them. With only three tubes, it was not extremely complex, so there were not a billion parts, and it was manageable. After a few nights, I ran out of parts and was done. I checked each resistor, capacitor, and connection to make sure it was all wired properly. Then came the moment to see if I could listen to music. I made sure it was turned off before I plugged it in. So far *nothing* happened! Good! I held my breath as I turned it on. I waited for the tubes to heat up, but after a minute, I saw no red glow in any of them. Hmmm, nothing! Not even a hum. I turned it off and called Dad. We tried it again, and nothing happened. We turned it upside down and went through the wiring again; he agreed I had built it properly. He said he had to go to Milwaukee the next week, and he had a friend who worked on radios and TVs. When he got home, he handed me the radio and said to try it. I took it to my room, plugged it in, turned it on, and in about ten seconds, I was listening to music. I needed to know why, so I asked. Dad said, "My friend told me to tell you to learn how to solder!" It *was* wired right, but all my solder joints were not electrically bonded together! All Dad's friend did was re-solder each connection! I turned about three shades of red from embarrassment, but at least I knew I built it properly!

In early spring, our junior high band put on a concert. Mr. Trumpke had a final dress rehearsal in the school's auditorium. One of the songs had a very cool ending: three very sharp short notes. Well, guess what, during this final dress rehearsal yours truly added a *fourth* short note! Mr. Trumpke went wild! He did a mock applause and repeated, "Bravo, Bravo, Bravo!" It was very obvious who did it, the kid with the bright red face! He made us play the ending three more times and always looked at me to see how many blasts I gave. Since I was so embarrassed, I only did one or two blasts and ended short just to be safe!

About this same time, Mom had health issues, and she was admitted to the Elgin Hospital under Dr. Abromitis's care. She had high blood pressure and other problems which they did not share with us. This worried me; after all, we lost Pronto only about three to four months before! I was scared! While she was in the hospital, Dad drove to Elgin in the morning, visited her, took the train to Chicago, worked, took the train back to Elgin in the evening, visited Mom again, and drove home. He left before 5:30 a.m. and got home about 10 p.m. and told us what was happening. On the weekend she was there, all three of us got to visit her. This routine was definitely wearing Dad down.

Unfortunately, this band concert was near the end of Mom's stay in the hospital. Dad decided to forego his evening visit with her to attend the concert. While I was happy about this, I knew he did not get to see her that night, which bothered me! The concert went well, and that song ended with *only* three staccato blasts, so I was off Mr. Trumpke's bad list! Several days later, Mom came home a little better; however, she continued to not feel well for a long time.

In the spring all eighth graders took a battery of tests to determine placement in high school. They tested for English, math, reading, science, and general social studies. Rog taught me a little basic algebra like 3X=15, solve for X! After I *finally* comprehended that X was an unknown (whatever that was), the rest seemed simple. One Saturday, all eighth graders went to the high school and took the tests; it was a long day! In math they had algebra questions; however, if it were not for Rog, I would have left them blank. The science and social studies stuff were OK, but reading and English, well—you can probably guess how easy (*not*) that was for me! A month later, we had an evening assembly with our parents. Most of my score were similar to others, but not in math; I thought I did really bad and became upset! A guidance counselor went through the general results and how to determine what classes we should take. First, it was mandatory everyone took gym and science/health. Next, my scores indicated I should be placed a general-level English class. When they came to math, my heart was racing. My scores indicated I should take algebra! I had actually killed the math portion and got a very high score; that made me smile! I also signed up for band since I was still playing (???) the cornet. Finally, I had to choose either a government/history/geography class, a foreign language class or industrial arts. As if I did not exist, Mom and Dad discussed in front of me what I should take. No thought was given to the first option; they only considered the foreign language or industrial arts options. They felt since I was so bad in English, I probably could not handle a real foreign language. Dad thought extra training with hand and power tools could be handy, so they signed me up for industrial arts. I was now set for the semi-big times at CLCHS!

In late spring, the first major change in our neighborhood took place. The lot behind our house was sold and an elderly couple, Mr. and Mrs. Ralph Jackson, built a small ranch house on it. This drastically changed our family, and in some cases, our neighborhood sports programs because many of our friends used it too. That was the bad news; the good news was, Rog and I got paid a lot more to mow the Jackson's grass!

Chapter 13

Summer 1958

THIS PAST SPRING THE *BOAT BUG* FINALLY LANDED Dad! He bought a slightly used sixteen-foot Molded Fiberglass (MFG) runabout with a 35 hp Johnson outboard engine. This boat was not a speed demon, but it did about 20 mph. He also bought a pair of water skis! Yes! Before I could learn to ski, I had to learn how to operate the boat. He told me this boat coasted much more than the old aluminum boat. The first time I operated it, I was in it alone (sound familiar?) and was bringing it to the boat pier at Gate 13. Dad stood on the end of the pier and kept warning me to slow down. I finally reduced the throttle to idle and put the engine in neutral; *however*, the boat kept progressing toward the pier at a rapid pace! I turned the wheel but my progress was still too fast, and I was going to ram the pier. As it approached and as soon as Dad touched it, he completely threw his whole body against it to keep it from crashing. It was a close call, and he let me know he was not happy about my operating skills, but I learned my lesson!

My initial skiing problem came in the fact I still did not like speed, but the good news was water was softer than snow-covered ground; thus, going 20 mph became a non-issue. Like most of the skiers on the lake, we wanted to ski on only one ski. As a result, it was not long before we graduated to dropping a ski after we got up and learned to balance ourselves. The best way was to only use one ski the whole time, so the next challenge was to learn how to *start* and *get up* on one ski. Starting took good balancing skills until the boat accelerated to where the ski supported us. Because of weight, Dad had a longer time to start. He finally found a solution; he bought a plastic curved ski tip, mounted it on the front of a wider board, added a deep fin and foot holders for his own slalom ski; we called it "Dad's surfboard!"

Sometimes Rog drove Dad, and other times I did. Dad quickly became comfortable with either of us handling the boat. He had two rules: (1) We always had to have two people in the boat when skiing, one driving and one watching the skier; and (2) The skiers always had to wear a life belt. We did these before they became national rules. By mid-summer, Rog and I were sharing the boat with many of our friends and using it daily, sometimes multiple times per day!

Dad did not want us charging our friends for the gas because as he said, "If you cannot buy your gas, then you cannot afford the boat." He even set up a charge account with a gas stations so we could charge it, and he paid the bill monthly. After all, the price of gas was about \$0.24[9], plus a quart of oil/tank, so how much could we use? Wwweeelll, one month he found out! Would you believe Rog and I charged almost \$100? That is about 300 gallons of gas plus oil! When he got that bill, he was not happy, and he told us to *ration* our time with the boat. We reduced the number of days we used it *and* stopped doing multiple fills per day, but you would not believe how much our waterskiing skills improved that summer!

Dad wanted to do a western vacation, and with Rog graduating from high school the next spring, we went to Colorado! He put one restriction on us; we were limited to one shoebox each for rocks, so we asked him for two of *his* shoeboxes! We angled up through southwestern Wisconsin into southern Minnesota. Since we did not have MP3s, DVD players, or iPods/iPads, we were *stuck* with listening to our car's AM radio and playing gin rummy. Road signs dotted the landscape; one set was the old Burma Shave sequence with a saying like: "Slow down, pa... Sakes alive... Ma missed signs... Four... and Five... Burma Shave!" Another we noticed which started in Minnesota were ads for *Wall Drug Store* which had souvenirs, postcards, boots, ice cream cones, T-shirts, and so on.

We initially headed for Rapid City and arrived the second day at the Badlands before lunch. The landscape grabbed us with its *deep ruts* dug in mounds of earth and all kinds of earth colors. After viewing this unique landscape, we came to Wall, South Dakota, but the western sky was pure black. The signs were accurate about what they offered; they even had hitching posts in case we showed up on a horse. We got a milkshake to go and hustled back to the highway. The sky let loose for a short time, and we continued to Rapid City. They had a new dinosaur park which had multiple full-sized dinosaurs, but they were still concrete gray; they had not been painted yet.

Our goal was to stay near Mount Rushmore. Because we did not have smart phones yet, we had to take potluck for motels. Dad rented a unit from a little *Mom and Pop* motel; it looked like an old railroad boxcar! After dinner I found a small cave; it was five feet high and wide and went about ten feet into a hillside, and I searched for gold. I was chopping away with my trusty pickaxe when Dad and Rog arrived. My enthusiasm outweighed my intelligence, imagine that! Dad saw me chopping on a rock and said, "Rick, it would be better to not chop on something directly above your head, so it doesn't fall on you!" Yep, I was hammering away at a rock on the ceiling! I switched to another location, chipped away, and did pick up a few rocks, which started my western rock collection!

The next morning, we visited Mount Rushmore. *Wow!* How neat was this! They had telescopes, so I examined the presidents' faces. What surprised me was they were not smooth; they had tiny groves in them. Somewhere in the back of my weird mind, I thought wind and rain had carved them out, not jackhammers and dynamite! Another Rick falsehood exposed! At Custer State Park, we were immediately greeted by herds of buffalo; some were beside the road and even came to the car, but we never encouraged them because they were *huge*! It was fabulous to see so many this close! Nearby was small Legion Lake that was picturesque because of its sandstone formations, and Rog caught a nice rainbow trout!

We cut through eastern Wyoming and entered Colorado and had our first look at the Rocky Mountains! They did not look like the Smoky Mountains; these were *real* mountains, and they had snow on them! *Wow*! At Estes Park, we stayed in a cabin on the Big Thompson River, which roared in our ears all night, but what a wonderful way to fall asleep! Rog and Dad fished the river, but it was too swift for me, so I just did rock hunting. In one store they even had pyrite, *fool's gold*, so I bought a small piece, which I still have. The movie *Around the World in 80 Days* was showing, and we thoroughly enjoyed it; the next morning everyone was humming or whistling the main theme to it.

Leaving, we took the highest road in the United States, the road through the Rocky Mountain National Park. It was curvy, which did not delight Mom, especially when Dad was viewing the scenery instead of only focusing on the road as we neared the edge of 1,000-foot cliffs! We saw numerous spectacular mountain peaks, waterfalls, and small rivers or creeks. Dad stopped often at overlooks and at piles of snow, where we made and threw snow-balls at each other! What a drive! We stayed two-nights in Granby. The first morning Dad and Rog went fishing. When they returned, Dad treated us an afternoon of horseback riding!

I never rode a horse before, so once I got up on mine and looked around, something bothered me; I was a long way off the ground! After basic instruction on how to handle and guide the horse, like it was going to obey me anyway, we set off. Dad started us by just walking and then increased the pace to a slow trot. The bouncing during the trotting bothered me since I did not feel stable because my feet did not reach my stirrups; I just pretty much hung on! We entered and went through a beautiful valley before going back to the ranch. All was well, except I had a problem; my butt was sore! I complained at dinner, but everyone ignored me. At the motel, I took my pants down and sure enough, I had a big blister on my seat! So, the first time I ever went horseback riding,

I ended up with a blister on my butt! Not much of a cowboy! Everyone laughed, except me! *Ugh!*

The next day we headed for Leadville, an old cowboy town, and toured a mine. At Buckskin Joe, we watched a gunfight show and then went to the Royal Gorge. The colors of the gorge's walls were awesome reds, oranges, purples, and grays! We walked the bridge over the gorge and could see the Arkansas River below through the spaces between the boards and, when the wind blew, it swayed! *Terrifying!* We took an incline, which hugged the side of the canyon, to the river and looked back up at the *tiny bridge* that was around 1,200 feet above us. What a sight! The next morning, we went through Colorado Springs as we started toward home. I looked out the back window and saw the 14,000-plus-foot Pike's Peak fade in the background as we left the Rockies. *Wow!*

The trip home had its own adventures. The fun started in eastern Colorado, which was flat and unimpressive, unless you are a wheat farmer! Rog and I were bored and started playing gin rummy; however, this time we argued about each other's cheating—can you imagine that!? When we stopped for lunch, we took the cards into the restaurant and kept at it! Dad finally had all he could stand, grabbed the deck, all fifty-two of them, and tore it in half! Did you get that!? The *giant* tore an entire deck of cards in half at one time! We were impressed! After lunch, Rog and I continued to play cards, but with only half cards *and* not arguing!

Dad took the straightest shot home, which meant going across Kansas. These two-lane roads were very straight except when they had to curve around a farm! We were making good time, doing about 65 mph, when we heard a small explosion, and the car began to shake. Dad fought the wheel as he let the car coast to a stop. The right front tire blew, so Dad had to change the tire. Unfortunately for him, everything had to be taken out of the car to get to the spare! Dad installed the spare, we reloaded the car, and took off. A simple job, right? Oh, did I not mention the grasshoppers!? Yep, when we got out of the car, we were inundated with grasshoppers, much like we were with mosquitoes on Alligator Alley! They were on us, on the stuff we pulled out of the car, in the car—basically everywhere! On the road again, we threw them out the window when we caught them. We had no other problems as we went through Iowa and western Illinois, except I did not get any lemon meringue pie this trip!

To make Star in Boy Scouts, I had to have five merit badges, but one had to be in citizenship, which I had, and another in aquatics. Each summer Camp Lowden held an aquatics school, and I went, but I was the only one from my troop, and I worked on three merit badges: (1) Swimming because I could already do all the required strokes; (2) Rowing because I had done lots of rowing over the years; and (3) Lifesaving because I was a reasonably strong swimmer. They worked us to death that week! Rowing was on the Rock River, and twice a day we waded to an island where the boats were. I wore tennis shoes in the water, so I did not cut my feet on glass being pushed by the current; however, this current also caused sand and gravel to enter my shoes, so when I walked the half mile back to the pool area, my feet and toes became *mincemeat!*

The rowing itself was easy; however, lifesaving was a different matter. Our instructors were all men over six feet tall and weighing 200 pounds! I was about five-foot, three-inches tall and weighed 110 pounds; *under matched!* They taught us how to break strangleholds a victim might get on us if they panicked, how to swim victims in, how to carry a person once in shallow water, and so forth. The last day was very hectic; we had to save the four instructors three different ways, twelve saves, to pass, then break all potential strangleholds! I was exhausted, but I did survive and made all of my saves, breaks, and carries. That Saturday with my three merit badges, a Red Cross Junior Life Saving Certificate, and almost skinless feet and toes, I was *very* happy to see Mom and Dad when they picked me up!

Freshmen band kids got an early taste of high school. Our band participated in two summer events: a parade at Riverview Amusement Park in Chicago and an hour-long concert at Veterans' Acres. Since the freshman never marched while playing and all had to learn new music, our band director, Mr. Clay Harvey, started practices in early August. We marched through the streets near the high school two nights each week while playing marches or our school song. Two other nights we practiced new music in the band room. I did not like marches because I had trouble quickly translating a note from sheet music into valves 1&2, 1&3, and so on. Slow music I could semi-play, well, not too great! The day finally came when we went to Riverview; after the evening parade, we headed for the roller coasters! *Yippy!*

Veterans' Acres is a Crystal Lake park that had a small pond surrounded by four or five wooded hills. The concert allowed band parents and others to enjoy an evening of music. This year besides a number of marches and the school song, we also played Ferdi Grote's "Grand Canyon Suite." There were about 200 people in attendance, and it went well.

This year, a third event was added; we went to Soldier's Field in Chicago and played in the pre-game show of the College All Star Football Game against the defending National Football League Champion Detroit Lions. This was quite a treat since our family always watched the game, but to see it live with nearly 50,000 people was amazing. As we marched onto the field and the crowd cheered, the hair, or should I say fuzz, on the back of my neck and arms just stood up on end! There were 100 bands on the field, but it felt like ours was the only one! It was too bad I really could not play any of the music! *Oh well.* We had great seats near the top of the stadium in the end zone! Hey, most never even got to this game, and it was one of the few times the College All Stars won!

Chapter 14

High School, Freshman Year

I WAS NOW A STUDENT AT CLCHS! I COULD NOT believe I was finally here; it seemed like a major step! I met kids from Algonquin, Lake in the Woods, Cary, Fox River Grove, and Trout Valley. We had 1,200 students and were called "Tigers." The class of 1962 started with 360 kids. Classes started at 7:35 a.m. and went until 3:05 p.m., having eight periods. Fourth and fifth periods were longer because they were divided in half and made up our four lunch times. We had six, six-week grading periods. As freshman we were given grade books, which lasted our entire time here; they even had pages for the fifth year! Hmmm, I wonder if that was meant for me?

My first course was Industrial Arts. This was broken into four sections: metals, mechanical drawing, wood shop, and electricity. Mr. Leon Richards taught the metals and electricity, and Mr. Edward Chinn taught the other two. My first project was a nail set. Mr. Richards showed me how to mount it onto a lathe and shape it. I was only to take 0.001 inch off on each pass, but that seemed too slow, so I upped it to 0.01 inch. As the first cut started, there was a loud crack, and the lathe died! He asked what happened; I just shrugged my shoulders! I then took my time.

I was switched to the acetylene torch. He showed me how to light it, add oxygen to get the very hot blue flame, and welded two two-inch square pieces of steel together. He handed me the torch and watched me weld a set of steel pieces; he thought I did a pretty good job. The next several weeks I tried to get the right kind of flame, but never managed it. He helped me again get the proper flame and welded two pieces together. One time I was using too long of a flame, it ricocheted off the metal and started a brush's wood handle on fire! I could not see this through the shield and felt a tap on my shoulder. Mr. Richards suggested I might want to put out my *brush* fire! After four weeks with the torch, he asked me to turn in samples of my work. All I had were the two he did for me and my initial try while he watched, so I turned these in. He thought I did an excellent job on them; I guess he liked his *own* work!

I never had problems drawing or interpreting mechanical drawings; my problem went back to my early days of—penmanship! I could not write legibly; therefore, even though my drawings were accurate and accomplished correctly, my written notes looked horrible! With a week to go in this section, I had done all the drawings Mr. Chinn had, so he gave me a 3-D drawing of a Boeing 707 aircraft and asked me to translate it into the three-view mechanical drawing format. While this was a challenge, it showed me how useful this skill could be.

Wood working permitted me to use several new tools to me. One of them was a wood lathe, which allowed me to sculpt a bowl. I learned from metals and took it slowly! I gave my bowl to Mom, and she had it for years, but it was dropped, or maybe was thrown, and broke into pieces. During electricity, Mr. Richards had us do many small experiments, and we learned basic electricity fundamentals like measuring voltage, amperage, or resistance, how to calculate the impedance, and so on. This was fun for me because of my interest in radio building, and I broke or burned *nothing* in class!

In General Science, Mr. Howard Harris lectured and did simple, fundamental experiments. Our paths crossed several more times before I left CLCHS. This course was for only one semester, and the second semester I had Health with Mr. Russell Larsen.

Next, I had my favorite subject (*not!*), English I. Miss Stephanie Sanders was my teacher, which was a problem. My weird little brain had problems converting her thick German accent into plain

English; it was as if I was taking German to learn English! Not a good situation! During her class, I realized if I memorized the twenty-word spelling list each week and got a 100 on it, this could help me raise my grade, like from a D to a C! I memorized the spelling lists; however, if I used any of them the next week, they were likely misspelled!

Mom could not understand why I read so slowly. She said, "Can't you look at a phrase and comprehend it?" I said, "No, I read one word at a time. I read, 'See... Spot. See... Spot... run... and... play.' I do not read, 'SeeSpot. SeeSpotrunandplay.'" It is the way my weird brain is wired! Due to Miss Sanders' urging, I was signed up for a *speed reading* course the second semester. My baseline said I read between 250–300 words per minute with 50–60 percent comprehension.

My book went underneath a device which had a shield that slowly progressed downward covering the page. Its rate of progression could be increased to force me to read faster. They also used a projector which flashed phrases on a screen. They started with two- and three-word phrases and slowly increased the length to eight- or ten-words phrases *and* shortened the time each was shown. After a semester of these exercises, I was retested. I now read between 200—250 words per minute with comprehension between 40—50 percent; the speed-reading course did not help me, but reduced what little reading capabilities I had! *Ugh!*

My last core class was Algebra. Rog said I was lucky to get Mr. Howard Tingleff because he was the best math teacher, and I would learn a lot. I learned about his mannerisms quickly. He might assign twenty problems, and the next day he picked twenty students to put their work on the board. Everyone did their homework as best they could because there was a good chance, we had to show our work on the board. If he saw something he did not like, he made a sucking, hissing sound through his teeth and said, "My boy, that's not right." To emphasize it was wrong, he took his big right hand, flattened it with all five fingers together and gently *speared* us in our side ribs or back. His words and *spear* were simultaneous. While not extremely painful, it did get your attention, and I learned to make sure I knew where he was always. I had problems with algebra and spent many nights at the kitchen table with Dad as we went over problems. Word problems were the worst; you know:

> "A train leaves Chicago at 8 a.m. and is traveling at 50 mph. Another train leaves Los Angeles at 10 a.m. and is traveling at 60 mph. The distance between Chicago and Los Angeles is 3,000 miles; when, where, and at what time will they pass each other?"

Dad always made me draw a picture depicting the two trains to understand the situation. Then he made me write down my conditions like: "Let X equal the distance the Chicago train traveled, and Y equal the distance the LA train traveled," and so forth. The first time I put my work on the board, Mr. Tingleff asked me where I came up with my methodology. I told him it was from my dad and he was a chemical engineer. He said, "OK," but presented it to the class the way he was teaching it so that there was no confusion. Outside of class, we snuck up behind each other, did that sucking, hissing sound, and said, "My boy, that's not right," while *spearing* our victim in the ribs with our extended fingers. Obviously, Mr. Tingleff made an impression on us!

All high school students had to take physical education (PE), or as we called it, "gym," all four years. We had first-class athletic facilities. I was told when our fieldhouse was built in 1950; it was the second largest one in the state! Each period had fifty percent of a class's boys, about ninety. Mr. Roy Nystrom was the one stuck with my half of the freshman boys. We lined up on numbers along the boundary of the basketball floor; these were alphabetically assigned for attendance. When the weather was acceptable, we spent our time outside playing soccer or doing track events. When the weather turned bad, we stayed inside and usually did gymnastics or tumbling.

My one optional class was band. We had a large band room, which had small practice rooms across the back. The good players were in the Concert Band; those like me were in the Cadet Band.

The Marching Band was made up of both, which gave us about 120 members. We did a show for all four home football games, and we practiced the music during our class periods. Jim and I were lucky since Carol Beber was a senior and drove us to and from our field practices. While I had trouble playing marches, I marched well!

During the winter, we practiced for a Cadet Band Concert for our parents. Occasionally, Mr. Clay spent his time in his office, and we were on our own. This usually entailed splitting up and using the small practice rooms. Whenever we got snow, we opened the windows in the practice rooms, grabbed snow, and packed it into snowballs. There were more than a few snowball fights in the band room, but Mr. Clay never caught us, or maybe he just did not care! In the spring, we practiced marches and marching again because on Memorial Day, we participated in parades at Cary, Fox River Grove, and Crystal Lake, and it was always hot!

Our lunch period was one half of an extended period. One thing, which was quite noticeable, was everyone sat with their classmates; almost no cross-class seating existed. Also, we also sat by sex, all boys at some tables and all girls at others. Again, very little cross fertilization! (Pun intended!)

One unique thing about being a younger brother was I knew a fair number of seniors. Many visited our home so I probably knew thirty seniors, and they knew me. At this time, we still had Rocky, and several of Rog's friends, especially Bob Birchfield, started calling me "Rock." Bob even got several others to participate. Between classes as I walked with a classmate, a senior like Bob or John Hess, who was six-feet, four-inches tall and our star basketball player, said, "Hi Rock!" My friends looked at me in awe and wondered how I knew these guys. This gave me celebrity status; not really, but it was cool to be recognized by seniors!

Near the start of the school year, Ken Kies moved to Lakewood. His house was opposite the seventeenth green. Many times, we played this hole because we could quickly exit it! Their downstairs recreation room had a pool table, so we frequently played Eight Ball. His dad worked at a record company, and Ken often got records and he gave them to us for free. They were usually not the big hits, but he gave me Johnny Horton's "North to Alaska," which was a favorite of mine. There was also a field behind their home where stickball was our favorite game. Somehow the two athletic kids, Ross and Jim, were always against Ken and me. We took an old broom handle and hit an eight-inch blown up rubber ball. One of us always had a transistor radio, so whenever I hear a song like, "Alley Oop," I think of stickball!

Following all home football and basketball games, we had an after-game dance. It was a sock-hop because they did not want scuff marks or damage to our basketball floor, and the lights were turned off except for the *Exit* signs. I walked around the basketball court many times with Ross, Jim, Ken, and others. You might ask, "Did you ever dance?" During my freshman year, the answer is "No!" I do have to admit whenever I hear certain songs like Percy Faith's "Theme from a Summer Place," or The Platters' "Smoke Gets in Your Eyes" or "The Great Pretender," my weird mind shuts down, and all I can see is that dark gym with the *Exit* signs lit, and lots of kids slow dancing! Why is this burned into my memory? Probably for the same reasons whenever I smell bread or cookies baking, I think back to the little bakery shop in Elmwood Park, or if I smell cinnamon, I am back in Brookfield school's basement cafeteria! It is like a "read-only-memory" chip has been inserted deeply into my brain. Will it ever go away? Actually, I hope not because they are great memories.

When the dance was over, we walked the three miles home. Ken got firecrackers, and we made time-delayed fuses which gave us a minute to remove ourselves from the scene before it *popped*. They worked because we were never stopped by the police! Occasionally, we had time to stop at a new establishment in town: McDonalds. It opened two or three years before and was the sixth or seventh one ever opened. If we stopped there, we got one of their fifteen-cent hamburgers or nineteen-cent cheeseburgers, and/or a twenty-five-cent milk shake! Such a deal! Their lit sign said, "Over 100,000 sold!"

In early spring, Ross ran for sophomore class president. His mother came up with neat slogan and Jim, Ken, and I were the first to don his new buttons, which said: "Ross ANnABLE President." The person running against him was Helga Massier. She was a pleasant girl who I met in fifth grade at South; she was usually one of the last survivors in the spelling bees! This election really divided our class; the boys were for Ross, and the girls were for Helga! At an assembly, each candidate gave a speech; their supporters were equally loud and enthusiastic. Fortunately, neither ever attacked the other but just pointed out their own strong points and capabilities. I suspect the margin of victory was razor thin, but in the end, Ross was declared the winner. While I voted and campaigned for Ross, I always felt sorry for Helga and thought she was worthy of this recognition, too.

Dad bought a car to replace our station wagon. He visited and dealt with Mr. Reichert directly and settled on a red 1959 Chevrolet Biscayne. He bought the one with the smallest engine (110 hp)! I believe it did zero to sixty mph in fifteen minutes, thirty-nine seconds, give or take a few seconds! I guess he knew I would be driving the next year, and he wanted to get a car that had *zero* zip! The only accessories he had installed were power steering and automatic transmission to help Mom drive, and an AM radio!

In the spring I went out for tennis. I had zero experience in tennis, had never played before, but I did not want to play baseball or run around a track, and from my experiences on the seventeenth hole, I knew I could not play golf. Mom gave me her old wood racket with its original cat gut strings! Ross, Gene Bacon, and Steve Mudgett were the other freshman trying out. Mr. Don Hymer was our coach, and I knew the two seniors, Bob Kaufman and Bob Birchfield; Birchfield was our number one singles player. We had only four courts and, of course, the varsity guys had the priority. There were times when six or eight of us nonvarsity players were on one court. Mr. Hymer gave us basic instructions, and during the spring I played a few singles and double matches with my classmates. Eventually, Gene and Steve teamed and played doubles throughout high school. Ross and I played doubles together, but I think he felt I was not good enough to hold up my end, which was probably true! Ross and I never played a match against another school because our conference had no underclassmen matches. Once in a while, Birchfield pulled me aside and gave me private lessons and even played a set with me. Of course, he never played hard, but it was fun!

Chapter 15

Summer 1959

I N J U N E T H E C R Y S T A L L A K E R E C R E A T I O N
Department held a tennis tournament for kids, and I signed
up for singles. For my first match, one of my eighth-grade football coaches, Mr. Johnson, was the administrator. My opponent
was a kid who was two years younger than me, who said he had
been playing for several years! *Uh oh!* We were evenly matched,
and we each won a close set. As we went into the third set, the
heat was getting to me, but I knew if this kid beat me, I would be
ridiculed forever. I finally won the third and final set 8–6 or 9–7.
Mr. Johnson asked if he could give me constructive criticism. He
told me when I started to play, he did not think I had any talent
for tennis! After that comment, I was about to die! Then he said
what impressed him most was I persevered even though it was a
hot and grueling match, I was able to pull myself together, correct
earlier mistakes and finished on top. He suggested I spend a lot
more time practicing, which I already knew. Two days later I had
my next match, Mr. Johnson was not there, and I got clobbered by
an older kid; thus, my first-ever tennis tournament ended!

Mr. Battles had an old non-working TV set, but I could have
it, so I put it in our lower level because Dad would not allow me

to have it in my bedroom. I turned it on; the picture was snow, and there was hissing coming from the speaker, but I thought it might be fixable. I pulled the tubes and tested them. I had used tube testers before with Dad, so I knew what to do. Several were dead, and some were weak, so I replaced the dead ones. When I turned it on, I was able to pick up a station fairly well. *Shazam!* I had my own TV! Eventually, all tubes were replaced, including the high voltage tube. This one had a big pin on its top which connected to a cable, so before I unhooked the cable or pulled this tube out, I made sure it was discharged by touching the side of a screwdriver blade to the top pin and touching the end of the screwdriver to the chassis. I learned to do this because when I first started to work on this TV, I accidently touched the high voltage tube when the TV was on! I did not get bit—I was picked up and thrown across the entire basement! OK, it jolted me badly, and I ended up sitting against the wall behind the TV! Since I survived that episode, I learned to be *very* careful where I put my hands and fingers when working on electrical things. I did not have to be thrown across the room twice to learn!

My relationship with Rog became closer. First, we fought less, which was a big relief to me as the *little* brother. Second, we spent quality time playing new sports like whiffle ball and frisbee, and he often gave me tips about school, what teachers were like and what to expect in classes. He applied to several colleges and picked Iowa State University (ISU) in Ames, Iowa. This got me thinking maybe someday I would also attend college. Hmmm! Third, we grew closer in work. This summer he picked up a lot of new mowing and clean-up jobs. What surprised me was if he needed extra help, he asked me instead of one of his friends. One job was to clean out the attic of an elderly lady who lived in an old three-story house. She had no air conditioning, and we had lots of stairs to climb each trip. She was boiling meat on her stove, and as the broth got thicker, the smell got worse! On the way home, I took the deepest breaths I could to purge that awful smell from my lungs! I will never forget it; neither will Rog! Also, I inherited his neighborhood mowing jobs when he left for ISU. Finally, right before he left, he gave me his bank. He said I could have the money, about $12, if I used it on a date. I said OK and was completely surprised! Maybe there was hope for us to become friends!

This year was a mixed one for scouts. Mike and Mr. Price pushed us to advance. I had all the requirements to make Star, but to get it, I had to go in front of a Board of Review at the American Legion. This also required letters of recommendation; one was from my minister. Mike gave me the form and I stopped by Rev. Dalrymple's home. His wife answered their door, I gave her the envelope, told her what I needed, and said I would be back in a few days. When I returned, Mrs. Dalrymple immediately handed me the envelope and said, "My husband said he didn't know you, so he didn't fill it in." I guess when you only come to church on Christmas Eve and Easter, that is not enough! We had several weekend camps to hone our skills. As we sat around a campfire, we got on the subject of *winning*. Mike said his wife did not like to play cards or board games with him because he always won. When she confronted him, he said, "I always play to win! It's the only way I know how to play!" That comment *stuck* with me, and it did *change* how I played games and sports.

By the time I attended Camp Lowden, Mike named me the Senior Patrol Leader. The week went well, and on Wednesday night, Mrs. Peterson brought Mom's letter of encouragement along with money, which I planned to use at the gun range the next day; however, that never happened. That night we did skits for our parents and had the calling-out ceremony for the Order of the Arrow (OA). This is an honorary achievement given to scouts who showed leadership and service to other scouts. This was always scary to me because the scouts stood in a big circle around the bonfire while three senior leaders, dressed in full Indian attire, marched around the circle to the beat of drums, occasionally stopped in front of a scout where the chief shot an arrow into the ground near the scout's toes, and continued until all OA candidates were identified.

My heart raced a little as they came by me. Suddenly, the chief stopped in front of me and shot an arrow near my toes! I was shocked and, will admit, scared. Next time around, they did the same to Mr. Price. After all other OA candidates were identified and attendees left, we were told, "You are forbidden to talk for the next twenty-four hours; go to your campsite, gather your sleeping bag, and return here in fifteen minutes." Mr. Price and I complied. We followed the leader into the woods. Occasionally he stopped, pointed in a direction, and said to a scout, "Take twenty paces and return to the lodge at seven in the morning with your gear." In the morning as it was getting light, I looked around and would you believe I slept the night in a poison ivy patch!? A few minutes later, Mr. Price came over, I pointed to the poison ivy, and he gave me a big smile! We had breakfast and were paired off; my partner was nice, and we got along fine as we built a small cottage. At dusk, we had an OA Induction Ceremony. Afterward, my partner and I instantly asked for names and returned to our troops.

On Friday, the troops competed in pool events. A scout could compete in three events. Since I was a *lake rat*, I was picked to do the diving and underwater swim. Tom Peterson and I teamed up and became our troop's horseback fight representatives; we ended up being in the top three out of the fifteen troops present. In diving they did not allow splash dives, but I ended up in the top third. For the underwater swim, we had to go as far as we could on one breath. The pool was Olympic size (50 meters/164 feet long), and many did one full length and stopped; the rest did shorter distances. Only last week's winner and I were left. We looked at each other for a long while, but I blinked and went first. I did a length and a half which assured me of second place, but I watched as he passed me and swam another fifteen feet. *Ugh!* So ended my times at Camp Lowden.

Dad heard about a new place to fish, Crane Lake, Minnesota. The bad news was it was above Duluth and 630 miles from home! We had the boats; Mr. Albertz had the tent and camping equipment, so a neighborhood marriage was arranged. Our aluminum boat was on top of the car and we pulled the MFG boat on a trailor as we left well before sunrise! Dad probably wished he had bought a bigger engine since it took a long time to accelerate to pass! On the way, Mr. Albertz told Rog and me to call him Bill, not Mr. Albertz! At the town of Crane Lake, Rog and I loaded the boats with our stuff while Dad and Bill bought food. We had a three-mile trip to our campground, which we had to ourselves. Bill picked the spot for the tent and he reminded us of his one tent rule: *no food inside the tent!* "Why?" Because food attracts bears!

They bought a steak, so Bill greased his frying pan, but Dad objected and said, "We'll cook it over an open fire!" After dinner, Bill said he never had a steak taste so good! We packed our food into a big tarp and hoisted it fifteen feet high to a tree branch. About midnight, we went to bed but, unfortunately for Dad, Rog, and me, Bill took a small snort of whiskey, went to sleep in a tenth of a second, and snored enough to keep the bears *far* away! This became his nightly ritual! We started fishing close to our camp and slowly worked outward. We caught quite a few bass and even several northern pike. What was neat was how light it stayed. We fished until almost 11 p.m., and the sky was still slightly light; however, the bad news was those blood-sucking mosquitoes! Dad had a new repellant, OFF, so we survived!

We had a spell of two days where we caught very little, so we did water skiing. Bill did not ski, but it was hard for us to turn down the opportunity to ski on *quiet water* and never see another boat! On the second day of slack fishing, near supper, I saw a swirl, took one cast, and caught a nice bass. Another swirl, I produced a second bass. By this time everyone was casting, someone caught a third one. We thought this might be like Big Siss when walleyes hit the same place and time, so every evening at this time we fished, but we never had another strike; the bass must have just been swimming past. We always had a campfire and roasted marshmallows, at least I did. We lay back and looked up at the Milky Way that was dazzling because of the clear atmosphere and no light pollution.

East of the camp and going north out of Crane Lake was the start of a passageway, which went to International Falls and beyond. One evening a couple canoed down it and joined us for an overnight stay. They told us about a trading post up the passageway. We warned them about bears, but they had a metal Coleman cooler and said they never had problems with them. That night, a black bear chewed through the cooler and ate their food. We were glad our food was tied well off the ground! We went to the Canadian trading post and were shocked at how nice it was! They had the usual souvenir stuff, but they also had nice jackets, pants, and shoes. Dad bought a pair of seal-skin boots for Mom, Bill got something for his wife, and Rog and I bought a few trinkets. When we got home, Mom was thrilled with her boots; they were pretty and very functional, especially in the winter with snow. She used them forever!

Weather interested me, so I ordered a ten-foot weather balloon. It had an extremely thin rubber material encased with white powder to keep from sticking to itself. The question was, "How to blow it up!" Mom suggested we use the exhaust port of her vacuum cleaner. As the balloon was growing, the wind picked up. Finally, one last gust pulled the balloon out of Ken's and my hands, and it reached the awesome altitude of twelve feet when it exploded! An elm tree's branch punctured the skin! So ended my attempt at being a weatherman!

The dynamics of our family were about to change; Rog was about to strike out on his own and enter that great experience called *college*. Mom always said, "My years at Purdue were the best; however, I would not want to repeat them!" After an early breakfast, Dad and Rog departed. While backing out of the garage, there was a horrible bending metal sound! Unfortunately, not all the doors were closed! The rear right door was left fully open so it caught the inside of the garage and bent the door forward. Not a good start! Dad did body blocks into the door, and inch-by-inch the door eventually closed and latched. He backed out again and had no problem *this* time! When Dad returned, he had an empty car with a wounded back door which Reichert's fixed. Our house was amazingly quiet! Conversation between the three of us was definitely lacking the first few nights. It took about a week to get into a routine without Rog, then we found whenever he came home, he disrupted our lives! What I just observed was the start of the *end* of the Hunziker family as I had known it!

Chapter 16
High School, Sophomore Year

W E WERE NO LONGER THE BOTTOM RUNG ON THE ladder, but I also did not have a big brother to watch out for me. First period, I had "Bugsy" Baker, also known as Mr. Arthur Baker. Guess what he taught? Yep, biology! Our laboratory time consisted of cutting up ~~Kermit~~ (Oops), I mean frogs, trying to grow things in Petri dishes, learning to use microscopes, and conducting field trips. Sitting next to me was Bonnie Rau; Judy Flood sat in front of her, and behind her was freshman John Woodman. When the class did lab experiments or field trips, the four of us were in cahoots, but if the experiments had anything to do with *cutting*, John and I did the dirty work! One of the more interesting experiments was about how effective, or not, toothpaste was against bacteria. Each student brought a tube of toothpaste from home, and everyone set up two sterile Petri dishes; one from before brushing and one from after brushing. After three days, we inspected the Petri dishes and saw a big difference in the number of bacteria. *Amazing!* Toothpaste *really* did work, and this was before fluoride was added to it!

After Plane Geometry came my favorite subject, English II! By now you know this is not true, and English was my nemesis. I was sitting next to Karen Baker and behind her was Tim Frisch. I got to know both much better during this class; however, Miss Reinecke daily reminded one of the three of us to quit talking to each other. Finally, in April she tired of us and said, "Rick, would you please stop talking and move up to the desk right in front of me!" *Wow!* This was the first time a teacher ever disciplined me! It was a shock, but it was probably well deserved. My saving grace again was the spelling tests. She had a passion about everyone spelling one word correctly before the end of the year; it was "all right." It drove her nuts when someone spelled it as the single word, "alright!" Every week we had twenty-one words instead of twenty; finally, in mid-April, the whole class got it *all right*, and we never had it on another test. In my newer dictionary, the second preferred spelling of this word is now *alright!* I hope she did not have a heart attack over this!

While not directly involving Miss Reinecke's class, another similar event happened to me! That fall I found an article that was very interesting and I shared it with Mom and Dad. As I read it out loud, it became obvious I struggled reading it. As a result, each night I was required to read to them for ten minutes or more; this lasted until I left for college. Every night when Dad got his martini and sat to relax before dinner, he gave up his time to listen to me read. He did not care if I read from a newspaper, magazine, or book. If he was traveling, Mom listened to me. At first, I really hated doing it, but after a while I got used to it and tried to pick articles I thought were interesting. While I never became a great reader, there is no question these sessions helped me. Thanks, Mom and Dad!

My last class this year was World History with Mr. Harmon Peaco. Sitting next to me was a senior, Judy Mercurio, and we talked quite often before class. She understood the Babylonians, Medes, Persians, Greeks, and Romans. My problem was I questioned, "Why are we studying them anyway?" One time I received a quiz back, she saw I got my usual low grade, and said, "I don't see why you are having trouble with this material, it's the same as what's in the Bible!" OK, that may be true, but if I do not go to church, Sunday school, or study the Bible, I am no better off, right!? In April, Judy and I were talking, and Mr. Peaco stopped the class, looked disgustingly at me, and said, "Rick, would you please move up to this front desk." Does this sound familiar? It should because this happened the *same day* when Miss Reinecke moved me to the front of her class. In fact, it was *two periods in a row*! I do not believe I ever told Mom and Dad about these actions!

Six weeks after Rog went to ISU, we visited and had lunch with him. I saw the pageantry around their football game and ISU won! We took him out to dinner and to breakfast in the morning before heading back home. The *biggest* thing I learned this weekend was Rog was happy at ISU, and he loved being there. Cool! I guess it was maybe something I could look forward to!

By October, I had earned about twenty-eight merit badges, but I needed several special ones like Canoeing, and the rest of the Citizenship ones to become an Eagle scout. While I had all the merit badges needed for Star and Life, I still had only earned First Class! Since I could not get a letter of recommendation from a minister, Mike said he was willing to write a special recommendation for me to go in front of the Board of Review; we discussed the pros and cons. Because I did not want to put Mike in a difficult position, and I was finding less and less time available to spend on scouting, the next week I told him I think it was best if I quit scouting. He did not like my decision, but he understood it. So, I left scouting. When I look back on all of this, no one, including myself, ever proposed another alternative—to get active in a church!

Dad was closer to Rog, so he decided we needed a *boys' night out!* This was the first time I can ever remember where just Dad and I spent an evening together, other than at the kitchen table doing homework! We went to Andy Griffith's movie, *No Time for Sergeants*, and it was hilarious! We both laughed hard and several times were crying from laughing so much. However, I was also embarrassed. Dad laughed *sssooo* loud, everyone in the theater was looking at him. After it was over, we went for a Tastee Freeze treat. Like father, like son; I inherited Dad's laugh and have been accused of being a *very loud* laugher too!

Late this fall, wrestling season started, and I participated, not as a wrestler, but as the team's manager. You may ask, "What does a wrestling manager do?" Whatever the coach wanted! Mr. Roy Nystrom was the sophomore wrestling coach, and I became his *flunky!* The best parts were I was close to the action and I got to go to away matches. During practice, most of my time was spent just watching! Whenever Mr. Nystrom was distracted, I feebly wrestled with my friends like Ross, Jim, Mike Gunderson, and Jeff Gulley; however, when he caught me, he kicked me off the mat because of my lack of strengthening my neck muscles. One varsity match I tried to watch was Ron Paar's. He was a senior, who went to state last year; so much was expected of him, and he did not disappoint! He won all his matches before the state tournament, went to state, but lost the final match; therefore, he was second in the state of Illinois! Ron was a class act to watch!

I was involved in two incidents. First, we were at an away match in the middle of the flu season, so they were short on workers. They asked Mr. Nystrom if he had anyone who could help. Guess who he volunteered!? Yep, me! When our wrestler was in control, I was to start the clock to time our wrestler's *riding* time. I had to stop it during timeouts or when his opponent gained in control. I still spent much of my time cheering for our wrestlers, and several times I realized I was late starting my timer. When it came to Jeff Gulley's match, it was a *doozy!* They fought hard, and it ended tied, but Jeff had dominated on top and had riding time. Mr. Nystrom appealed to the referee, he came over to examine our times and awarded *no points* because Jeff did *not* have the required extra minute of riding time! Why? During the period Jeff started and stayed on top the whole two minutes, I forgot to turn the clock on, so Jeff was missing two full minutes! Mr. Nystrom was livid and gave me the ugliest face he could muster to show me how he felt. He never said anything to me later, but there was a definite chill! What worried me more was what Jeff thought about me! I let him down; he should have been credited with a win! Did I mess up our friendship!? He said nothing to me that night, nor any other time and we were *still* friends! *That* is called *forgiveness!*

The second incident happened at a home match. Mr. Nystrom had laryngitis, told me to sit next to him so I could relay his instructions, and told the wrestlers to listen for my voice. Through all twelve matches, he whispered instructions, and I yelled them to our wrestlers! We won the match, and for once I felt like I had a *small* part in it. He even smiled and patted me on the back as we walked out of the gym. Maybe I made up for my goof with Jeff, but probably not. At our awards ceremony, Mr. Nystrom commented on my *loudmouth* and the problems it caused! Everyone laughed! I did get my class numerals: 62!

The second semester Dad wanted me to sign up for behind-the-wheel driver training at school, so, being the obedient son I was, I signed up and Miss Frances Brand, who was a spry sixtyish woman, was my instructor. Half the time was spent in a classroom learning the rules of the road and the other half was spent driving their Biscayne! The second semester was delayed two days due to a major snowstorm, so the day school reopened, I was our group's first driver! After going over some basics, Miss Brand asked me to start the car, put it in "drive," and start driving. I negotiated the school's driveway and a few nearby roads and even skidded a little on the snowy/icy roads. She wanted me to turn right, so I put on my right turn signal, but the snow was not fully cleaned off this corner, so the side of the car swiped a pile of snow, and scratched the right back door as I turned. Hmmm. There must be something wrong with this door on Biscaynes! The first time I *ever* drove a car, it was on snow and ice-covered street! My parents were happy my first six weeks of driving was all done on the school's car and not ours!

After I turned sixteen, Dad took me out driving on weekends. He provided me with different venues, including unfamiliar roads and high-speed tollways. Sometimes he yelled at me and I got upset, but most lessons with him went well. When our classroom and driving activities were accomplished, we took our written and driving tests at CLCHS. After the four of us received our driver licenses, Miss Brand said she had her own test she wanted us to experience. We met after school and I started out in the driver's seat. She had me drive to Elgin. I had been on this road many times before, but I had never driven it, so it was neat to experience another *virgin* road. Elgin probably had 50,000 people, *and* they had the Elgin Watch factory. She wanted us to experience a rush-hour situation by encountering the Elgin Watch factory shift change, the closest thing she could find to congestion. How cool was that? She was a complete instructor; she was patient with us and never yelled, got mad, or disgusted with us (like Dad)—and she gave us great driving experiences. Miss Brand was a class act! And, look out! I was now a licensed driver of that powerful Biscayne!

During spring break, Jim, Ken, and I signed up for our school's annual trip to Washington, DC. There were about fifty students, but we were the only sophomore boys. We bussed to Chicago, caught a train to Richmond, and had tours of the Virginia State House. The next day, we headed to the revamped village of old Williamsburg. This was quite interesting since we got to see how dentistry, horse shoeing, cooking, candle making, and so on were done in the 1700s. It made us appreciate today's conveniences! Next, we visited Mt. Vernon and saw President George Washington's wonderful estate along the Potomac River. Our last stop was our main objective, Washington DC.

All the white buildings and memorials were impressive! After touring both chambers in the Capitol Building and its Rotunda, we visited the Jefferson and Lincoln Memorials; however, since we were from Illinois, special emphasis was placed on the latter one! Finally, we got to visit the 555.5-foot-tall Washington Monument! The line to take the elevator to the top was long, so we, feeling physically fit, decided to take the stairs to the top! After all, how many steps could it be!? Actually, 879 steps! We attacked the obelisk with vigor and started by running up steps. After we ran up for what seemed like a long time, we looked upwards, but could see nothing but marble and *more* steps! Ugh! We took the rest of the steps at a much slower pace! The view from the top through the small windows on all four sides was worth the effort! I took pictures, but when the film was developed, my camera was not working properly, so I had nothing to prove I was at the top of the Washington Monument in April 1960; therefore, I guess it did not happen! We took the elevator down, and the train ride home was uneventful. What an experience to see our nation's capital!

This spring, tragedy struck! We got word Mike Arakelyan's pregnant wife was killed in an auto accident. This was to be their first child, and the baby died, too. This was devastating for Mike, and for the troop. She attended all ceremonies and events and was the primary one arranging and serving refreshments. She was truly an integral part and an honorary member of our troop. If Troop 165 had *a scout mother*, it would have been her! I had never been to a funeral, so Mom prepared me and answered my questions. The afternoon of her viewing, we walked up to the casket and when I saw her, I had a queasiness in my stomach, and felt faint. I settled down and after a few minutes, we met Mike. This was the first time I had seen him since I quit scouts, so it was a little awkward for both of us, especially under this situation. I had no idea what I should say. We had a good visit under the circumstances, but I could see this was crushing for him. As Mom and I slowly walked out, I took one look back at Mike; he was crying as he talked to another visitor! Our drive home was very quiet; it was a *horrible* day!

Mom and Dad wanted me to take aptitude tests to help determine possible areas of study or work. Mr. Richard Whitt, our sophomore guidance counselor, gave me a series of tests during study halls. I answered about 200 questions like:

> "Which of the following do you like doing the most: (a) Reading a book; (b) Playing a card game; (c) Watching TV; or (d) Working a jigsaw puzzle?"

I could give no right or wrong answers, just answers. My answers were compared with the aptitudes of about 100 types of professions. A positive score meant my likes were similar to those working in a given field, and a negative score meant the opposite. Out of all of the potential types of occupations, only *one* was positive—dentist! I hate going to dentists and had absolutely *no* desire to look into people's mouths! I had a negative score for *every other* work occupation! Since Dad was an engineer, I figured I would be one too. For electrical engineering, I had a *minus six* score which was one of my higher negatives scores. I showed Mom and Dad my scores, and again, their attempt to help me define and improve myself failed! About this time, I had to sign up for my junior year's courses. First, with Mom and Dad's blessing, I gave up band. As far as the core classes, Mr. Whitt suggested I take *no* math or science cources! When I told him I was planning to go to college and be an engineer, he was stunned! Much to Mr. Whitt's chagrin, I signed up for intermediate algebra/trigonometry and chemistry!

Tennis my sophomore year was great, but not *too* great! Gene and Steve were solidly our number one doubles team. Ross and I played doubles and participated in over half of the varsity matches! Challenge matches between two upper classmen and us determined who was the number two doubles team, and we typically won about half of them! Also, many teams had a third doubles team, or they would combine some of their single players to form another doubles team. Our best win came against North Chicago who had their number one and two singles players teamed. In the past we could jump while serving, but this year at least one foot had to be touching ground. Mr. Hymer indicated these guys jumped every time they served and suggested we call foot faults! There was no question in our minds they were the better players, but as time went on, they became quite frustrated. Apparently, no one had ever challenged them on their foot faults; they never argued about our calls but just accepted their foot faults. Due to their numerous violations, we were ahead when the match was terminated and declared the winners! The frustration for Ross and me was when it came down to winning a *varsity letter*. The school required we played half the matches, which we did, and in either the conference or state tournament, which we did not; however, we won our challenge match to the state tournament, but Mr. Hymer decided to take the upper classmen because they had more experience. So, Gene and Steve got their varsity letters, and Ross and I only got minor letters. We were frustrated, but there was nothing we could do. Life is not always fair!

Chapter 17

Summer 1960

W HEN ROG RETURNED FROM ISU, DAD WANTED
to reward him for completing his first year, so the fearsome four headed for Crane Lake. Another group was at the campsite, but we used the same tree to hang our food, which was good since we encountered black bears twice! We fished previous spots, and Dad caught a northern pike over thirty inches long! On several nights by the campfire, we observed a bright star, the US Echo satellite, slowly progress across the sky. Cool! Of course, Bill took his snort of whiskey right before bed, and the three of us listened to him snore! We went to the Canadian outpost. Bill's wife liked Mom's seal-skin boots, and we tried to convince him to buy a pair, but his stubbornness won!

One night about midnight a small boat was coming southward down the channel. The little motor was *put-putting* steadily, and the operator started singing. He was not a good singer, and it was obvious he had had more than a little snort of whiskey; we thought he drank the whole still! As his voice and motor were slowly faded, we heard a big crash, and he started cussing loudly. The motor stopped, then started again, and he went on his way southward. About a half mile across the bay from us was a big island whose northern point consisted of granite! Our little friend apparently *did not see* this island and ran right into it! We laughed a long time, and this became the highlight of the trip!

Because of his engineering schooling, Rog got a cooperative job at Pure Oil, and I became my brother's chauffeur for work. This gave us daily quality time together. For myself, I had Rog's old local lawn-mowing jobs. I owned my lawnmower and charged more if I used it versus when I used the lawn-owner's mower. Dad told me if he ever saw a sloppy job, I had to mow it again for free! With that motivation, I was careful how I mowed. Over the years, Mom and Dad became closer to Chet and Florence Battles, so I also acquired mowing their double-lot yard and cleaned around their shrubbery. I found that Mr. Battles was quite particular about what he wanted done, so I had to be careful. Mid-summer Mr. Battles's lawnmower died. He went back and forth whether he should buy a new one or let me mow it with mine. After I mowed it a couple of times with mine and he paid me the higher price, he decided to buy his own. He asked what he should get, and I picked one that had *bells and whistles!* Hey, if I was not going to make some *big bucks* on his lawn, at least I was going to have him get me one that made my job easier!

Construction started on the empty lot south of the Albertz's home. One Saturday, I was working in the backyard of the lot south of this construction. Her young children were with me when the owners of the house under construction visited to see its progress. This family had five kids, three older ones and two younger ones. The boy with me made a snide comment about the new owners, and I said he might want to be careful because their youngest boy might become his best friend! He just grunted and walked away. Later I found out our new neighbors were the Archambaults.

Chapter 18

High School, Junior Year

A s Dad took Rog back to ISU via a company plane, I became an upperclassman at CLCHS. My junior year would be interesting, frustrating, and fun. First, I had no band, which made Mr. Clay and me happy. Next, I was surprised that my schedule indicated I had a new teacher, Mr. Sickal, for English III. Our first semester was devoted to studying outstanding authors from the US and England, like Wilder, Bunyan, Dickens, and so forth. Mr. Sickal was mesmerized by the Pulitzer winning play by Thornton Wilder entitled *Our Town*. So thrilled was he that we recreated it in our classroom! It took place in the early 1900s, focused on two young kids, George and Emily, who fall in love in high school and marry. She died during childbirth and then came back to discuss life and death. Guess who Mr. Sickal picked to be George? Yep, yours truly! Poor Gerry Wolf was picked to be Emily. I did not mind that match at all, but to do their *dating lines* in front of the whole class, I was embarrassed and blushing! Remember what a great reader I was!? Well trying to read *and* act at the same time was *way beyond* my ability, and he constantly had me reread my lines!

After three days, he fired me, and someone else played George. I felt bad I was no longer Gerry's partner in crime, but I was glad to get back to my desk. Mr. Sickal became the junior class sponsor and guess what play he picked? Yep, *Our Town*! By the way, he did not pick me to play George for his stage production, nor did I try out for *any* part! Next, we studied John Bunyan's *Pilgrim's Progress* which is about a man name Christian and his family's journeys from Earth to Heaven. Again, had I gone to church and read the Bible, I might have had a better appreciation for this literature. This first semester with Mr. Sickal was disastrous! It was the first and only time at CLCHS that I got a D for an entire semester! Ugh! The second semester emphasized writing and grammar and, as hard as it is to believe, I survived it with all Cs and even got a B on the final exam! I was happy when English III was over!

Math was split with a semester of intermediate algebra and one of trigonometry. I had a very energetic teacher named Mr. William Faellaci. Rog had him and really liked him, so I was looking forward to his class. I still struggled with certain algebra concepts, and Dad had to help me at night! Trig was interesting, and from the start, I was able to grasp the concepts of sine, cosine, tangent, and so on. Trig turned out to be one of my better classes.

For American History, I had Mr. George Hartung, Rog's *favorite* teacher at Crystal Lake! When class started, he spent a few minutes just talking and getting to know us! The girl who sat right in front of him was Susie Schenk, who was very outgoing. There were many days Susie and Mr. Hartung bantered back and forth, and the whole class was laughing. It was delightful to see a teacher who really liked students! I did find Mr. Hartung to be a fascinating lecturer, and it was a subject I could understand and *was* interested in because it only went back several hundred years, not thousands! So, I understood why Rog liked him!

This fall, the US was in a very heated election for President; Richard M. Nixon and John F. Kennedy were the candidates. Mr. Hartung never hinted who he liked, but he gave us an important lecture! After describing the whole election process, he said, "While this is all well and good, what bothers me the most about our process is that when the new president gets to the White House, he is already tired and worn out!" Every election I think about this and figure it is even worse now because most of our candidates run for two to three years before the election! Is there not a better way!? I do have one side note about the 1960 election. Everyone knows Mr. Kennedy won; however, when the *Crystal*

Lake Herald published the county's presidential results, the last person listed, who received *one* vote, was Otto Hunziker! People accused Dad of voting for himself, but he swore he did not. A few months later, it came out Mom's best friend, Mrs. Albertz, voted for Dad because she said, "He was the smartest man she knew! If anyone could fix our country, he could!" What a tribute!

Another surprise was Mr. Howard Harris was my chemistry teacher! The first day of class, Tuesday right after Labor Day, Mr. Harris passed out a sheet with the names, symbols, and valences of all the elements on the periodic table. He told us on Friday we would be tested on them! Everyone groaned but me! Why? Dad, being a chemical engineer, knew everything in chemistry was based on knowing symbols and valences, so he had me make flash cards in June! I used those flash cards every day all summer; I even took them up to Crane Lake, and Dad questioned me around the campfire or while fishing! I could have taken Mr. Harris' test that Tuesday and gotten a 100! As promised, on Friday, Mr. Harris passed out the test. He taught two sessions of chemistry, and I was the only who got 100! *Shazam!*

We had a chemistry lab twice a week. On the lab days we sat at worktables. Each table had chemicals, glass instruments, Bunsen burners, sinks, and so forth. Linda Johnsen, a senior, was my lab partner. In my yearbook, Linda wrote, "It's too bad you got stuck with me for a lab partner. I hope our little system of completing experiments isn't revealed. We had a lot of fun this year, but I am going to get a better tan than you." As I think back, I can certainly explain being quite tan when we entered class, but I am not sure what "our little system of completing experiments" was! Maybe we *dry labbed* them; you know, not doing the experiment and guessing what the results should be and reporting that to the instructor. From my grades, we must have guessed more right answers than wrong ones if that was the case!

I also had Mr. Harris for study hall. I was unhappy because I was one of the few juniors that had it in Room 105 with all freshman and sophomores! The first day he seated us alphabetically. One of the girls who sat in or near to the first seat of the first row was tasked with taking the roll and marking who was absent each day. On Monday after his test, he tapped me on the shoulder during study hall and said, "Rick, you did really well on Friday's test." I replied, "Mr. Harris, someday I will tell you a story about it," and we both smiled.

For gym, we had Mr. Owen Metcalf. He was a legend at CLCHS. He was short, of slight build, old, and wore gray glasses which had built-in hearing aids. He was a great guy and loved working with kids. In the fall, he had us doing soccer. I volunteered to be our team's goalie since I was pretty good at punting and fairly good at catching kicked balls, thanks to Dad's training. We played on the football practice fields, so the goal post structures were our goals. Jim Harwood and Mike Gunderson were the deep backs with me. We had a good bunch of forwards, which resulted in the ball mostly being on our opponent's half of the field. The three of us spent most of the period just visiting. Once or twice the ball came to our half, but Jim and Mike were adept at kicking it back across the mid-field line, and we went back to visiting. When it did get by them, thanks to Mike Arkelian's comments about being aggressive and wanting to always win, I came far out of the goal and literally dove on and wrapped myself around the ball, quickly got up, and punted it away. I think only a few goals were scored on us in the six weeks we played, and most were penalty kicks from right in front of our goal. I got an A from Mr. Metcalf!

This fall we had a major change within our home. Mom and Dad always promised me Rog's bigger bedroom when he moved out, but I was quite comfortable in my smaller room, so I never moved to his room. But then in September, Grandma Alexander sold her house because she struggled to keep it. She kept her bedroom suite and moved into Rog's bedroom. Mom and Dad were happy to help Grandma, but Mom was upset I did not get the larger bedroom. She mentioned it when Grandma moved in and several times later. I tried to assure her it really did *not* bother me; I was happy with my room! Personally, I thought it was cool having Grandma living with us!

For Homecoming, we decided to *pull* our float. No class had ever used *boy power,* to pull a float. We were playing the Zion-Benton Zee Bees; our float's theme was, "Whip the Zee Bees." Dave Thompson, who lived at Gate 20, volunteered his garage for our construction facility. We had a tiger seated on a chair, one of its hind legs was draped over the chair's arm, and in one of its front paws, which was raised over its head, it had a whip. Laying on top of the wagon were several *dead bees*. Attached to the front of the wagon were two hefty twenty-five-foot-long ropes which the junior boys held over their shoulders while pulling the wagon. We were dressed in white togas with "Zee Bees" written on the front; like we were being whipped by the tiger. One of the more popular songs recently was Sam Cooke's, "Chain Gang," so we pulled while singing, "Working on the chain gang, chain gang, chain gang," and then we *grunted and groaned* like in the song! The person leading us was Don Grivett, one of the smallest boys in our class. On slight downhill grades, we dropped our ropes and let Don pull the float by himself while we cheered! We had a ball doing this, and it was one of my fondest memories at CLCHS!

We set one weekend aside to see Rog and attend an ISU football game, and Grandma even went with us. Rog introduced us to many of his friends before going to their game against Oklahoma University. It was quite a struggle, but ISU prevailed and beat them for the first time in twenty-eight years! We took Rog out to dinner, and then he had a treat for me; I could stay overnight with him in his room! He introduced me to more of his friends, and every few minutes someone came through the hallway making a war whoop. We went to bed well after midnight, but I had problems sleeping because of the noise and celebrating. We got up early for breakfast, ate, and headed home as I dozed. At lunch, I just kept breaking down crying. Why? I am sure some of it was due to the lack of sleep, but mostly I think it was because for the first time I *really* realized our family, as I knew it, was *broken up*! I saw first-hand how happy Rog was, and he had replaced his family with a new one; that realization got to me! Over the years, Mom, Dad, and Rog asked me about what was wrong with me, but I never could say it was because of this. After all, how could a junior in high school admit he *missed* his older brother!?

When Rog came home for Thanksgiving break, it was also the end of the fall quarter, and he decided to change majors. He originally was in mechanical engineering; however, this fall's physics class had become too much for him. I guess Mr. Curtis's physics class did not prepare him well for upper-level physics classes. He switched to something entirely different: Forestry. He always enjoyed the outdoors and decided why not make it his living. He flourished in this new endeavor and had much better grades. So, in the end, Mr. Curtis did him a favor!

Rog also provided us with a nutritious tidbit that plagued our family for years. The only specific canned vegetable Dad insisted on was Le Sueur Early Spring Peas. One dinner Mom served us peas; Le Sueur, of course. As Rog served himself, he said, "I read where peas make you sterile!" We laughed, but Mom tucked this little jewel of information into the back of her mind and never forgot it, as you will see later.

The much-awaited wrestling season arrived. Mr. Buck Wheeland was our coach. The first week of practice was mostly conditioning; we did lots of running, pushups, leg lifts, and bridging. Bridging developed and strengthened neck muscles, which were essential to a wrestler. Next, we worked on take-downs, escapes, reverses, pinning combinations, and how to counter each. As our first match approached, we held challenge matches. There were only two of us at 127 pounds, Ron Kimura and me. Ron was a senior who had won several varsity letters, so he had lots of experience and was quick and strong. I wrestled my first-ever match against him, and the results showed who was in charge; it was not me! The score was 9–0! Not a good showing, and I knew I had a long way to go. If a wrestler won his matches against other schools, they could not be challenged, so it was a while before I could challenge him again. When our next challenge match came, I improved a little, but lost 7–2!

Rog was home over Christmas, and since I had learned a lot more about wrestling, we went to the basement with Dad officiating. Even though Rog was bigger, heavier, and stronger, I now understood leverage and knew holds. This also included pinning combinations, which I successfully applied every time I was on top. I pinned him three times in a row! I beat my big brother fair and square, three times! *Wow!* Dad laughed so hard he had tears running down his cheeks!

Mr. Wheeland held practices the week between Christmas and New Year's, and while not mandatory, we were encouraged to participate. On Wednesday, December 28, only twelve of us attended, and I was paired with a 154-pound senior, four weight classes above me. Mr. Wheeland showed us a fireman's carry takedown. I had to duck under my opponent, lift him onto my shoulders like a fireman carried a victim, and rotate and lay him on his back on the mat where I could apply a pinning combination. The key was to keep my back perpendicular to the mat when I had him on my shoulders. My partner slowly went through the process of learning it, and I found myself easily put on my back! This was cool because Ron was not here and did not know about it! Mr. Wheeland helped me through the "take it slow" process to make sure I was doing it properly.

When doing it with my partner, it was more difficult for me to bring him over the top of me because of his weight. After many slow and medium speed tries, I tried it at full speed. I ducked under him, got everything right to hold and lifted him off the floor to bring him over the top, but the next thing I remembered was Mr. Wheeland waking me up with an ammonia packet! Something went horribly wrong, and I was out cold, and the small of my back hurt excruciatingly! Apparently, I did not keep my back perpendicular to the mat when I picked him up and rotated him over me! After a couple of minutes of not moving, I got up and gingerly walked around, but my lower back was *very* sore, and I also had pain down my legs!!! I showered and called Mom to pick me up.

She asked me what happened, so I told her what I could remember, and she immediately drove me to Dr. Abromitis's office. He took X-rays which showed no broken vertebrae, but my spine bowed to the left for four vertebrae! He suspected the muscles and tendons on the right side of my lumbar got torn, which caused the ones on the left side to pull the vertebrae that direction and pinch my spinal cord, which caused the pain down the legs. He told me that as the damaged muscles and tendons healed and strengthened, they should pull my spine to where it should be. His solution was to come every day for several weeks and have deep-heat ultrasound treatments. What a way to end 1960 and start 1961! Every night after school, Mom took me for treatments. Ten days later, it started feeling better.

While not taking gym because of a medical excuse, I was shooting baskets, and I tried a layup, but landed and jarred my back; the pain was awful! I went to the doctor's office and explained the pain was worse but did not tell him or Mom how it happened, so he continued with more ultrasound treatments. At night, the pain down my legs was so bad, I cried and was afraid to move for fear it would *get* worse! The pain did not subside, so he took black goo, which he called "Sputnik," placed a four-inch strip of it on a long bandage and taped it along the right side of my spine. He told me in the morning I would have a long blister, put Vaseline on it, and tape gauze over the whole area. Then he told me if this did not work, he would have to inject medication all along the right side of my spine to stimulate the growth of the muscles and tendons. That did not sound appetizing so, "Come on, Sputnik, *work!*"

When I woke the next morning, my bed was wet. During the night, the Sputnik formed several blisters which broke. Mom removed the bandage, put Vaseline on the area, placed gauze over it, and taped me up. Guess what? The pain was substantially reduced! About a week later, he did another Sputnik, and the third week, he did another. After a total of about two months, he released me but gave me lower back strengthening exercises to do; I regularly did them for about a year. In all I had twenty-one ultrasound treatments and the three Sputniks!

Mom and Dad went to a Continental Can meeting in Miami, Florida, and stayed nine days while Grandma oversaw me. The good news was I got to pick up my friends and drive them to school! Near the end of the week, Dad called and said they would be a day late getting home because he was buying a new car! He came across an English Ford he liked called an Anglia. On Monday they arrived home with a cute little green car about the size of the Volkswagen Beetle. The bad news was, it had a stick shift! Dad taught me how to shift this car, and I really liked driving it. About the same time, Ross's folks bought a VW Beetle, and he learned a trick! He showed me how to make it backfire! His VW did a *pop*, but when doing it with Dad's Anglia, it made a *bang!* I was always the *backfire* champ! I remember Dad saying a few years later he never had to replace a muffler so soon! Hmmm, I wonder why?

We had our usual Class of 1962 boy's table at lunch. People like Don Johnson, Jim Harwood, Corky Iverson, Frank Church, Steve Heiman, and Muley McGuire shared lunch at the same time.

You might ask, "Who is Muley McGuire?" Rog told me he was at the movie and his older brother, Murray, who was one of Rog's friends, asked him to move, and he said, "No!" He refused to budge for a long time, and his brother said, "He was more stubborn than a mule;" hence, being dubbed "Muley." His real name was Powers McGuire. You may remember him as the kid who sucker punched me in the stomach! Since we were now in the same school, our brothers were friends, and we had a few classes and time together, we became friends too—although, I would not have minded hitting him just once in the stomach for old time's sake!

There was one major event being held over our heads, especially for our class. Two years earlier, they started construction on a new high school between Cary and Fox River Grove, so we knew this school split was coming our senior year! The new school, Cary-Grove High School (C-GHS), and CLCHS would be combined for football, but all other sports were separate. We could participate in each other's social activities since we spent three years in the same classroom, sports activities, and socials! This was not an ideal situation since twenty-five percent of us were going to be siphoned off!

I ran for Student Council. When I turned in my petition, I found out sixteen filed for our class's eight slots. Each candidate had to give a speech, and I had never done one before, so this was a daunting task. I had to decide what to say to make students vote for me and then figure out how to say it. I really did not have any traits that stood out, and I was pretty much just an average kid. Hmmm, that ended up being what I used, being "Mr. Average!" Since I was not outstanding academically or athletically, why not appeal to *the masses or the middle* of the class. I wrote, rewrote, and revised my speech and practiced it in front of Mom and Dad often, so I felt ready.

They took us alphabetically, so I had to follow a funny and likeable kid named Earl Hansen. I do not remember his speech because I was trying to concentrate on what I had to say. I delivered what I felt was a pretty good speech, especially since it was my first-ever one in front of a large group. One thing I included was something our class could shoot toward. Last year, we were the first class to ever *pull* a Homecoming float, so I proposed the Class of 1962 should be the first class to ever *carry* a float! About this time our 1961 CLCHS yearbooks came in, and I passed mine to classmates to get their good wishes, comments, and signatures. To my surprise, several even commented about me *not* being "Mr. Average!" Because I ran around with many who would attend C-GHS, I was worried the split would cause me to lose much of my base support! The election was held, and the winners were announced at a "sock hop" in the gymnasium on a Friday night.

They started with the upcoming sophomore classes of C-GHS and CLCHS results, then the upcoming junior classes, and finally the senior classes. By this time my heart was beating hard and fast! They announced all in alphabetical order, so I knew when my name would be announced, or not. The Class of 1962 Student Council Members elected were: Ross Annable, Craig Brown, Carol Boysen, Judy Conley— As each one was announced we clapped. The next name given was Earl Hanson! I clapped, but was very nervous since my name was to be next, but the name announced was Janice Lundahl! I clapped, but my heart *skipped* a beat. It was over; I had lost! I went home devastated! At that point I felt "politics" was not for me!

On April 12, the world changed drastically! That was the day the USSR put a Russian cosmonaut, Yuri Gagarin, into space. He would do one complete orbit of the earth. What a shock! We put satellites in orbit, but never a man! The USSR beat us, *again!* What a blow to our country's esteem. On May 5, on a Mercury capsule flight, the US sent Alan Shepard in a suborbital flight of about fifteen minutes. While he did not achieve orbit, he was certified as the second man and first American to fly in space. This helped our country's ego, but it was still not in the category or prestige of what the USSR did!

We had a new tennis coach, my math teacher, Mr. Faellaci. Ross worked part time and was somewhat out of the doubles picture. There was also a question about how well my back was healed, and I was not sure it could take all the running and stretching singles required. So, what to do? Because of bad weather, most of our early practices were spent hitting the ball against a brick gym wall! During my "wall playing," I found out I had a problem serving. I always had a problem serving, but this year it was even worse because when I stretched to smack the ball, sharp pains shot through my back! Not good! Somehow, I got teamed with senior, Jack Weightman! We were the number two doubles team behind Gene and Steve. Jack was over six feet tall, so his presence at the net was intimidating, and his net game was quite good. I did finally develop a method for serving while not ruining my back. We won over half of our matches and even had fun. I do have to say, "Thank you, Jack, for putting up with my injury and faulty tennis play!" Mr. Faellaci awarded Ross and me our varsity letters!

The end of the school year was a sad time because of our split. During the last three years, we had made *good friends*. We knew we could go to each other's events, but really, how often would we do that? One night after tennis practice, I was in the locker room with Tim Frisch and Mark Bear. We had a real heart-to-heart talk about what we each planned for our future. We talked about getting together over the summer since Mark had a boat on the Fox River; maybe we could ski on it or on the lake with our boat. Guess what? Summer came and passed; neither of us called the other to set something up, and we only saw each other *one* time! Unfortunately, this was true with so many of our friends at CLCHS who moved to C-GHS. It was a *very bitter* departure at the conclusion of our junior year!

Chapter 19

Summer 1961

LATE SPRING, SUMMER, AND EARLY FALL MEANT lawn mowing, trimming, weeding, and/or leaf raking, and I had six lawns to manage. Rog was basically not home this summer. When he switched to forestry, they required a summer camp, so he was going to school in Colorado. This was the first summer the Hunzikers did not have one of its members, except for a few weeks in August. I will have to admit I *missed* him a little. OK, a lot!

Much of the summer was spent using our boat and hanging out on the Harrington pier. Dad traded up to a used 50 hp Johnson outboard. While our speed only increased to 23 mph, it had more power; Dad could now easily start on one ski! My friends liked it because one evening, the Lakewood four decided to go for a ride after dark. I accidently took a turn a little too quickly, the boat's bow dug in, and the motor just whipped, or fishtailed, itself almost instantly ninety degrees! Nothing like this ever happened before, *sssooo*, being upcoming studious physics students, we tried it again, and the same thing happened!

Only two of us were in the front seat, so we tried it a third time with all of us up front. This time the bow dipped deeper, causing water to come over the front deck and windshield, and the backend fishtailed quicker and farther than before! It was so exciting, we probably did it another five times! Back at Gate 13, we covered the boat and went ashore. As we walked up the embankment, I could see the outline of two people sitting on the infamous green bench, but could not determine who they were. As we walked past them, I heard a voice I knew all too well say, "Did you enjoy the boat ride boys?" It was Dad! *Oops!* My heart stopped, and no one replied. Dad never asked me what we were doing, and we never did this unique maneuver again!

Harrington's diving board became a place for social activity as well as being the apparatus for perfecting our splash dives like cannon balls or can openers. Ken accomplished the all-time best splashes. His tall, lanky body pushed the greatest amount of water to the side, so his following concussion factor was the greatest. He often produced massive splashes over twenty feet high! As a result, people watching and/or sitting on the bench at the end of the pier were often susceptible to being soaked, especially if they were wearing street clothes instead of swimsuits! This happened often!

Since my senior year was approaching, I started to think seriously about college. I was interested in working with electronics, so I figured electrical engineering is what I would study. Dad told me I could go to any school within 300-miles of home except for Northwestern and Wisconsin: Northwestern because it was a private school that cost many times what a state school cost, and Wisconsin because he felt it was too liberal and thought Continental Can never hired a *good* engineer from there! My big question was, *where* do I want to go? Because Mom and Dad went to Purdue and I had heard about it all my life, it was on my list, but I knew my *average* grades might be a problem. I had no idea how well I might do on ACT/SAT admission tests, so for a safety net, I considered the University of Illinois because of being in-state. I came across an admissions book about Michigan State

University, so I also added it to my list. I had never visited or seen any of these universities, so how was I to choose?

Dad had to visit their plant at Elwood, Indiana, and suggested Mom and I go with him, and we could spend the day at Purdue while he worked. We stayed in the Purdue Memorial Union and that night I had problems sleeping, so I looked out my window onto the campus, and was amazed I was at *the* place where Mom and Dad met and where many Hunziker and Alexander events occurred! The next morning, I got a campus map and headed out on my own; regrettably, I had made no appointments. I entered the Electrical Engineering building where I saw a big lecture hall and stood on a balcony overlooking a huge bay filled with large electrical motors! I walked past Kappa Delta Rho where Dad and Uncle Bill lived and even went in the south entrance of Ross-Ade Stadium and saw the beautiful field and the box offices. *Wow!*

I got out of there before someone saw me and walked past an old dormitory called Cary Hall. All the windows were wide open, and each had a big fan in it, so I made a mental note, "You do *not* want to live here!" I went into a new men's H-Hall and happened to run into one of its officials who was kind enough to give me a tour of the entire facility! I made another mental note, "This is where I wanted to live if I came here!" Inside the Co-Recreational Gymnasium, I spent about half an hour examining the various activity areas of this impressive facility. I also walked past Alpha Chi Omega, where Mom stayed, and saw the E. C. Elliot Hall of Music.

I came to a monument about ten feet tall which had lion's heads on its four sides. Mom and Dad told me that if a virgin walked past it, the lions would roar, but since 1903 when it was built, there had never been a virgin on campus since they had never roared (college humor)! Leaving Lions, I entered the Stewart Student Center and immediately saw a huge mural depicting the US Government establishment of Land-Grant Schools; Purdue was one of fifty. I looked through all its display cases as I walked through this building on the way back to the Memorial Union where Mom was sitting and reading under the watchful eye of a statue, John Purdue. I really enjoyed the walk and seeing things, but I wish I had talked to academic people. I was sold on Purdue but, more importantly, would Purdue be sold on me!?

Shortly after this visit, Jim Harwood and I visited the University of Illinois. Again, we had no appointments and just visited many buildings and a couple of residence halls. It was an impressive and large campus. We got to see a room in one of the men's dorms; there were two beds, two desks, and two closets. Jim pointed to one of the beds and said, "I'll take this one, and you can have that one." What went through my mind was Rog telling about how many *new* and wonderful guys he met at ISU, and I wanted to have the same experience. I was afraid if I went to Illinois, I would room with someone from Crystal Lake and might forfeit opportunities and experiences, which made Rog so happy at college. I did not want to do that, so I pretty much decided Illinois would be my last choice. For the record, I never did see Michigan State's campus that summer, so I would have been *flying blind* if I attended there.

In August, Rog came home from Colorado, and he was excited about his new course of study. Dad felt since he went to school for a full year, it was time for a fishing trip! We rented a cabin on a lake near Eau Claire, Wisconsin. On Saturday, we pulled the boat out of the lake and gathered our fishing gear. On Sunday morning, the three of us took off, and by mid-day we were in our cabin. We cooked a quick dinner and made our first fishing excursion onto the lake. We fished all the next day, but that night Rog was up the whole night vomiting. Dad and I fished from the cabin pier the next morning, but since he was not vomiting anymore, we later fished nearby from the boat. We had one more day with Rog laid up, then all of us got to fish together the next day.

On Friday, we did a twenty-plus-mile float trip down the Chippewa Flowage. We met our two guides early. Initially, Dad and I went in the lead boat; it was overcast, but ten minutes after we shoved off, it rained. River float fishing is quite different because you only had one shot at the spot you liked, and I could cast on both sides of the boat, so opportunities abounded! Earlier, I bought a two-inch, spin-cast, single-jointed frog with a single treble hook for fifty cents; it was the only lure I used all day! Even with the horrible weather, we caught lots of bass, small northern pikes, and others.

It stopped raining, so we had lunch, and then Dad went with Rog in the second boat. About an hour into the afternoon and during heavy rains, something big hit my little frog lure when it was only six feet from the boat. I set the hook and it took a few minutes to get the fish where the guide could net it, but once he got it into the boat, I knew I had just caught my biggest fish ever! It was a thirty-inch northern pike! What a thrill! About a half hour later, I caught another northern pike, this one was *only* twenty-two inches. Fifteen minutes after we arrived at the end point, Dad and Rog appeared and I asked how they did. They said OK; then they asked how I did. I said nothing, but just held up the stringer with my two northern pikes and some bass! They said, "Wow!" I was the champion fisherman and had been vindicated and was smiling from ear-to-ear!

We got adjoining motel rooms, showered, went to dinner, and were in bed before 10 p.m. About midnight I awoke, barely made it to our bathroom in time, and tossed dinner and more. I was super miserable. Rog got up and tried to help. As things started to settle down, I looked for something to remove, or at least cover up, the smell I caused. I came across a bottle with what looked like a wick on the top. If I could light it, it might help the room's smell. As I was opening drawers for matches or a lighter, Dad's door opened, and he asked what was going on. We told him about my bout with the *porcelain throne*, and I asked him if he knew how to light this bottle so we could eliminate the smell. He just laughed and said, "That is an air wick—you do not light it!" Laughter broke out, and it was something Dad kidded me about the rest of his life! In the morning, my stomach still bothered me, so I slept in the back seat all the way home.

While we were gone, Mom and Grandma had been busy. Rog had a girl friend at ISU who sent him daily letters. Much to his chagrin, he had to search all over the house until he gathered his letters. I walked into my bedroom and found a big stuffed dummy sitting in my lounge chair, and I loved it! Why? Guess what it was wearing? It showed off my orange-and-black letter jacket! Cool!

Chapter 20

High School, Senior Year

S ENIORS! THE CLASS OF 1962! AFTER THREE LONG years, this was finally *our* year: Head of the class! The Top Dogs! The Big Cheese! The Kings of the Hill! The Big Men on Campus (BMOC)! *Wow!* We made it! We were a little excited about being at school this year!

When Ross and I picked up our schedules and books, I got three surprises! First, we were in the same physics class! This was the first time I was in a real class with Ross, one of the *accelerated* guys! Second, we had Mr. Harris for physics! Wow, what a change! Third, my schedule said, "Hall Monitor" instead of study hall for the half period before eating. I guess for thirty minutes every day I was going to be Tom Batiuk's cartoon character Funky Winkerbean sitting at a desk with a World War I machine gun mounted on it! Oh, my!

When walking into Mr. Harris's physics class our first period, we *big seniors* were loud and boisterous; however, he quickly quieted us down. He sat us alphabetically at our four-student lab tables; mine consisted of George Harrington, Jim Harwood, and my main lab partner, Don Johnson. Mr. Harris held up our physics textbook and said, "Over the summer, I examined your textbook and found it lacking; therefore, I will be adding tougher problems to bring you up to the standard I think you should have! They will be called 'Harris Problems!'" We wanted to ask, "What does that *really* mean!?" We found out what it meant right away! For me, it meant *lots* of evenings at our kitchen table with my exasperated chemical engineer father trying to explain physics to stupid me! Later, I found out it was *really worth* the struggle!

Mr. Tingliff's solid geometry and advanced algebra classes were run like his freshman algebra class. Students still put every problem on the board, and sometimes we were *speared* as he said, "No, no, my boy, that's not right!" From my earlier experience, I learned to quickly go to a corner, so I could protect part of my backside!

Late morning, I had our obligatory physical education class under the ever-watchful eyes of Mr. Metcalf. We started the year playing football on the practice fields; however, there was a *twist*, literally! The field was *rotated* ninety degrees; the original goal lines were now the out-of-bounds sidelines, and the sidelines were now the goal lines! While we did not have far to go to make a touchdown, we could go *very wide*! Thanks to Dad throwing me a million passes, I served as an end. Ralph Stoerp was our quarterback. During huddles, I stood thirty or forty yards off to one side. Many times, the other team never realized I was there, so Ralph just lofted a pass to me, and we scored a touchdown! Cool! Until spring came when we did outside track events, the winter was spent participating in co-ed activities.

Lunch time was next, but for the first half hour, I was a hall monitor. My station was right outside of Mr. Harris's physics room near double doors, which were to remain closed until the bell rang. I had a desk for studying, but it had no machine gun! *Darn!* My first duty day, I sat at the desk reading, but as students gathered on the other side of the double doors, the noise increased, Mr. Harris came out of his room, waved at me, and shut his door. I went outside the double doors to quiet the students down, but this was a forever problem! After a couple of days, Tommy, the freshman who moved into the house built next to the Albertz's, came up and talked to me. Over the year we got to know each other fairly well, and it was nice to have someone to converse with. I never did get any studying done during my hall monitoring!

At lunch we had two male seniors' tables. One consisted of all the *super accelerated* guys like Craig Brown, Jerry Wendt, Ron

Burritt, Roger Schneider, Tom Shalin, David Knaack, and others. These *geniuses* invented a new student, Harry Glick. Harry became a full-fledged member of our class, checked out books, was mentioned at our class activities, was always "missing" in yearbook pictures, and must have been an *accelerated* guy since I never had him in class! Our yearbook had a complete page dedicated to him.[19] It included a blank picture of Harry, a picture of his birthday party, which included members of the faculty and even Principal Mr. Buchner, and the following poem, "An Ode to Glick":

> How he came, I know not,
> but he came
> and will remain
> Harry Glick.
>
> His ID and library card,
> his seat in study hall
> recall
> Harry Glick.
>
> His name is on the honor roll
> (how I do not know),
> but here it is–
> Harry Glick.
>
> Will he stay on
> or be gone?
> To us he will be
> in eighty-three
> Harry Glick.

Our table was more down to earth. We had dummies like myself, *accelerated* guys like Randy Schulze, Don Johnson and Powers "Muley" McQuire, and some jocks like Mike Gunderson

---

[19] *1962 Tiger Tales*, Crystal Lake Community High School, Crystal Lake, Illinois, 1962, p 23.

and Jim Harwood. We mostly just told stories, harassed each other, and joked around. Hey, what else are senior guys supposed to do!?

After my economics/sociology class with Mr. Reber, the next-to-last period of each day, I was lucky to have my favorite subject, English IV—*not*! Because of our school's split, one of the new-hired teachers was Mr. Gene Penland. He seated us alphabetically, which put me behind Jim Harwood and in front of Lynn Keck. I chatted with both before class, but when the bell rang, we quickly learned Mr. Penland was ready to work. I think he was one of the strictest English teachers I had and emphasized writing correctly. While that certainly was not my strong suit, I was able to actually learn some (*not* many) English rules and guidelines. His manner was great, gentle, and fair.

My main goal this fall was to apply and get accepted into college. Fortunately, CLCHS was a testing center for the ACT and SAT college entrance exams, so I gave up two Saturday mornings to take them. My first choice was now Purdue University; their out-of-state student application was due by October 1. It was the first one I accomplished, but I also submitted timely applications to Michigan State and Illinois. It took four weeks to get the results of my ACT/SAT tests, and I submitted them to all three universities. The test results were pretty much the same; I did great in math/science (the top 2–3%), and horrible in English (the bottom third). I guess this was a premonition that, "I are a Engineir!" In early November, Purdue wrote me saying I met their minimum qualifications, but it would be sometime before they could offer me a slot! In late-November, I heard back from MSU, and they said "Yes!" We sent in a $25 deposit to save a slot for me. Right before Christmas, I was accepted at Illinois but rejected it in favor of MSU. I was still waiting to get my *yes* or *no* from Purdue.

In late September, Dave's home was again our homecoming float's construction site, so I went to help. We were to play the Libertyville Wildcats, so our theme was, "Wildcat-er-killer!" We had a tiger's head, four appropriately-sized body sections of a *caterpillar*, and a tail section with a black "62;" all which were *carried!* The head's frame used a slew of 2x4s and 1x2s, which held the chicken wire for its shape, and it was about ten feet high. When the parade started, about twenty of us went underneath, knelt by our brace, and on command, lifted the entire float. Don Johnson, Jim Harwood, Bob Frenz, Dave Thompson, and I were in the head, the Fanter twins were right behind us, and girls carried the body and tail sections. David Langdon and Tom McEwan led, carrying a big three-foot high by twenty-five-foot-wide sign stating: "BEWARE! WILDCAT-ER-KILLER!" Pat Dewey guided us because we could not see out! Being seniors, we were near the front of the parade, and everything started fine. After about 100 yards, *disaster struck!* The head's braces disassembled and/or broke! While we were grabbing things and trying to figure out what happened, we ended against the curb! Other classes' floats passed us and yelled, "Hey seniors, what's wrong! Cat got your tail?" We had to hold the head together while carrying pieces the rest of the parade! *Ugh!* Once there, we repaired the head. Saturday's before-the-game trek around the quarter-mile track in front of our Homecoming crowd was a chore, but we did manage to make it, and "Mr. Average's" prophecy last spring came true: *We were the first class to carry a Homecoming float!*

One Saturday night in early November, Ross, Jim, Ken, and I decided to visit C-GHS. They had a dance, and we wanted to visit our old classmates. It was dark and raining as we entered their driveway, the pavement was partly flooded, so it was difficult seeing exactly where to go. Suddenly, the pavement turned into mud! In the middle of the parking lot, they planned a grass area; however, there was neither grass nor any kind of barrier indicating where the blacktop ended! All four wheels were in the mud. A police officer outside the school literally shouted at me to get the car out of the mud! I could not go forward, so I tried reverse. Eventually, the car came to the end of the *mud/grass* area.

The officer again yelled, "Get out of the mud!" Since both rear tires were hitting the pavement's edge, I rocked it and the back tires *jumped* up onto the pavement. After backing, the front tires got hung up on the pavement lip, so I again rocked the car. When the front tires exited the mud, the car lurched backward, and I hit something! This is when I noticed a car parked behind me! The officer yelled at me again and got the owner of the car. He was another police officer! So, I hit a policeman's car! Great! I hit his front driver's door with the back-left corner of our Chevy, so it had two major dents, one from my bumper and one from my fin; there was zero damage to Mom's car. After taking my license and insurance information, he handed me a two-foot-long ticket! Before we left, many of our ex-classmates were exiting the dance and yelling at me, "Way to go Crash Hunziker!"

The next morning Dad contacted our insurance company, we drove to C-GHS with a camera, and parked our car where the officer's car was parked. Several Saturdays later, I appeared in court. On the way there, Dad asked me two more times to recite what happened. When we arrived, the police officer who yelled at me and a judge sat at a table. The judge called the case to order and swore me in. He asked what happened, and the officer gave a brief explanation of what he saw, but never mentioned his constant yelling! When it was my turn to tell what happened, Dad stepped in and did all the talking.

Dad talked about the rainy conditions, flooding, and no markers showing mud versus pavement. Then he produced our photos showing the ruts, how they led to the officer's car, and finally how the hit car was parked in the "No Parking" zone! The judges looked at Dad's pictures and said, "What kind of camera and film did you use because the pictures are so clear and brilliant?" I kid you not, *that* was his first comment about the case! He eventually agreed it was an *accident*, dropped all charges, fines, and points against me, stated we *were* responsible for fixing the damage, and asked me to pay the $25 court cost, which I gladly did. I hired a good lawyer and he got me off. Thanks, Dad!

Mr. Hymer held a pre-wrestling meeting and told us about the upcoming season and what he expected as our new coach. I noticed I was the only one at 127 pounds; I had a good chance to get in a number of varsity matches. At dinner, I told Dad about this meeting, and he immediately said, "You're not wrestling!" I did not push it any further. We lived near Dr. Abromitis, and many weekends he and his wife shared before-dinner drinks with my folks; this happened to be one of them. I mentioned wrestling practice was starting, Dad reiterated his "No." So, I asked my doctor, "Could I wrestle?" He said, "Sure!" I said, "See! He said I could." At that point Dr. Abromitis interjected, "But, if you have the same injury, you may never walk again!" I was stunned! In my mind I saw an old-fashioned balance scale with "Wrestling" on one tray and "Never Walk Again" on the other. When one went up, and the other went down, and vice versa. Even at seventeen, I was smart enough to realize, I did not want to live my life in a wheelchair! I never asked Dad about wrestling again.

OK, since I could not wrestle, was there something I could do to get in shape for tennis? Mr. Kloepfer started a new indoor track team, so I thought running could give me extra endurance; however, it would not help my backhand! I figured I could do a quarter mile, and he paired me with a junior named Chuck Porter. I knew him because he lived in Lakewood and ran track the last couple of years, so I had no problem letting him set the pace, and I just kept in step. There were about five pairs of runners, and we took turns doing our laps. Each pair ran about eight sets of two laps with five minutes of rest between them.

The second week, Mr. Kloepfer said I could not do just one event; he suggested low hurdles. I was not a strong jumper, and being only five-feet, seven and a half tall; clearing a low hurdle was a major accomplishment! I started slow and by the end of the second week, I was doing about sixty percent of full speed. The third week, we ran the full quarter mile, and I kept up with Chuck but really struggled with the hurdles. One night after doing our quarter-mile sprints, I was tired and tried to increase my speed significantly. I cleared the first two hurdles all right, but when I came to the third one, my lead foot was too low, went under the top bar, and I tripped over it, *badly*. That ended my indoor track journey because my knee was wrenched, and my calf muscle was pulled. So much for trying to get in shape for tennis!

I needed to impress the Purdue admissions office and, thankfully, classes and grades were going well for me! My time at the kitchen table with dad was paying dividends. Mr. Harris's tougher problems were challenging, but I was able to collect straight Bs from him until the final for the first semester. I thought I did pretty well on it, but when he handed it back, I had an eighty-eight. As it turned out, it was the highest score in our morning session, and I beat Ross by four or five points—*a miracle!*

Mr. Tingleff's solid geometry class was rockier. I got an A the first six weeks, but the second grading period, I had a 92.5; exactly halfway between an A and a B! He gave me a B+; I talked to him, but he would not give me the benefit of the doubt! *Ugh!* The third six weeks, I got a B–, but I had one more chance to improve my grade via his final exam. After I turned it in, I literally thought I got all 100 questions right! I even had time to check most of them twice. When he handed the tests back, my heart was pounding; I did not get 100, but a 99! The second highest score was Ron Burritt, who graduated fourth in our class. I beat an *accelerated* guy by 11 points and got my A for the semester!

In economics, I ended with a B, but Mr. Penland's English class was a very big challenge for me. I still struggled with writing, spelling, and reading. I barely squeaked out a C that semester and was *very* happy to walk away with it. So, for the first semester, I ended with a B+ average: one A, two Bs, and one C, plus an A in Physical Ed from Mr. Metcalf.

The first six weeks of the second semester was amazing. I was able to earn an A from Mr. Harris, and it was on February 20 while sitting in his physics class, we heard the lift-off of astronaut John Glenn starting his journey as the first American to orbit the Earth. What a tribute to physics! I made an A in advanced algebra from Mr. Tingleff and a B in sociology from Mr. Reber. For English, I worked extremely hard and was on the border between a B or C, just like I was with Mr. Tingleff the previous semester for an A or B. If I got a B–, I made our school's honor roll for the first time ever. Our parents offered us $50 each time we made it; however, they did not have to drain their saving account to pay us off! I wondered if I was going to be rich, or be the same old *average* student.

Mr. Penland gave us a short writing assignment while he annotated our grade books. I knew I would be the fourteenth to get my grade, so I watched carefully to see if he was writing a B or a C. My heart sank because it looked like he just made a half circle. Before giving us our grade booklets, he said many came very, very close to the next higher grade, and if they put a little more effort into it, we could improve. That seemed to seal my doom! When I got it, I opened it and saw B–! I had made the honor roll and was $50 richer! I did not take the bus home because Mom picked me up. When I got into the car, I asked for my $50, and she praised me for my hard work! This was also my birthday, so we celebrated by going to Woodstock, where I went into the Selective Service Office and signed up for the draft! Hey, that was what you did back then on your eighteenth birthday! We forwarded all the grades to Purdue, and I held my breath!

In mid-March I got mail from Purdue. With trembling hands, I opened it and read the short letter. It stated I was *admitted to the School of Electrical Engineering* starting in September 1962! *I made it*!!! I was *ecstatic* to be going! There were three of us going to Purdue next fall: Janice Lundahl, Pam Visin, and me. Both of these girls were near the top of our class, and then there was me! I missed being in the top quarter of our class by one (61/240) with my 2.5/4.0 grade point. Purdue required all incoming freshmen to take another battery of tests to determine class placement. From my standpoint, these test results were the same as the ACT/SAT tests, so why did we do them? I did well in math, so I was to take calculus. I filled out an application for a residence hall, but I remembered to *not* list Cary Hall on the application, figuring that would protect me. *Wrong!* A short time later I got my assignment, Cary West, Room 108, and my roommate's name was William Conrad.

During spring break Don Johnson, my physics partner, planned a trip to the University of Iowa, Iowa City, Iowa, because he was interested in a possible baseball scholarship, and he asked me to join him. I thought it would be neat to see another Big 10 school's campus, and Mom and Dad had no problem with it, so we took trains to Chicago and Iowa City. It was cold those days, but we walked all over the campus, and Don had his meeting with Iowa's baseball coach. (NOTE: I do not know what happened in that meeting, but he went to Illinois!) On Saturday night, we got tickets to the Iowa/Wisconsin basketball game. It was a special night for the Iowa fans since it was the great Don Nelson's last career home game. Iowa won which made it even a greater night for the Hawkeye fans!

Mr. Hymer replaced Mr. Faellaci as our tennis coach. We had challenge matches, and I ended up playing Number One Singles. What this *really* meant, I was the *sacrificial lamb!* I had to play the *best* from rival schools so others could compete against less-skilled players! Our conference's best player was a freshman, Wittman, from Zion Benton; he even beat Libertyville's senior, Marlin, who dominated the last three years. On Wittman's first serve, he used unbelievable top spin; I was lucky to just get my racket on it! Let me spare you the suspense; I was skunked 6–0 and 6–0!

We went to Libertyville, and Marlin beat me almost as bad: 6–0, 6–2! My best match was against Barrington, who had the third best player in our conference. He arrived in a black limousine, wore an expensive warm-up suit, and carried seven rackets! He won the first set 6–4, and we continued in a contested match; however, I lost the second set, 7–5; at least I was competitive! The conference tournament was held at Crystal Lake, and since my record was horrible, I drew undefeated Wittman. The game scores were closer, but the outcome was the same: 6–0, 6–0! A week later, Mr. Hymer took Gene, Ross, and me to Rockford for the state tournament; Steve had to work, so Ross teamed with Gene in doubles. I had to played the number one seed! So, what's new? I tried a different strategy! I hit to his backhand, rush the net, and force him to put it past me or lob it over my head. My strategy was not working because I never realized until late in the match, he was a lefty! My shots to his backhand were really to his forehand! He skunked me both sets, so my high school tennis career ended with a thud!

High school graduation was in our fieldhouse. We lined up alphabetically, so I was between two girls I knew well, Karen Hughes and Chris Hurley. With our black gowns and black caps with orange tassels, we quietly marched in as our band played. We stood at our chairs, had prayer, and then sat. Valedictorian Marcia Ekstrom and Salutatorian Ross Annable gave speeches I do not remember. We walked single file past the main podium, were given our diplomas, returned to our seats, and moved our tassels to the other side of our hats; with that we were graduates of CLCHS!

At home, Mom and Dad gave me two presents. First, was a card with money. Second, they gave me a waterproof Timex watch. They thought I needed a good watch to help me get to my classes on time; they had no idea how important it was to make it a waterproof one. Judy Flood had an after-graduation party. It was neat to go around and talk to so many classmates. The depressing part about the graduation ceremony and this party was it would be the last time I *ever* saw, talked, laughed, or shook hands with most of my high school classmates! We spent four, six, or even eight years together, doing common things, and then literally, went *separate* ways! *Wow!* There were many classmates I did not mention. This was not intentional but because space and time were limited. Our yearbook shows we had 177 in our class, but the graduation ceremony program[20] listed only 170; this, of course, does not include those who became the first-ever graduating class of C-GHS. Unfortunately, I had no contact after graduation with too many of my wonderful classmates. This is not what I wished!

---

[20] *Crystal Lake Community High School Baccalaureate Service and Commencement Program,* Crystal Lake Community High School, Crystal Lake, Illinois, June 3 and 8, 1962, Respectively

Chapter 21

Summer 1962

THE SUMMER OF 1962 STARTED OUT LIKE PRE-
vious ones. Roger left, this time, for North Carolina. For me, it was more lawnmowing and yardwork; I still had my six regular customers. Doing lawns allowed for waterskiing time; however, that was limited because many of my fellow skiers were working regular hours.

The third week of June, I received a phone call that changed the rest of my summer and the three following ones. Mrs. Hartung taught lifesaving lessons and because of my Red Cross Junior Lifesaving course, she wanted me to again serve as a *drowning victim*. A couple of days later, I was surprised at how large her class was. She also recruited another *drowning victim*, Jim Rosulek, who graduated in 1961. For the next two hours, Jim and I alternated *drowning* while a student *saved* us. After class, Jim asked if I would be interested in being a lifeguard at Grafton Beach. I knew Ken and Dave were going to work there because Ken approached me this spring about it. I told Jim I could not do it because I only passed the *junior* lifesaving course.

Mrs. Hartung asked me if I remembered how to do releases from various victim's holds. I said, "Sure," so she asked me to demonstrate them on Jim, which I did. She then said if I *saved* Jim via three different approaches and used three different carrying methods, she would give me my senior certificate, and I could guard. Fifteen minutes later, she certified me! Jim suggested I come to the beach the next day and meet his boss. I met Mr. Neil Bennett, and he said on hot weekends when the beach was packed, he needed extra guards. Weekends sounded good to me since I could do the lawn work during the week. He asked me to come at 11 a.m. Saturday with the intent of working until 7 p.m. I was to be paid the same as the other guards: $1.50/hr.

With Grafton being close to Chicago's northernwestern suburbs, weekends could become nightmares! The entire Grafton Beach Park was about a quarter mile of beachfront along the southwest corner of the lake. An eight-foot-high wire fence separated the parking area between Lake Avenue and the fence from the beach. From the east end, there were two changing sheds, the main building, the main gate entrance, and to the west were outhouses, a second gate entrance, and a wooded park with picnic tables. The main building had a concession stand, a safe room, two "Employee Only" bathrooms, and a sitting area. The western half of this building was a rented apartment. Outside this building on the west side were a couple of very big trees by the main gate.

I did not sleep well the night before my first guarding day. It was going to be hot, which made me happy for the work. Jim, Dave, and Ken were the three main guards, but a few others and I worked peak hours. Neil gave me a whistle and put me on top of the main ten-foot guard stand adjacent to the seawall and followed me up onto it. He indicated the buoy-enclosed swimming area, which was about 150 yards long and seventy-five yards from shore. He pointed out what he considered were the dangerous areas: the slide shoot to the right, the two 6 x 10-foot separate piers to the left, and the two twelve-foot square rafts in deep water. He said the rafts were my responsibility if we did not have a boat between them. At this time, Dave was in a twelve-foot aluminum rowboat sitting between the two rafts. There were other guard spots along the seawall, and every hour we rotated to a new position and were given a few minutes to get a drink or eat. Sitting in the hot sun for eight hours was a chore, but at the end of my first shift, no one drowned, so I guess we did all right! On Sunday, I arrived the same time. When it was my time to be on the main stand, Neil joined me again. I thought I had done something wrong, but he asked me,

"Would you like to teach swimming lessons? It pays $3.00/hour!" I remembered that horrible summer taking my lessons at the main beach, so I said, "Sure!" That evening Dave and Ken went home at their scheduled times, but when it came time for me to leave, Neil asked if I could stay until closing since there were too many swimmers for just Jim to watch. I agreed because I wanted to let him know I was a team player. When closing came, Neil asked me to get the resuscitator, and I asked, "Where is it?" He pointed to a silver suitcase sitting next to the big trees, so I grabbed the twenty-five-pound suitcase. Inside, Neil instructed me on how to use it.

Eight days later, Grafton started its single, four-week session of three, one-hour swimming lessons between 1–4 p.m., Monday through Friday. I was given two beginner classes and one intermediate class. The beginners were typically five to seven years old and we had twenty-five to thirty kids per class. That was too many for me to watch; it was not like we were in a confined classroom; we were on a beach, and they could easily wander off.

The first day I took the beginners to a stretch of sand and we laid down in the shallow water on our stomachs while facing the shore; our feet were in the deeper water. The first thing I wanted to do was to find out who would, and who would not, put their face in the water and blow bubbles. Those who were afraid of the water, I named "Number 1s," a little psychology here, and those who were not afraid were named "Number 2s." At the end of each beginner's class, I met with their parents and said if it was OK with them, I am going to split the class in two, they only needed to be here for a half hour instead of a full hour; it would mean less exposure time for their kids on cold days, and I would be able to concentrate on each section better, based on their needed skill set. The parents liked the idea. Hmmm, does this sound like *accelerated* kids and others? I hated it when my instructors always stood on a pier or shore and never got wet. I liked getting *down and dirty* with the kids, and they seemed to respond too.

The intermediate class was cool because they knew how to do the crawl but had to learn the elementary backstroke, breaststroke, and sidestroke. These kids were usually nine to eleven years old and fewer in number, so I kidded around with them, which they thrived on. At the end of our four-week session, Neil said he was impressed with my work and suggested while at Purdue I should take a class and earn my Red Cross Water Safety Instructor (WSI) Certificate because it would come in handy. This year since I did not have my WSI; I had another instructor, Alice Hoeft, sign my advancing students' cards.

In late August, Rog was home. He walked up to Mom at the beach and said, "Mom, this is Sybil from school. She is going to stay with us for a couple of days!" Mom was speechless because she had no idea Sybil was coming and had never met her before, but she hit hyper-mode and had everything ready by dinner time. Guess what vegetable Mom prepared for dinner? Yep, *peas*! Those *sterilizing* little green peas! All of us laughed but Sybil! Somehow, the fact that *peas made you sterile* was finally mentioned. This was the first of several times Mom served peas to our girlfriends!

On Friday before leaving for Purdue, Ross and I went to the high school to see Mr. Harris. When we walked into the building, there was something different about it. I had a strange feeling; one I had never experienced before. I spent four years here, but now there was this feeling I was an *outsider*, like I did not *belong*! When first period ended, we knocked on the physics room door, and Mr. Harris was pleased to see us. Since both Ross and I were to take calculus this fall, we asked him what it was about. He showed us several examples. This was the first time we ever had a hint as to what calculus was or how it could be used. We left after a half hour and thanked him for his time and insight.

On Saturday morning, Ross, Jim, Ken, Randy Schulze, and I went to the McCormick Center in Chicago. There were many musical performers there, but we went to specifically see the folk-singing group, The Brothers Four. They sang classics like "Greenfields," "The Green Leaves of Summer," "Riders in the Sky," and more. Besides their songs, jokes were in abundance, and many were politically oriented. Several were steered toward the John Birch Society, but as they like to call them, "The Birch John Society!" Obviously, many involved toilets, bathrooms, or out-houses. We got to Crystal Lake late, so Ken dropped each of us off at our homes. It was my last night in Crystal Lake because in the morning, I was heading for Purdue! It was hard to believe the time was finally here. *Wow!*

Chapter 22

The Girls of Crystal Lake

Before I write about Purdue, I need to back-track. When writing to a specific point in my life, I had to decide how to handle a certain subject: dating. My decision was to pay special tribute to those who I will always hold dearly in my heart. This particular chapter I looked forward to writing, but at the same time, I dreaded composing it because I *really* wanted to make sure I gave distinct tribute to those young ladies who were gracious enough to ever go on a date with me in my formative years! Also, while never dating them, there are other girls who provided real meaning and friendship to me. It is for all of these I wish to pay this special tribute. I dedicate this chapter to all of those mentioned below!

You will remember I already talked about my childhood girlfriend in Elmwood Park, Laurie Heick. We did everything together! There were times years later when I wondered what would have happened had we never moved? I, obviously, have no answer to that question. In Brookfield, there were none who were extremely special to me.

In sixth grade, I mentioned I become fond of Linda Petrillo; I had a crush on her! She was much taller than me and, had there been school sports for girls, she would have been *the* star! She ran fast and was a good basketball shooter. In sixth grade, it was neat being on Safety Patrol with her and working together with Frank Sibr.

In the spring of our sixth grade, John Stephani planned his birthday party for our entire class; however, I think he just wanted a date with Debbie Durbon! He and *others* paired all our classmates. Eventually, everyone was paired up except Mary Kleeman, Forrest Hare, and me. Mary was fairly short, cute, but quiet. *They* decided she could pick between Forrest and me. Forrest was a good athlete and tough kid. Me, I was pretty fat in sixth grade and certainly was not an athlete. We both made pitches, and the next day she, surprisingly, picked me, the almost-nothing fat kid! While I was happy about this, I kept wondering who Linda was going with! Mary gave me her address, and a few days later I had my first official *date* at twelve years old! Dad drove me to her house. We just sat there, and when he asked if I was going up the house, I said, "No, just honk for her!" He looked at me weirdly but honked! Within a few seconds she came out to the car, opened the door, I scooted over next to Dad, she got in, closed the door, and we were off to John's house.

When we got there, the boys were sitting on one side of the room and the girls were on the other side, so I joined the boys. It stayed that way for most of the evening. After refreshments, John opened his presents, and *they* decided to play a game. It was announced we were going to play, "Spin the Bottle!" I never heard of it, but as they explained the rules, I knew it was not a game I wanted to play, so I, and many boys, continued to sit off to the side. At the appointed time, Dad was back, so I opened the front door, and Mary got in and sat between Dad and me. When we got to her house, I held the door open, but after she exited, I crawled back in and shut the door. Dad sat there to make sure she got safely inside, and then backed out of her driveway. After a bit of silence, Dad said, "Boy, I need to talk to you about how you should treat a girl!" He then proceeded to give me pointers about what to and what not to do. I filed this information in the back of my brain for what I hoped would be other dates. Because the boys and girls were separated most of the whole night, I never did figure out who was Linda's date! I do wish to thank you, Mary, for picking me, and I am *sorry* I was not a better gentleman! I should have been nicer to you and treated you more courteously! Thanks again and best of everything!

In eighth grade, Mr. Cherry and Mrs. Hartung often combined gym class; dancing was the main activity. We had to dance *every* dance and fortunately there were many girls I enjoyed dancing with: Gloria Stewart, Chris Hurley, Janet Akerman, Susie Schenk, Joyce Ayanoglou, and, of course, Linda. At the end of eighth grade, there was a formal dance, and I knew who I wanted to ask. Several weeks before the dance, I called Linda. When she answered, I nervously told her who I was and asked if she would like to go to the junior high dance with me. "Yes, that would be great," was her answer! After that terrible minute on the phone, my heart finally came back to a regular rhythm. Later, Linda told me what color her dress was, and Mom ordered a corsage.

Right before the dance, Mom dropped a bomb on me: Rog would be driving me on this date! I was not happy about this since he ran around with Jim, her oldest brother. To calm me down, Rog said he would not harass me, but could I trust him? As I walked to her front door and rang the bell, my heart was pounding hard when her mother answered and invited me in. We talked for a few seconds, and then Linda came into the living room, and I was floored! She looked *beautiful!* She had on a pretty dress with nothing over the shoulders, so when I presented her with the corsage, her mother quickly stepped forward and asked if I preferred her to pin it onto Linda's dress. Without saying a word, I handed it to her!

I helped Linda with her coat, and we walked to our awaiting chariot. I opened a back door for her, let her in, gently closed it, and got in the other side. We talked about school and teachers, but Rog never said a word except his initial, "Hi!" He kept his word! We danced, got refreshments, talked to other classmates, and had a pretty good time. When it was time to come home, Rog was waiting for us. At her house, I got out, opened her door, she got out, we walked to the front door, and I waited until she got inside before I returned to the car. I believe I followed Dad's instructions to a tee, and I think we both had a good time; I know I did! The only problem I noticed was when we danced, she was about a head taller than me even though she was not wearing heels!

In early August, Lakewood was holding a teen dance. About two weeks before it, I was walking and happened to meet Linda. We talked and asked her if she would like to go to that dance and she said, "Yes." None of the other guys I ran around with had dates, so when Linda and I got to the facility, my buddies were gathered in a corner. I spent time with Linda, danced a few times, and then went over to see my friends. After a few minutes, the DJ for the night, Linda's middle brother, Dick, came over and whispered in my ear, "You know you brought Linda to the dance, so you ought to spend your time with her!" I blushed and knew I goofed, so the rest of the evening *was* spent with her. I could not believe I had two dates with Linda! *Wow!*

About the time of this second date, marching band practice started at the high school. I realized many of the taller upper-classmen were always hanging around the drum section. Why? The newest drummer was Linda, and they certainly noticed her, and she seemed to respond as well. Observing this happening, I knew my days with Linda were over. This was a time and girl I will never forget! Thank you, Linda!

During my freshman year, I was so shy, it was very difficult for me to get up the nerve to ask any girl just to dance, especially if she was one I liked. Girls just scared me! I could talk to most girls in class, but as I just said, if I liked her, it was difficult for me to start the conversation. *Ugh!* My shyness was still prominent in my sophomore year; however, there was starting to be a glimmer of hope for me. Most of the time at after-game sock hops, there were a few girls I would ask to dance. Probably the most prominent one was Gloria Stewart. We shared many classes together, so there was a familiarity with her.

Another was Karen Becker. In eighth grade she was one of our basketball cheerleaders. Remember, she was the one who sat next to me in Miss Reinecke's English class until my talking did me in! Even with that set-back, during our coed time in gym, we had the opportunity to learn the polka, and somehow, Karen and I got connected! While we did not do slow or other dances together, when it was announced the next dance was going to be a polka, we sought each other to dance it. However, I never did get my nerve up to ask her out, and she moved away that summer!

I mentioned earlier that Bonnie Rau sat next to me in biology, but I did not know if she was dating anyone. She was very cute and slightly shorter than me and was a Junior Varsity cheerleader, so she obviously attended home basketball games. Toward the end of basketball season, I asked her to one of the after-game dances. She smiled, thanked me, and then said, "I cannot go to the dance with you, I've been dating Jae Edwards!" Shot down and in flames! Jae was one of the superstar junior basketball players, so I was nowhere close to his league! Afterwards, she was always nice and kind to me, and we got along fine during biology field trips, but I never asked her for a date again. By the way, in case you were wondering about my taste in young ladies, Bonnie was crowned our Homecoming Queen our senior year, and I voted for her! See, I did have good taste!

In the spring, several told me Linda Stack in Mr. Peaco's World History class was interested in me! I shrugged this off, but others said the same thing. She was cute, a little shorter than me, and this was the only class I had with her, but we did not sit close together. A dance was coming up and somehow, I got the nerve to asked her and she said, "Yes!" I used Rog's $12 to buy the tickets! She lived in Trout Valley, about ten miles east of Crystal Lake, so she gave me a map and directions to her house.

I had earned my driver's license two weeks earlier and this was going to be my first date ever where I drove, but as I was getting ready, Dad said he would drive, period! My balloon was busted! He drove but he did not follow her instructions and got lost! We had to restart at the beginning and truly follow her instructions; we arrived *only* fifteen minutes late! We danced most of the slow dances. We had never really talked to each other before this night, but somehow, we had no problems conversing; it seemed easy and our time at the dance went much too quickly. On Monday, I was back in my usual clamshell and could not get the courage to just say, "Hi!" This lasted for about two weeks and by that time she thought I did not like her. I was remorseful I had blown it with my second Linda! Sorry, Linda, you deserved more than my shyness!

Mid-August 1960, Ross wanted to date Nancy Roubik, but he asked if I would double date with them and suggested I ask Leslie Baughn. Leslie visited a friend in Lakewood and spent much of her time at our beach. Many evenings they were on the raft, and we played "King of the Raft" and playfully pushed them off. I was always pushing Leslie off, so we got to know each other a little. I was concerned about Ross's suggestion because she was a year ahead of us. After a few days, I concluded, "Why not?" Ross asked

Nancy, who said, "Yes," so when I asked Leslie, I also explained the circumstances. She said "OK," and our double date was set.

I first picked up Leslie. She lived just beyond Grafton Beach, so I did *not* need a map to her house! This was the first time I saw her when she was not wearing a swimming suit! She was cute, had braces, and was just a little shorter than me. We picked Ross up and then drove the 100 yards to Nancy's house. After putt-putt golf, we went to a movie. When it was over, we treated our dates at the Tastee Freeze and talked. I dropped Nancy and Ross off and took Leslie home; she said she had a good time and thanked me. A couple weeks later while on the raft, I asked Leslie out again. We followed the steps of the previous date, but without Ross and Nancy.

Once school started, I backed off since I figured other boys her age would pursue her. We saw each other daily since we had the same lunch period and sat about thirty feet apart. In December, we were bumping into each other more often, so I asked her to the Christmas Prom and to my surprise, she said "Yes!" We had a great time talking, dancing, and even had our portrait taken. The photographer told me, "Move closer to her; she won't bite!" My face turned bright red! The weather and roads were horrible, so after the dance, I suggested we eat locally at Breaker's right on Route 14. She liked the idea, and we had a great meal with little hazardous driving.

A week later I received our dance pictures, and her mother thanked me for bringing it. I gave Leslie my yearbook, and she signed it by her senior picture, "Can't thank you enough for going to the Breaker's instead of the Evergreens. Congrats for being original. Thank you again for Christmas prom." Near the end of tennis season, I heard two seniors talking about the senior prom. One said, "I'm taking Leslie!" I was happy to hear she was going with a good guy. Leslie graduated in the top ten of her class and went on to study at Northwestern University. The last time I *ever* saw her was at lunch the last day of school as she walked past me and smiled. Leslie, thanks for dating me and the fun times!

In the fall of 1960, the owners of the new house next to the Albertzes moved in, and when Mom and Dad had their annual Christmas open house, they invited this new couple. That night I was introduced to Mr. and Mrs. Archambaults, who had five children. Their oldest was Ed, who was a senior and would go to Illinois the next fall. Their oldest daughter, Mary Anne, was currently a freshman, and their second oldest son, Tommy, was in eighth grade, but next year was the freshman who visited me daily during my hall monitoring chore! They had two younger children, Larry and Nancy, who were probably six and five, respectively.

The summer of 1961, Nancy Roubik and Mary Anne were inseparable! Most nights when Ross, Jim, Ken, and I hung out at the Gate 13 beach or Harrington's pier, they visited us. Ross told me Mary Anne liked me! You must understand, I thought she was *very* cute! With her dark eyes and hair, and beautiful smile, I thought she looked a little like Annette Funicello, and you *know* what I thought about her! I could not understand why someone like her was interested in *average* me, so I ignored his information; however, she seemed to smile a lot when I was around!

One evening as we walked home from the beach, I got bold and asked her out. Her reply caught me by surprise! She said, "I'll have to ask my mother!" I was not sure how to reply, so I think I just said, "OK." We parted in front of her house, but the rest of the way home, I kept thinking about it; I finally concluded this was a parental requirement since she was only fifteen. The next day when we had a moment alone, she said she could go out with me. *Great!*

The day of our date, I washed the inside and outside of Dad's Anglia. Mom was not happy we were going on a date because they had quickly become good friends with her parents, and she was afraid I would spoil it! She warned me, "*Be nice* to Mary Anne!" If Mom realized how scared I really was around girls, especially ones I liked, she would have known I was not going to do anything shameful!

I was nervous as I drove those 500 feet to her home! Her dad answered the door and invited me in. He said she would be down in a few minutes. Mrs. Archambault came downstairs, with Mary Anne following her. *Oh my gosh!* She had on a light blue dress and *looked spectacular!* Since the movie *Ben Hur* with Charlton Heston was long, I said if it was all right with them, I wanted to take her to the Tastee Freeze afterward but planned to have her home by midnight. They agreed and smiled. I parked near the theater and put on the parking brake since it did not have "Park." After getting our tickets and snacks, we found seats without people in front of us so we could see.

Once settled, she reached into her purse and produced a pair of glasses. I never saw her at the beach with glasses and said something about it. She laughed and said she mostly goes around blind because she did not like to wear them. When she put them on, I looked surprised! She asked what was wrong. I replied, "You're the girl who took attendance in Mr. Harris's study hall all last year!" She said she was. Here I had seen her every day this past year, but I never *saw* her!

When the movie was over, we headed for the Tastee Freeze; however, I was having problems with the car. It drove OK in first and second gears, but whenever I shifted into third gear, the engine lost power and slowed down, so I drove the two miles to the Tastee Freeze in second gear! When we got there, a big blue cloud followed us into the parking lot! After parking and as I went to grab the parking brake handle, I realized it was *still on* and I had driven with it engaged! So much for impressing this girl I knew how to drive a stick shift! We got our refreshments and talked about the movie. I had questions about how people were healed of leprosy when rainwater touched them. Because of her religious background, she explained it was Jesus's blood *mixed* with it which cured them. I guess I got the idea and still had questions, but I did not ask them. Once our ice cream was finished, I *took the parking brake off* and had no problems driving her home!

A week later we had our second date; however, this was the weirdest date I ever had, not with her, but anyone! This time when she told me she could go, she added a twist. We would have four kids with us, her two younger siblings and a neighbor's two because she had to babysit them! The movie was *The Parent Trap* where Hayley Mills played both early-teen twins in this romantic comedy. When we sat down, with six popcorns and six drinks, Mary Anne and I sat in the center to split the kids up, the old *divide and conquer* routine. They enjoyed the movie, laughed a lot, and were quite attentive. At the Tastee Freeze, each got their own ice cream dish which did not get spilled. *Whew!* We asked them what they liked best in the movie, and each gave a response. Larry was last and said the part he liked best was when one of the twins had the back of her dress torn off which exposed the back of her underwear and legs! Even at seven, boys will be boys!

On July 21, US Astronaut Gus Grissom completed America's second suborbital flight. Upon splashdown the capsule's hatch blew early, and it sank. I usually read the *Chicago Tribune* each day, OK, mostly just the comics, and read "Line o' Type or Two" on their editorial page. They had a poem about Gus Grissom that ended something like, "Gus thought he saw written on it, 'No deposit, No Return!'" I thought it was clever, so I memorized it and recited it to Mary Anne. She thought it was funny too, so each day after that I memorized a short poem and recited it to her.

As the summer went on, we went out one night each weekend, and most days when the weather was nice, we spent time together. One late afternoon, we were the only ones on the raft and I lay on my stomach. She sat next to me, picked up peeled paint chips, and played Tic-Tac-Toe on my back. I often took her for boat rides and even taught her how to water ski. Most evenings I walked her to her house before bidding her good night.

After dark one night when we got to her house, she told her mom she was home, and we were going to talk for a while. As we sat on their front steps, we heard firecrackers exploding near my house. A few seconds later, footsteps came up the street, stopped in front of us, and we could hear two guys laughing and gasping for air. Ross and Jim obviously set firecrackers off under my bedroom window and ran; however, I was not home! I never confronted them about this, so if they ever read this book, it will be the first time they really know what happened that night!

As she and her family left on a two-week vacation, I said, "Goodbye" and took their picture. The following morning was when Dad, Rog, and I did our Chippewa Flowage fishing adventure. Mary Anne was my first *real* girlfriend because, besides lots of dates, we spent a lot of wonderful time together, and I easily connected with her. Some of my fondest memories of her are many of those unscheduled, impromptu times.

When school started, we only saw each other once while passing through hallways, and it was a very quick encounter, so I passed her a copy of a poem and headed off. When football season started, our first game was an away game, about a thirty-five-mile drive, and none of our parents were thrilled about us going to it; however, we got permission and went. It was a cool evening, so I wore my letter jacket in public for the first time! *BMOC!* After winning the game, we first stopped at her house to let them know we got safely back before heading to the Tastee Freeze.

Next, we won our first home game and went to the sock hop. We danced the slow dances, but the "Twist"was the big craze, and she wanted to do it. I never tried it before, so I was not sure what I was doing. About halfway through the second attempt, my back went out and it hurt badly! I apologized, but I had to stop. For that night and the next two, I bathed my back in Bengay ointment! The next weekend was another home game and sock hop and she wanted to do the *twist* again, but I said, "No!" I believe this disappointed her a lot!

After one of the slow dances, I did something completely new! As it ended, but while her right hand was still in my left hand, instead of releasing it, I held it! Our hand holding position was uncomfortable, so we each let go but quickly reconnected with our fingers intertwined! I had never held a girl's hand before! What a *mover*! It was an amazing feeling to walk beside her holding hands, and it only took me *eight* or *nine* dates to do it! She said she wanted to tell her brother something, so we walked over to where Tommy and a couple of his friends were sitting. They talked a couple of minutes, and then we walked back to the dance floor. Personally, I think she just wanted to show her brother we were *attached!*

I asked her, and she got permission to go with me to our Homecoming dance. Right before Saturday afternoon's game, they announced the float winners: the seniors *and* the sophomores! The sophomore class had a float with a tiger licking a lollypop entitled, "Lick Them!" I did not take her to the game because I had to work in the refreshment stand the entire game. Each night I had brought her home, a light was on in the Albertz's living room, and I worried Mrs. Albertz was spying on us! This bothered and stymied me, when I got her home; I thought this might be the night I could get up enough nerve to kiss her good night!

Her dad invited me in and when she came down the stairs, she was *stunning!* She had a beige dress, top, and a scarf wrapped around her neck! She also wore flat shoes, so she was not taller than me, which I appreciated. We went onto the dance, and did dance a lot of slow dances, but no *twists*. One of the decorations in the fieldhouse was the head of our winning "Wildcat-er-Killer" float; however, there was nothing present to represent the co-champion sophomore float. She was quite upset about this and brought it up often!

After the dance I took her to The Evergreens in Dundee. As we entered and were shown to our table, almost all the customers paused their conversation and watched us pass. It was not me they were looking at; it was Mary Anne! After we ordered our food, I wanted to tell her how stunning she looked, but as I started, she asked if I would do something for her. I said, "Sure," and she asked me to quit giving her poems at school. She dropped a book, a bunch of them fell out and the kids in the room laughed at her. I said I would comply, but the mood changed, and I never got back to telling her how stunning she looked. It was quiet between us as we drove home. When we got to her house, the Albertz's living room light was on, I lost my nerve, and just said good night at the front steps. Shyness killed me!

On Monday when we were to pass each other, she did not come by! It happened before, but on Tuesday when we did not meet again, I figured she was going a different way to avoid me. Ross said he was planning a party after this Friday's away football game and invited Mary Anne and me. On Wednesday, we did not meet again, so later I went to her locker and told her about Ross's party; the next day I got her, "Yes." When I got in the car for our date, I just sat there for a few minutes. I did not feel *excited and thrilled* about being with her thonight like on all our previous dates; it was like the *spark* was gone!

The drive to the game was quieter than usual. I did not know if she was upset about the floats, the embarrassment of the poems, or something else I did or did not do, but she seemed to have lost that *spark* too. It was a cold night, our football team forgot to show up and got killed, so everything seemed to perpetuate the same mood. We quietly drove to Ross's house and joined in with the other couples. We danced a few times, but because Ross and Randy and their dates were doing a lot of kissing, we spent most of our time looking at Ross's record collection. The bottom line was this was not a great evening for either of us.

Shortly after I became "Crash Hunziker," CLCHS held its annual Sadie Hawkins turn-about dance. I had never been asked before, and with Mary Anne and I not meeting regularly, I figured I would keep my losing streak intact. One day she suddenly appeared, told me she was hosting a pre-Sadie Hawkins party and asked me to both! I wanted to say, "I'll have to ask my mother," but instead I simply answered, "Yes!" She caught me off guard, but I was happy to have time with her.

Mom and Dad had another engagement that night, so I was home alone with Grandma when Mary Anne rang our doorbell. She had a few freckles painted on each cheek and wore a delightful straw hat with pigtails attached, all of which I thought were really cute! Also, she made me a corsage; it was about seven inches in diameter, and had blue and red ribbons with Hershey's Kisses in the center. Before leaving, I had Grandma take a couple of pictures of us. She opened the car's back door and let me in first! At her house, she opened the front door and had me sit on a couch with other guys. There were about forty in attendance, and all our girlfriends were very attentive, constantly bring us drinks, cookies, and other refreshments. This party lasted about an hour.

The fieldhouse was decorated with corn stalks, hay bales, and fence posts. The lights were turned off as usual, and we danced and talked to others. On a small stage, senior Jerry Wendt, who was dressed like a preacher, appeared and announced, "Marriage ceremonies commence immediately!" Mary Anne said, "Let's get married!" Who was I to turn her down!? We waited about fifteen minutes as each couple went up, said their "I dos," and were pronounced married by the preacher man. Also, the bride and groom kissed! Aaahhh, so here I am in line with her and thinking, we have never kissed, so will we do our first kiss in front of all these people!?

When it was our turn to step onto the stage, my heart was pounding. Jerry asked for her name since he knew me, and I told him. He then proceeded with a twenty-second sermon, turned to me, and asked, "Do you take Mary Anne to be your lawful wedded wife!" I could not do it straight, so in my best *Little Abner* voice I said, "I do!" He then asked her, "Do you take Rick to be your lawful wedded husband?" She said in her real voice, "I do!" The preacher then pronounced us married and I could kiss the bride! We kissed! It was about a millisecond long! (Note: A millisecond is 1/1000 of a second!) Actually, it probably lasted a whole half of a second, but we *did* kiss! *On the lips! Our first kiss!* Oh, and *my first ever kiss!*

Going home I was the first to be let off. Mary Anne walked me to the front door, and I just felt all eyes in the car were on me to see if I would kiss her. I wanted to—boy, did I want to, but not in front of others, so I opened our front door and said, "Thank you for inviting me. I had a *great* time!" When I got inside, I was sick that I had not given her a real kiss and let my *shyness* get to me! How *stupid* of me! She made major efforts to restore our relationship to where it was before Homecoming. She went overboard to make sure our turn-a-bout date went *perfect*; I think she wanted both of us to regain our *spark!* I could not believe I left her hanging at our front door without a *real* thank you! I just plain blew it! I thought maybe, just maybe, I could make up for a small portion of my *dumb* behavior by giving her a good picture from our date! A couple of days later, my film was developed, and I was flabbergasted! I thought Grandma would be able to get a reasonably good shot of us since we were only a few feet away; however, she took three horrible pictures! My hope of a peace offering went out the window! So, between me not doing a *real* good-night kiss and not having a picture for her, I failed miserably. *Ugh!*

The Christmas dance was in mid-December, and we had a date. Mom heard through the grapevine the type of dress she was buying and that she was getting new flat shoes so she would not be taller than me. I picked her up, and she was again *stunning!* We were still in an awkward relationship, but after the Sadie Hawkins dance, and even with my stupidity, I think we both were more in tune. The dance went well, and since it had been snowing, we ate at a local restaurant. When I took her home, their driveway was full of snow, and I pulled too close to the right edge. Before I realized how close I parked to the right edge or could open her door, she opened it and stepped out! Unfortunately, she semi-fell and partially slid down the side slope of their driveway. She quickly righted herself, her flat shoes were filled with snow, she became angry at me, and rushed to get into her house. I got back in the car and sat there for a minute, thinking: What have I done!? I just basically ended our relationship, for now! *Ugh!* I then noticed the Albertz's living room light was on!

This year CLCHS hosted their first-ever foreign exchange student, Jo Elsrud. She was Norway's Junior Ski Champion, so she probably gave up an opportunity to be in the 1964 Winter Olympics by coming and studying in the US for a year. Her Scandinavian heritage showed through her blonde hair, blue eyes, and weathered, but pretty face. She fluently spoke five languages and was very coordinated and athletic. She stayed at Polly Rosenthal's home, so when Ross started dating Polly, I got to meet Jo on several occasions. I remember attending a senior party, and we actually spent time talking. I had no classes with her except gym.

This winter I was primarily concentrating on one thing, getting decent grades so I could get into Purdue. Mr. Metcalf divided our PE class into groups of about eight, and I was picked to be one of the captains! In March we were to be teamed with an equal number of girls to form co-ed volleyball teams. Another captain was Ron Burritt. Both of us were interested in knowing Jo better, so Ron went to Mr. Metcalf and arranged Jo's group of girls to be teamed with his group; however, he made the mistake of telling me. I looked at the new proposed rosters and noticed that both Ron's boy and Jo's girl groups each had one more person than both my boy's and girl's groups. I pointed this out to Mr. Metcalf and said it was not fair they had two more kids, he agreed and switched Jo's group to mine, but I said nothing to Ron. The next day when the teams were made official, Ron just stared at me, and all I did was shrug my shoulders! So, for six weeks, Jo and I played volleyball together and got to know each other better.

In early April, the senior class presented the play, *Charlie's Aunt*, so I thought it would be fun to ask Jo to go. After PE class one day, I asked if she would like to go to this play, she blushed a fair amount, but said, "Yes!" The night of the play while walking to the auditorium, I noticed Jo was slightly taller than me, so I tried my best to *erect* myself to my full *awesome* height! At the auditorium, guess who was ushering, Ron! We talked and then took our seats. The play was very funny and our *acting* classmates did a great job, especially with the often-spoken line, "She's from Brazil, where the nuts come from!" Jo laughed as much as I did, and we enjoyed the evening. Afterward, we went to the Tastee Freeze and spent quite a bit of time talking. We talked about our families, our likes, and I asked many questions about Norway. She was very open and willing to talk about all of this. Before we knew it, I had to get her home by my promised time.

On Monday, since Jo and I had to go the same direction for our next class, I waited for her and the two of us walked together. About the middle of this week, I asked if she would like to go to a movie this weekend, and she said, "Sure." We laughed a lot during the movie and like last time, we had refreshments at Tastee Freeze. I again asked a hundred questions about her and Norway. The next week this scenario was repeated.

There were two more dances, one in early May and the Senior Prom in early June. After three dates, I *rolled the dice* and asked her to the Senior Prom about six weeks before it. I do not recall her exact words, but in essence it was, "Let me think about it," or, "Can I get back to you on that?" It was not a "Yes," but also it was not a "No." I kept wondering what was going on. There was another time each day where our paths crossed, so I thought that I should ask her on another date and decided to do it, but before I could say anything, Jo said, and I remember this, "You know the Senior Prom is a really big deal for a girl and I really want to go with someone taller!" *Taller*! I am too short! This reply really threw me for a loop!

When I got to my hall-monitoring station, my mind just went crazy! What was I going to do? I had no interest in other girls and only had about six weeks before the prom. I felt numb. Tommy came up to visit like he had been doing all year, and I thought about asking him if Mary Anne was dating anyone but decided against it. A few days later when Ross learned I had been turned down, he indicated he thought Jo was interested in a Norwegian exchange student at another high school. I understood that fully because I knew after the prom, she would be going back to Norway, and I would be here. Why did she not just tell me that instead of saying basically, "I'm too short!?"

I started going through ideas for a date for the prom. There were other girls I liked, but the one girl that kept coming to mind was Mary Anne. I went back and forth on this because I did not even know if she was dating or whether she would be interested in going out with me again after my *stupidity* last fall and winter. After about a week and a half of wavering, I got up my nerve, visited Mary Anne at her locker, and asked her out to a movie. As usual, I waited a day for the answer, which made me wonder what her mother might think of me. She did say, "Yes!"

The date went fine since there was no snow, and I pulled much farther to the left side in their driveway! By the way, every time I came home from a date with Jo and drove by the Albertz home, their living room light was off; however, on this night when bringing Mary Anne home, it was on, *again!* As a result, she got no kiss! In the middle of the next week, I asked her out again, and it went pretty much the same as the previous date. It was now about three weeks before the prom, so I figured I better make my move. I met her at her locker and asked, "Would you like to go to the Senior Prom with me?" Her face lit up and she said, "I'd love to, but I have to first ask Mom!" The next day I had her positive answer, so plans were set in motion, and we went out once more before the prom.

Gene Bacon and I were talking about our prom dates after tennis practice, so we decided to double date for the after prom. He was taking Melon McGough, and over the next couple of weeks, our two dates talked and decided who was going to bring what for our after-prom trip to Lake Geneva, Wisconsin. Mary Anne indicated she was going to be wearing a pink dress and preferred a wrist corsage, so I ordered an appropriately colored and configured corsage. The night of the prom, her dad met me at the door and let me in. As usual in a minute or two she came down the stairs and was *beautiful!* I slipped her corsage onto her wrist and told her folks I thought it would be sometime near 6 a.m. when I got her home from the school-sponsored after-prom event. As we headed for the car, she commented on my cummerbund and bow tie, and said, "*Red* ones! They don't go well with my *pink* dress!" I had ordered my Tux shortly after she said, "Yes," but before I knew the color of her dress and forgot about the colors! *Ugh!*

The fieldhouse was well decorated. As the sun set and the floor got darker, more people entered the dance floor, including us. We occasionally talked to other couples, including Gene and Melon so we could discuss last minute arrangements for the next day. We stood in line to get our picture taken, danced, and just walked around while enjoying the music. At midnight, the dance was over, and we were ushered onto school busses to go somewhere else, which was *top secret*!

The bus was well decorated with ribbons and bows, and each window had a rock and roll 45-rpm record cover. She picked out one she liked! Initially, I think everyone was a little disappointed when the bus stopped in front of the movie theater. We got out and walked through a beautifully decorated lobby into the theater. After everyone was settled, they introduced our entertainer, Mr. Sound Effects! He did all kinds of sounds like train noises, ship's horns, guns firing, doors opening, windows breaking, and the like. Once we heard his repertoire, he told many funny stories which tied his sounds together. He was on stage for almost two hours and pretty much had everyone in stitches. After a break, we boarded our busses and headed to the Cary Country Club. The room was elegantly decorated, and all the tables had linen, candles, and well-polished silverware for a formal breakfast. We took our seats and over the next ninety minutes were treated to a variety of breakfast delights. About 5 a.m., when we were full, we reboarded the busses to go back to school. Five minutes later, I looked at Mary Anne as she was leaning against the side of the bus sound asleep, like 90 percent on the bus. Between watching the blinking police lights escorting us and having too many scrambled eggs, I started to develop an ache! I was happy when we got to school, and I could get fresh air on our walk to the car. The ride home was quiet, and as I drove into her driveway, I noticed the Albertz's living room was light on!

When I got home, I immediately sat before the *porcelain throne*, seeing my breakfast a second time. I was to drive us to Lake Geneva, so I had to get better! I nursed ginger ale and packed my supplies and left about 10 a.m. We loaded Mary Anne's baskets of food and took off. I then made a *really foolish mistake;* I told her what happened to me when I got home. She was displeased, and this set our tone for the rest of the day! Stupid me! We picked up Gene and Melon and their contributions, and drove to Lake Geneva. We picked out a couple of picnic tables, walked along the shore, watched ducks, skipped stones, and eventually ate a wonderful lunch the girls prepared; however, I ate lightly and kept nursing my ginger ale. After lunch, we rented a rowboat and guess who did all the rowing? Unfortunately, I had to sit with my back towards Mary Anne to row, tried to turn around often, but this did not bode well with her. I even used the oars to splash everyone a little just to liven it up. We then packed everything into the car and headed home. Within minutes all three were asleep. I was extremely tired too, and for the first time ever, I had to really fight to stay awake while driving. I knew I did not want to become part of a headline about four teenagers being killed in a car accident! We dropped Melon and Gene off, and about 4 p.m., I helped Mary Anne carry her empty baskets in and said, "Goodbye." A few days later, I got our prom pictures, which turned out very nice, and dropped one off at her home.

The weekend after the prom was graduation and parties, so I did not see Mary Anne. On Wednesday after graduation, I was sunning myself on the raft when she swam to it and invited me to join her and two other girls on their boat. We sat in the front seat while the other girls lay on its deck. I heard their conversations but did not add much to them. I was thinking, she asked me to the boat, so maybe I should ask her out again! Someone asked about the time so I looked at my new waterproof watch and said, "Its almost 4:00." Mary Anne indicated she had to head home, and I said I would join her.

We got to South Shore Drive when I realized I left clothes on the green bench. I said I would be right back as I left for the bench, picked up my things, and turned to head back for the road. I looked southward, and Mary Anne was nowhere in sight! I stood there for a moment, trying to figure out what happened. I concluded she probably felt I had already *shyly and stupidly goofed or messed up too many opportunities* with her, so it was now time for her to move on. Who would not have done the same!?

What I did not know is that this was the last time I ever saw her at our beach or in our neighborhood! A few days later, Mom said she took a job at the Tastee Freeze and over this summer and the next two years, I occasionally saw her there. She always gave me her big smile and was friendly, but our social life was over! I hoped her life would be fulfilling and wonderful. About two weeks later, I got that call from Mrs. Hartung, which changed my life and set me going in a different direction.

I received an invitation from the Rosenthals to attend a going-away party for Jo; it was to be held right *before* graduation because afterwards, she was leaving. Initially, I was torn between going and not going. We had communicated little the last month, so I was apprehensive, but I did go. That night, the Rosenthal house was packed, so again it was also another opportunity to interact with my classmates. As the party wound down, Jo and I had a very enjoyable conversation, talking about the past year and what we saw in our futures. We exchanged addresses, promised to write, and said "Goodbye," but I told her I would be there Tuesday when she left.

That morning about eight of us were there, and we were gathered close to Jo. When the time came for her to leave, she gave each of us a hug and she even kissed my cheek. Tears were shed; after all, she had been a well-involved classmate for the most important year of our high school experience. She, Polly, Ross, and Polly's folks got into the car and drove off as we waved. When the car disappeared, we just stood there for a moment and quietly stared in that direction. Finally, we said our goodbyes and headed in our own directions. As I drove home, I wondered if Jo and I would write or ever meet again; only time would tell. It was the next day that Mary Anne and I had our last moment together, and she disappeared. This was not a good start for the first week of my summer vacation! I just lost two very close and wonderful friends within thirty hours, both of whom were young women I was very fond of! *Ugh!* Thank you both for sharing wonderful and memorable times with me! They *are* treasured!

During swimming lessons, I spent more time with the instructors; one of them was Charlene Fay, who was the same age as Mary Anne, cute, had fairly long curly dark brown hair, and was about two inches shorter than me. Ken mentioned Charlene liked me, so now being just a little smarter about girls, notice I said a *little* smarter, I took the hint and asked her out; she immediately said,

"Yes," and she wanted to go to the drive-in. I had never done this before, so I was intimidated. When I rang her doorbell, Charlene opened it, and it was the first time I ever saw her in real clothes! She immediately introduced me to her mother, who was very gracious toward me. Then she called for her Dad and said, "Dad, there is someone here that I want you to meet." He was a big husky guy, and it seemed like he *charged* at me as he came into the room with an extended hand. We talked for a few minutes and then we left.

We talked throughout the first movie and were in a silly mood that night, but we decided to watch the second movie which was Bob Hope and Bing Crosby's *The Road to Hong Kong*. There was one sequence in the movie, which is too complicated to explain, that just put us into stitches! We laughed for five minutes and had tears running down our cheeks. I took her home, and she said she had a good time and went inside. She had the early shift the next day, so when I showed up a few hours later, I blushed when my co-workers said, "Hey, we heard you and Charlene had a good time!"

Our second and third dates followed the same pattern, except on the latter one when I walked her to her front door, she turned, leaned in, and kissed me on the lips! It was not a millisecond kiss, but a *real live kiss*! I was caught off guard but I was quite happy! So the next weekend, I thought I would take the initiative. When I leaned in, I closed my eyes too soon, and kissed her on the end of her *nose!* She immediately, lightly grabbed my chin, redid the kiss, and then smiled. For the rest of the summer, all our goodnight kisses were done with her holding my chin!

As summer came to a close on Labor Day weekend, we stored all of the equipment at the beach, and high school classes started. That Friday morning when Ross and I met with Mr. Harris, we hung around and waiting for the bell to end second period. Ross ran into Polly while I ran into Charlene. She smiled and was wondering what I was doing at school. I told her as I walked her to her next class and confirmed that night's date. Because of *the guys* upcoming trip to Chicago on Saturday, and I was leaving for Purdue Sunday morning, this night would be the only chance we had to be together. We went to a movie, exchanged addresses, and when it came to saying "Goodnight," our kiss was much longer than usual, *and* it had to last us almost eleven weeks!

OK, you are now up to speed on my *love life*, such as it was. I just thought those seven young women, Mary, Linda, Linda, Leslie, Mary Anne, Jo, and Charlene, deserved special recognition for their understanding, patience, and perseverance for even going out with me. There will be other women, which also served me well, to develop that final relationship which would last for the rest of my life, but these seven were the first ones to set my life in the right direction. Thank you, all! From now on my *love life* will be incorporated with other activities.

Section 4

Purdue University

Chapter 23

Freshman Year, Fall Semester, 1962

I T TOOK US JUST OVER THREE HOURS TO DRIVE THE 180 miles around Chicago to Purdue. I followed signs to Cary Hall's check-in, filled out paperwork, and bought my Cary Club green freshman pot (i.e., beanie), which I had to immediately wear. The guy who took me to my room was Jim Shutt, the first person I met at Purdue! He escorted Dad and me down the south first-floor hallway of West, pointed to a door and said this was his room should I have any questions. When we came to Room 108, the door was slightly open, so we stepped in and there was a guy sitting at a desk who stood up and introduced himself. He was a little taller than me, had dark-rimmed glasses, and his name was Bill Conrad, just like I expected. We unloaded the car, and Dad invited Bill to go to lunch with us, but he had already eaten. After lunch, I said my goodbye to Mom and Dad. It did not bother me to see them drive off because I saw how Roger flourished in his college environment, and I assumed I would too.

Our room was old and small. West was built in 1937/38 and was the largest unit in Cary with 235 men. We were now using the furniture Dad used! Our room was about nine feet wide by sixteen feet long and had a closet, bunk beds, two desks with wood chairs, a small dresser, an upholstered sitting chair, and a trash can. Conrad, what I would call him from now on, took the top bed and bottom dresser drawers to make it easier for me. Between the desks on the far wall was a window looking out onto the courtyard, and a steam radiator sat under it. We also had a locked door, which led to the next room. That was it! *Home Sweet Home* for a year!

As I unpacked, we talked. Conrad recently left the Navy, so he was twenty-two. He served as a radio operator decoding messages, and his last station was in Adak, Alaska, where he spent sixteen months. I told him a little about myself, but it was dull compared to his life. We both signed up as electrical engineers.

At 5:00 p.m., all incoming freshmen had a required meeting at the Edward C. Elliot Hall of Music. Purdue's president, Dr. Fredrick L. Hovde, welcomed us and others spoke. The Purdue Symphony Band concluded the meeting. Their director announced, "Today's first number is going to feature one of your own class-mates playing on the xylophone. She is Janis Lundahl from Crystal Lake, Illinois!" I was flabbergasted! One of my two CLCHS class-mates was being featured on the first day at Purdue! I told Conrad we were classmates and I knew her well, but he did not believe me until I showed him my yearbook! After the short concert, we were to go to our preferred church, so I looked for a sign saying, "Congregational Church." When I found it, one of the freshmen waiting under it was Pam Visin. What was the probability I would see both of my high school classmates the first day!? After all, there were *only* 18,000 on campus!

At midnight, upperclassmen came through the hallway banging on the doors and ordering us out of our rooms. Conrad lay there and said, "Go back to sleep!" Eventually someone opened our door, turned on the light, and ushered us to the downstairs dining room. We were to bring our green pots, too. There was a tall kid yelling at us, another who had a pronounced southern drawl, another blowing a trumpet, and so forth. Some of the guys had beards, but most did not. One of the guys making noise I recognized; he was Jim Shutt! The President of West, John Pickett, introduced him-self and told us the rules about our green pots which we basically had to always have on our person. They taught us the Cary West cheer and the first verse of our school's song, "Hail Purdue!" About

2:00 a.m., when we could somewhat sing "Hail Purdue," we went back to our rooms and slept.

The next morning, I went to Deac's Bookstore and purchased my pre-ordered books and materials. They asked if I needed a slide rule; I said, "No, I have my Dad's engineering slide rule from the mid-1930s!" The bill was $150! Upon returning to West, I passed an opened door, and the guy sitting at the desk was the trumpet player from last night. We introduced ourselves; his name was Tom Hintz, an Indianapolis entomology junior. I commented about his *horrible* trumpet playing, he laughed, and said, "I borrowed it from a friend and he just showed me how to produce a noise from it!"

I spent most of the rest of my morning getting to know my freshmen co-corridor residents. Rick Rozelle, from New York, and Larry Jones, his muscular roommate from Indianapolis, lived across the hall from us. Jerry Gochenaur was in the room on the other side of the locked door between us. Down the hall were Rex Hedegard and Mike Hatch. These were the freshmen I most hung out with my first year.

That afternoon, upperclassmen began to arrive. A sophomore electrical engineer, Marvin Estes, was Jerry's roommate. He was very tall and skinny but had a stroke while in high school; it cost him most of the use of his right arm, hand, and leg. In the end room next to Rozelle and Jones was another entomology junior, Gary "Bucky" Buckingham, who was fairly tall and muscular. In the corner room next to us was our sports director, sophomore Tom Bartels (Bart), the guy with the pronounced southern drawl. His roommate was Ron Wenzel, another sophomore. These were the older students I had the most interaction with. Oh, there was one other person. In a room next to Hintz's was our graduate-student counselor, Mike Long. It was his duty to keep us quiet after dinner for studying. Since I had a loud laugh, he visited me almost nightly!

On Wednesday, September 12, our classes began. Classes started at 7:30 a.m., each period lasted fifty minutes, and we had ten minutes to get to our next class. The last class ended at 5:20 p.m., but at 12:20 p.m. on Saturdays. Our longest session was the ten weeks from now until Thanksgiving; our total semester was sixteen weeks. The bad part was we had to study over Christmas break because we had two weeks of classes afterward! *Ugh!* The second semester had two eight-week sessions, with spring break in the middle.

Freshmen engineering students started with eighteen credit hours: calculus, chemistry, English composition, engineering graphics, an engineering lecture, and Reserve Officer Training Corps (ROTC), Air Force in my case. All eight semesters the schedule was somewhat similar: Monday, Wednesday, and Friday were my heaviest days, and Tuesday, Thursday and Saturday were generally lighter. This semester, I had a particularly heavy Friday schedule; eight hours total which included the chemistry lab from 2:30–5:20 p.m.! Also, I had a two-hour engineering graphics class on Saturday! Yes, I had classes on Saturday *every* semester; not that I always attended them!

The first class I attended was differential calculus. The lecture was in the Electrical Engineering (EE) building, Room 129 (EE129). It held about 500, and I had many classes there. When the bell rang, the professor introduced himself, turned to the four large green chalkboards and started writing Xs, Ys, Dxs, Dys, and so forth. I had no idea what he was doing, but I copied every one of them! I ended with five pages of *stuff* but did not know what it meant! He was *horrible!* As I walked out, I heard two students commenting, "Why are we doing this stuff about ranges and domains; we did all that in high school last year!" I felt sick and wondered, "What am I doing here?" He assigned even-numbered problems, but I had no clue how to solve any of them.

The next day in my recitation class when the grad-student instructor went through the assigned problems, I started to see where this was going, but to do the homework *before* that recitation class—I was lost! The first half of that semester, I was drowning! I got an F and managed a D on the second test! Then by accident, I met my savior! I was talking to Marv, my EE sophomore neighbor, and he mentioned calculus. I told him I was lost in it, and he said he would help! Oh man, the times I spent with him were enlightening! If it was not for Marv, fifty-eight years later, I would still be in that first calculus class! Really! I did not ace the rest of this course, but at least I salvaged a C for the semester!

My chemistry and graphics (mechanical drawing) courses were a continuation of Mr. Harris's and Mr. Chinn's classes, respectively, if I kept up with the work. In my English composition class, well English was English, and I was happy when it was over, and I did not have to repeat it! AF ROTC was going OK. Since Conrad was ex-Navy, he taught us how to spit-shine our ROTC shoes. He usually did one shoe to demonstrate how to do it and then let the guy do his second shoe; however, he never did either of mine; I had to do both. I guess that came as the privilege of being his roommate, but he did a good job instructing us, as you will later see. Pam Visin and I passed each other twice a week between classes. The first time we met, she told me Janis received a *million* phone calls for dates after her appearance on stage! With a men to women ratio of 5:1, well *duh!*

The first Saturday evening, the freshmen put on our required show for the upperclassmen. We mocked those overseeing our orientation meetings, but I am not sure those we mocked liked it, but the other upperclassmen really enjoy the razing. I did a rendition of the "Birch John Society" jokes I remembered; they laughed almost as hard as we did! The following Saturday was our upperclassmen/freshmen flag football game. I won a kickoff contest, and as we lined up for our initial kickoff, a teammate told me, "Do not kick to the guy with the blue shirt, that's Dave Mills, who won the Big Ten 440 last spring; he's fast." Based on my tip, I angled it toward the opposite side of the field. Whoever fielded the ball, lateraled to Mills, and we watched as he took off and scored. On their kickoff to us, I was in the center of the field, so I thought I would block their kicker, Gary Buckingham. When I body-blocked him in the chest, he lost only a millisecond getting down the field because my size was no match to his! The referee was our sports director, Bart, one of the guys we mocked the weekend before; all penalties went against us! The final score was a million to 0!

All year long, there were sport competitions between the eight units within Cary Hall. The previous year West won the All Sports Trophy, which was based on competitions throughout the entire year. Bart often talked to us during our early *orientation* sessions, encouraging us to participate. As a result, when they started a fall tennis tournament, I signed up. I had not hit a ball the last four months, but to my surprise, I won my first match and reported it to Bart; he was quite happy! A few days later, I had my second win! There were actually two brackets of sixteen singles being played, so I was now in the top four of my bracket. I lost the next match; however, we won the fall tennis tournament. Bart was given gold medals, but there were not enough to go around, so he decided to give them to those who won matches. He came into my room and handed me one of them, but I said, "I did not win my section of the tournament." He explained his philosophy and said I earned it. When he left, Conrad thought it was cool Bart rewarded those who deserved it!

As the weather cooled, I wore my only medium weight jacket. I brought my CL letter jacket; however, I removed the varsity letter and class numbers and sent it to the cleaners so the outline of both did not show; others wore similar jackets. Once when leaving West, someone behind me said, "There goes a guy from Crystal Lake!" I turned around, and it was the loud, tall sophomore who harassed us during *orientation*. I said, "Yes, and where are you from?" "Dundee," was his reply. His name was Sheridan Miszklevitz, better known as "Clevitz."

One day as Conrad and I headed to classes, we noticed John Pickett was wearing a mostly black pot with a small gold front rim, and from one hand via rope he dangled a foot-long wooden object. Later, we learned he had been tapped by the Purdue Reamer Club to be a pledge. The Reamers were an activities and services honorary for independent male upperclassmen with an academic standing of at least Junior 5. Also, they had to prove their leadership abilities; Pickett did this by being West's president. The wood object he carried was a replica of a reamer. Like Dad told me, one of the big things they were responsible for was the care and feeding of Purdue's official mascot, the Boilermaker Special (BMS). The Reamer Club started in the early 1920s, and in the early 1940s, Purdue got their first Special. I saw the BMS 2 in 1956 at Northwestern; in 1960 they got the BMS 3. No other university had a 7,000-pound mascot that can go 70+ mph on the highway! The fact Pickett was picked to be a Reamer really impressed us about who he and the Reamers were! We also noticed Bart was wearing a maroon and gold hat and carrying a tomahawk. He was tapped to become a member of The Tomahawks, which was a sophomore independent men and women service and leadership honorary. There were also chapters at Indiana University and the University of Illinois. In fact, Purdue's and Illinois's football teams play for a Tomahawk trophy, a small cannon. We were likewise impressed about this recognition for Bart.

Purdue was picked to win the Big-Ten football title, and our first game was at the Pacific 8's projected champion, Washington, but the game ended a disappointing tie. The next weekend was a bye week, so all the freshmen were summoned to the north end of Ross-Ade stadium. This was the card section, so for a couple of hours we practiced. After beating Notre Dame in South Bend, we finally had our first home game; we were heavily favored against Miami (OH)! This was also Senior Cord Day. Traditionally, senior men returned in the fall with beards; hence, why some of our *orientation* upperclassmen had beards. In addition, all seniors participated in a parade to the stadium while wearing their painted cords (corduroy pants or skirts). It was led by the Boilermaker Special and the Purdue Marching Band. At the stadium, they filed onto the field and formed a tunnel in the southeast corner for our team to run through as they entered the field. It was a unique tradition to observe. Miami kicked off to us. Our first play from scrimmage was a long bomb for a touchdown, except our All-American end dropped it! The game went downhill from there, and we lost my first home game! *Ugh!*

There was another exciting event during football season, and it had nothing to do with a ball. All home-game weekends had a show called "Victory Varieties." They had two shows on Friday and Saturday nights in the Hall of Music, so 24,000 tickets were available; it usually sold out! The entertainment was top-notch: Bob Newhart, The Kingston Trio, The New Christy Minstrels, Nate King Cole, The Beach Boys, and so on. The cost was horrendous, $2/ticket, and I always found a single seat down front and center. My favorite group was the New Christy Minstrels who did a timely skit in their performance. The stage was dark, a single light came on, and there was a boy and a girl standing alone. For about a minute, their conversation went: "I don't know if we should do it!" "Oh, come on, no one will know!" "I am worried something will happen, and we'll get caught!" "Don't worry, we'll be careful!" "OK, so you think we should do it?" "Yes, I think we have a right to do it!" There was a pause, they bowed their heads and jointly said, "Our Father who art in heaven …" A short while before, the

Supreme Court of the United States had *banned* prayer in schools. The audience stood and cheered!

Mom and Dad came for Dad's Day against Michigan. It was not much of a game, but "Hail Purdue" got played a lot since we won big! They asked how classes were going, and I told them calculus and English were my bad ones. They had one thing to tell me, and it was a *bomb*! Since this was probably our family's last Christmas together because Roger would graduate in early December 1963, they decided we should go to Florida for Christmas break. They planned to leave home Saturday morning, pick me up after class, and head south! *Ugh!* This meant I had no time to see Charlene! I was not a happy camper at this announcement!

Correspondence was something I wanted to do. I will admit, Charlene was probably on the top of my list. We wrote weekly; however, in mid-October I got a disturbing letter from her. As I read it, I could picture her being in tears and the paper being sopping wet. Two of her classmates were on a double date with two older boys. They were traveling the backroads we used to the drive-in where one set of railroad tracks existed; it had a signal, but no gates. Something happened; their car tangled with a train, and the two girls were instantly killed. Both boys survived with extremely serious injuries. Charlene lost her best friend, Gerry Bigham, who she had known for years and had even come to Grafton several times this past summer. Not knowing what to say or how to say it, I wrote back, but I doubt I was able to comfort her very much.

I also corresponded with many of my classmates. Like me, Ross and Randy had access to tape recorders. We agreed to communicate via audio tapes, and every three to four weeks I got a tape. Another classmate I corresponded with, as promised, was Jo. She told me while going to school in Oslo, she worked at the Kon Tiki Museum and especially liked talking to US visitors. After passing a couple of letters back and forth, I bought a small Norwegian dictionary and a sweatshirt with Boilermaker Pete on it. I used the dictionary to find salutations in Norwegian to use in my letters. One time I wrote out a three or four sentence paragraph and substituted the appropriate Norwegian word for each English word. She wrote back laughing! She said she figured out what I was trying to say, but direct word-for-word translation was not very good Norwegian grammar. It was probably my initial horrible English grammar that messed it up! The sweatshirt cost me $3, but the postage to send it to Norway set me back $7! A little while later, I got a letter back with a picture of her wearing it. On the back, she wrote, "Do you see I have your sweatshirt on? I have Ross's blue jeans on! I guess I will see you this summer, Rick." Two things about her inscription. First, I never got a straight answer from Ross why he sent her blue jeans! Second, if Jo came back to the US in the summer of 1963, I never heard about it or saw her! Darn!

During the last two weeks of October, there was this thing called, "The Cuban Missile Crisis." The Soviet Union got caught sneaking ballistic missiles into Cuba! These could quickly destroy the southeastern part of the US, including Washington, DC, with little or no warning. Conrad met another ex-Navy guy, Dick Cartin, and they became friends. Both were on edge, especially when President Kennedy ordered a blockade of Cuba. They both made plans to leave for active duty, and I was about to lose my roommate! Fortunately, the Soviet leader backed down, and the world backed away from a major nuclear confrontation. Conrad and Cartin let out a big sigh of relief!

I went by Hintz's room and noticed a guy talking to him. I recognized him; however, I do not believe he knew me. His name was Bill Reichert, CLCHS Class of 1960; his dad owned the Crystal Lake Buick/Chevrolet dealership! I introduced myself and asked him how he knew Hintz. He said he used to live in Cary near Hintz. Since he was a junior and had a vehicle, I asked him if I could get a ride home at Thanksgiving break. He told me when his last class ended, which coincided exactly with mine; I could not believe my luck! After Thanksgiving when Pam and I met between classes, she asked how I was getting home for Christmas. I told her I was going to Florida, but mentioned Reichert, so for the next year and half, we often traveled together with Reichert!

When Thanksgiving break arrived, my priority was to spend time with Charlene. Wednesday night, both of us were excited to see each other since there were no quiet moments as I drove to the movie. We saw *West Side Story*; the music and Romeo and Juliet plot were enchanting. On the way to the Tastee Freeze, I told her I had a little surprise. She gave me a questioning look! I asked her if she would like to go to Saturday's Purdue/Indiana football game. She liked the idea, but said she better ask her folks; she got an OK from them.

I picked her up at 8:00 a.m., the traffic was good, and time passed quickly as we constantly talked. We had won the Old Oaken Bucket the last fourteen years, were heavily favored, and scored quickly! We stopped IU and were driving deep into their territory again when we tried a pass in the flat; it was picked it off, and they ran it back for a score. Now tied, our team deflated, and the rest of the game belonged to Indiana! I was devastated! We walked to West to freshen up, and she asked if she could see my room, which was allowed on afternoons of football games. She was surprised at how small it was, but quickly noticed my pictures of the guards and swimming instructors on my bulletin board. Once on the Illinois Tollway, I finally told her about my parents' decision to go to Florida for Christmas, which meant I would only be able to see her for a few minutes on Sunday before I went back to school. She was not happy, but there was nothing I could do about it. It was a long day, and it ended with our usual nice soft kiss.

One thing I hated about not ending the semester over Christmas break was we had assignments; I had an English theme and calculus problems due when I got back. Mom, Dad, and Rog picked me up about noon, and it took a day and half to get to the motel on Treasure Island, St. Petersburg, so I used part of that time to do my homework. The weather at the beach was warm and pleasant, and the surf was gentle, so it made for great shell collecting. I bought postcards and sent one off to Charlene. After ruining my back, I sought ways to strengthen it, so on Christmas day, I got an exerciser I wanted for my back. About the fourth day at the motel, I got the flu and started vomiting. *Ugh!* On New Year's Day, our tradition was to watch the Rose Bowl. Wisconsin had a great year and one of their starting guards was CLCHS's Ron Paar! It was a close game, but in the end, Wisconsin lost! Before we left, I wanted to get Charlene something "Florida-ish!" Finally, I got her a carved coconut head; do not ask me why! We got home late Saturday night and on Sunday about 1:00 p.m., I went to see Charlene. I gave her my present; I actually think she liked it! I said I would be home in only two weeks, and we would then have two weekends to go out. She kissed me, and we said our goodbyes. On the ride back, I kept thinking about the time I missed with Charlene while in Florida, but I could not turn time back!

Sunday night, Marv and I visited, and he was quite excited because his folks bought a boat, but they told him he could not take it out unless he learned to swim. I said, "Marv, for you a deal! Since you singlehandedly are getting me through calculus this semester, I will teach you how to swim!" He was excited, so a couple days later, we went to the co-rec pool. He was not afraid of water, and we invented a semi-side/crawl stroke for him. He improved to the point where he did several laps. When he completed my *swimming course*, he wrote home and his parents were excited for him.

Scholastically, finishing this semester was tough, especially when doing regular daily assignments at the same time I was taking final exams; Purdue did not have a finals week, but they had finals! My last test was the last Saturday of the semester; a two-hour test in graphics and an A was at risk because the final would determine my grade. That morning, I stopped by my mailbox and found a letter from Charlene. I had written her about when we could get together, so I figured this was her reply. I got to my classroom early, so I decided to read her letter before the test. A *bad* idea! Her letter started, "Dear John …" I knew I was in trouble since my name is Rick! She dated someone right before Christmas and would not be able to go out with me over semester break! *Wow!* As our instructor distributed our tests and I started working on it, my mind was 180 miles further north, and I struggled to concentrate on the task at hand! A couple of days later, I got my first set of final grades, and none were an A, so I was quite disappointed with myself. Had I not opened that letter until *after* my test, my grades might have been better!

Semester break was a dud! I slept in, read a novel, and watched my TV in the basement. On Friday, our high school had a home basketball game. When I entered the balcony, Mr. Harris was collecting tickets. He asked how college was going, and I told him what happened in calculus and how Marv bailed me out. I also mentioned this coming semester was the big flunk out one because we had organic chemistry *and* physics. Since I mentioned chemistry, I told him my story on how I made flashcards to learn the elements. He told me I was the only one who got a 100 on that test!

Chapter 24

Freshman Year, Spring Semester, 1963

THE ADMINISTRATION TOLD US AS FRESHMEN, "Look left. Look right. Understand, one of you will not graduate!" This coming semester would separate graduates from nongraduates. I had integral calculus, organic chemistry, mechanics and sound physics, speech, and Air Force ROTC; however, based on Neil's suggestion, I also took Technical Water Activities for my WSI certification, giving me nineteen credit-hours! I had to meet Mr. Agnew to arrange my WSI class. He said the best way to learn how to teach swimming and lifesaving was to just teach the classes, and he would occasionally observe! He introduced me to my thirty students, and I was left in charge. *Gulp!* There were freshmen through juniors, students from other areas of education, and jocks who needed credits to stay or become eligible for a varsity sport. Half the class could swim and the other half were beginners. I had those who were swimmers do four laps each of the four main swimming strokes so I could observe where improvements were needed. I took the beginners to the shallowest end, which was still eight feet deep, and had them get in and do floating exercises. Each session, I split my time between the groups with each focusing on whatever their weaknesses were, and often Mr. Agnew sat on the top bleacher observing. A month before spring break, I progressed the advanced group into lifesaving. The second group progressed to swimming the crawl; however, improvements were needed on their swimming technique, like kicking!

This semester's biggest difference was calculus! My lecturer was Dr. Spalding. *Oh my gosh!* What a joy to have him do our lectures. The first half of each period, he did basic derivations and carefully explained each step. The second half he did selective problems within our assigned homework; thus, we had examples to follow when doing homework! Marv won the biggest benefit; he was not bothered much by dumb me!

Physics was known as a separator of boys from men. The lecturer was pretty good, so I was able to pick up good tips and clues as to what was expected. I had a foreign graduate student for the recitation class, and he had real English problems. Even though he reviewed the classroom assignments, he did a very poor job explaining things. Within two weeks, only one other student and I regularly attended! When we had tests, he published the class's scores, and I was usually in the top two or three. Thank you, Mr. Harris, for your difficult and horrific "Harris Problems"!

Dad prepped me by warning me that organic chemistry was the toughest course he ever took as a chemical engineer! This class was *the* class that killed many prospective engineers *this* semester. I was able to keep up and got reasonable lab grades, but I was having problems when it came to solving chemical reaction equations, so my tests scores were on the low side. This class forced me to plow my way through and push as hard as I could. Dad was right; it was tough!

Speech class was my easiest class. We had to make different types of speeches; one was how to do something. We had a Purdue football player who drew a play on the board using two letter abbreviations for each player. He said, "We used to use Xs and Os, but the guys kept forgetting which they were!" Everyone laughed. Another time we had to do a speech that brought emotion to the surface. My swimming class was right before speech, and the chlorine was quite strong, so my eyes were usually watering. Tears easily came forth and were handy for this speech. Finally, we had to do a sales pitch, so I *sold* my stereo tape recorder. While the speech went all right, getting the forty-pound recorder from Cary to the swimming pool, to the classroom, and back to Cary did tax my arms! I never got lower than a B, but it seemed impossible for me to get into the A range.

The Wisconsin wrestling team came to Purdue for a dual match. As Conrad and I went to see it, I told him one of Wisconsin's wrestlers was a guy who went to my high school, and last year he finished third in the NCAA at the 171-pound weight class. When the teams came out to warm up, I elbowed Conrad and pointed to Ron Paar. I could not believe how big he looked. Remember, he just finished a very successful football season as a starting guard, so obviously, he bulked up for that, and he was now wrestling at 191 pounds. Ron beat our guy 5–2, and it was cool to see him in action again!

As March approached, I walked by Hintz's room and heard Johnny Mathis singing. I asked why he always played this music on Thursday nights. He replied, "It's because my girlfriend, Susie, is coming up this weekend." They had been dating for a while, and most Saturday night and Sunday afternoon dinners at West involved Mike Hatch, Hintz, Susie, and me eating together. She was a small, petite redhead from Indianapolis, and they were getting serious and appeared to be very compatible and happy.

Spring break was welcomed! In fact, it was a busy one. The first weekend of our break, I visited several of my CLCHS classmates who went to Illinois. When I got there, I met up with Jim Harwood, Don Johnson, Paul Koch, Steve Mudgett, Dave

Thompson, and Bob Frenz; the latter two were attending other colleges. Saturday night's state championship game turned out to be a two-point victory for a Chicago high school. As we walked back to the dorm, Dave pulled me aside and asked, "Why did you quit writing Charlene?" He and Charlene apparently communicated, and she must have mentioned I no longer wrote her, which was true. I told him about her *Dear John* letter, and he seemed surprised, so she must have not mentioned it. We watched the two-time defending national champion University of Cincinnati get beat by two points in overtime by Loyola University! Two exciting game in one night!

Randy Schulze was also home, and we decided to visit Ross. He lived in a private, two-story home with a back entrance we used to get to his room. His room was about the same size as mine, but he did not have a roommate. After talking, Ross navigated for us as we toured the campus sites. The last place we visited was their Student Union and Ross showed us where we could buy beer. Wisconsin allowed anyone over eighteen to buy it; however, since I was driving, I did not have any. We bought food, went back to his room to eat, and then drove back to Crystal Lake. This was the first time I saw either of them since Thanksgiving, and old friendships are precious!

Back at school, there were noticeable changes. We no longer had to wear white shirts and ties to dinner! However, *the big* change was Cary Northwest and West would be closed for two years for renovations! *Wow!* Questions: Who is going to be my roommate? Where would I live? I knew Conrad and Cartin wanted to room together where Cartin lived, so I was slow asking others. By the time I did, they were already paired with someone; therefore, I took potluck again. That brought me to: Which Cary unit? Notice, I did not even think about one of the newer resident halls, I *only* considered Cary. What a difference twelve months made! Hintz and I talked, and he said he was going for a single room on East's first floor. Being only a sophomore next year, I applied for a double in the same area.

I wrote to Neil that I was taking my WSI certification class. I also sent a letter to Mr. Willis, who oversaw swimming lessons at the main beach. I explained I taught last year at Grafton, was in the process of getting my WSI, and would like to teach at his beach. I received positive responses from both, so I was now set for summer. In addition, Neil told me Ken and Jim were not coming back. What a surprise!

During ROTC, we had a special inspection by the Air Force Angel Flight. This was an all-female supplemental group that supported and promoted Air Force ROTC. I could see out of the corner of my eye three Angels coming my direction. Occasionally, they stopped in front of a cadet, turned to face him, looked over his uniform, made a comment, turned forward, and continued. As they approached, I recognized the Angel doing the inspection; it was Janis Lundahl from CLCHS! When she got to me, she stopped, turned, looked up and down my uniform, and said, "Give this man a merit for his shoes!" The Angel following her made a notation while Janis turned forward and marched on. During our four years on campus, this was the *only* time I ever remember being face-to-face with Janis, and she *gave* me a merit! *How cool was that!?* Conrad's shoe-shining instructions worked!

The call from Bart for spring tennis players was issued, and I stepped up. In my bracket, I repeated what I did last fall, winning the first two matches to get to the final four. We won the spring tennis championship, and Bart gave me another gold medal! At the end of this semester, West also won Cary's All Sports Trophy for the second year in a row. Much of the credit this year goes to Bart's enthusiasm and constant push for participation!

As the semester was ending, I needed a final push to get respectable grades. My Air Force ROTC, speech, and calculus classes moved along well, but I did not slack off. Since I had done so well in my physics recitation class, I thought I had a chance for an A; however, I found out our recitation class had the lowest grades in the entire physics section; therefore, what I thought were *top* grades, were really in the B range; I had no chance for an A!

I did not know what to expect in my swimming class. I had seen Mr. Agnew watching me several times, but one day when we were done early, I gave the guys a chance to blow off steam. We did all kinds of acrobatic splash dives for ten minutes; however, as I walked to the locker room, I saw Mr. Agnew watching! *Did I blow it?* A couple days later we met in his office, and he told me I had to make out their grades! In the back of the Red Cross book there were 250 questions we could use for written lifesaving final exams. My final was to answer each question *and* put the reference page number! The answers were easy, but it took me about ten hours to find all the reference page numbers. I turned in my grade sheet and Red Cross book; a couple of days later, he gave my book back and said, "Good." I did not know what I got until the grades came in the mail.

The course I was worried about was organic chemistry. We were told there would be 1,000 points which including daily assignments, lab reports, and tests; the cut-off for pass/fail was 600. I breathed a sigh of relief after the final since I had 639, so I knew I passed! We were told over 60 percent did not have the required 600 points, and it was fixed! Remember, I told you this was the flunk-out semester!

Dad said I could use his Anglia to bring my stuff home. Since Rick Rozelle and I were caught up on our classes, I invited him home two weekends before Memorial Day. Neil had others scheduled to set-up the beach, so at 10 a.m. on Saturday, we went to Grafton to help. Chuck Porter was there, too, since he was the new guard. I introduced Rozelle to Dave, Chuck, and Neil, and the five of us started to get things deployed. There was one change in our strategy; instead of using the boat near the rafts, we had another ten-foot stand, which we floated and sank into the muck somewhat beyond but between the two rafts.

About halfway through this process, Charlene walked onto the beach. This was the first time I saw her since I got her *Dear John* letter, and I was uncomfortable. I did introduce her to Rozelle, and we went back to work. She hung around until we were done, but we talked very little. The beach was prepped for opening and we said, "Goodbye! See you in a couple of weeks." I finished everything at Purdue by Thursday before opening day, packed Dad's car, and drove home.

Chapter 25
Summer, 1963

R OG SPENT THE SUMMER IN SOUTHEASTERN IOWA
and visited Sybil at Cedar Rapids on weekends. It was a hot
Memorial Day weekend; the beach was crowded, popsicles and ice
cream bars were sold, and all hands were on deck. Dave, Chuck,
Charlene, Janet Russell (Class of 1963), Bill Speechley (same class
as Charlene), Sandy Zimmerman, and I were guarding. Midge
Junroe and Elve Seims worked the concessions, and Midge and
Neil worked the main gate. No one drowned because there was
standing room only in the water, and no one could fall over!

Monday evening, Dave went back to college and starting on
Tuesday, all the other guards had classes, graduation, or prom/
after-prom activities. Neil set me up to work twelve hours each
of the next four days, and Midge, whose parochial school was out,
worked until Neil could relieve her. Three days were warm, so I
guarded, but one day was cool and no one came to swim, so I raked
the park and moved picnic tables. Since we had few swimmers, I
could sit in a chair on the seawall, which allowed Midge and me
to talk a lot; we became like *big brother* and *little sister*. Also, while
the summer started edgy between Charlene and me, we quickly
became good friends again!

The second weekend, I was working Saturday's late shift. The
beach was crowded, and many co-workers were there. On weekends, Dad brought me the same dinner they enjoyed. He told the
workers at the main gate there was a note for me on my dinner

tray. When I came to eat, everyone started joking with me about how smart I was. I could not figure out what was going on, but then someone handed me the note Dad left. It was my grades: all Bs, except for one A and one C! They all thought I was smart, but I knew differently, and it would show later! My two surprises were the A in my WSI class, and my 639 was good for a C in organic chemistry! *Wow!*

In early June, Neil suggested two guards should be qualified scuba divers in case we needed to search for a lost person. Dave and I instantly volunteered and were set up with lessons with Carl, a certified scuba instructor at the main beach. The first ten hours of lessons were in a private pool where we learned the basics. Upon completing this, he took us to a quarry in Racine, Wisconsin, where we did dives. We put on wet suits, but Carl only had two pairs of gloves and boots, one set he kept, and the other set Dave used. We could easily see thirty-five feet and observed fish. After swimming near the surface for ten minutes, he signaled us to head deeper.

Our ears started hurting, and we had to valsalva (i.e., holding your nose while forcing air into your inner ear to equalize the pressure) many times as we went deeper. When we got to about thirty feet, we came to the thermocline where the temperature changed from about 55° F to 38° F in two inches! Once we went below it, I quickly noticed how my feet and hands got much colder, and they ached. At forty feet, Dave and I went through the buddy breathing process without any difficulty. A couple of days later, we came back; this time Carl wanted to take us all the way to the bottom, about 110 feet deep. He said there was a car there that we could climb in, but there was no way I was going to get into something that might trap me! Again, Dave used Carl's extra gloves and boots, so my hands and feet got very cold. We saw the car with the driver's door open, but neither Dave nor I got in! After being there for what seemed like an hour and freezing, I tapped Carl, made a sign like I was shivering, and pointed up. He understood, and the three of us ascended. Passing through the thermocline going upward felt *sssooo* good! With that dive, Dave and I were certified and received our dive cards.

Late June, we had a very drunk and belligerent guy. He threw everyone off one raft! Usually, Neil could get their attention with a bull horn and have them come in. Not this time! He sent Chuck to tell the guy to come in. When Chuck got on the raft, they started to argue, so Neil sent me too. As I climbed onto the raft, the guy took a swing at Chuck and semi-missed, but he caught him on his collar bone. I was already crouched, so I ran across the raft staying low, grabbed him at the waist and drove him into the water. Once in the water, I had the advantage! When he surfaced, he yelled at me! I told him in my sternest voice, "Swim in and see the deputy sheriff waiting for you!" He turned and started swimming, and Neil ordered him off our property. Chuck was OK, so we went back to work.

July was an especially busy month for me. For the first time I was going to teach three, one-hour classes for six weeks in the morning at the main beach, three one-hour classes for four weeks in the afternoon at Grafton, plus guard when needed in the evenings and weekends, and mow four lawns! At the main beach, I had a beginner, advanced beginner, and junior lifesaving class. When they started, I did what I did at Grafton by dividing the beginner's class in two, and many of them progressed to the next level, and *I got to sign* their Red Cross cards! In the afternoon, I had a beginner, intermediate, and swimmer class. All went well, and the parents were pleased when I was able to provide them Red Cross advancement cards. I will admit, I was tired at the end of each day and was glad when swimming classes were over!

Bill Speechley, one of my co-workers, had a boat which did 44–45 mph. He learned at that speed he could ski barefoot! I saw him tumble into the water many times; however, he persevered and eventually did it! By the end of the summer, he barefooted around the entire lake! In August when he was proficient, he volunteered to teach me. Since I always skied at *slow* speeds, I had to learn how to *high-speed* ski! It took several days before I had the confidence to go to the next step. Bill did his transition from the ski to bare-foot by using a slalom ski that only had two front-foot binders. Once skiing, he backed both feet out of their front binders, then put his back foot into the water, and while all his weight was on it, he slipped the front foot off the ski, and put it into the water too. *Voila!* He was skiing barefoot, except he took tons of falls before he knew the exact angle, body placement, and way to hold his first foot when putting it into the water.

I had to also find that careful balance, and *trial and error* was my method. After what seemed like a billion falls, I put my rear foot in the water and felt the needed support before trying to set my forward foot into the water. Unfortunately, as I was quickly transitioning my forward foot from the ski, my small toe caught the foot binder and pushed the ski forward and across my path. When the ski hit both shins, I tumbled forward into the water. Bill came around and said, "Hey, you almost had it; try it again!" I said "No!" and never did try it again, but for about 100 feet I was semi-up!

Another skiing adventure involved the fastest boat on the lake, Reichert's jet boat. This dude did 65–66 mph, and skiers had to use a 120-foot tow rope, so they would not be drowned by the jet wash when starting! One morning, John Reichert and Tommy asked if I would like to ski. Since I had been doing high-speed skiing with Speechley, I said OK. When I got outside the wake, I signaled John to open it up! The water was like glass, so I was literally *flying* along. As we approached the main beach, John did a slow 180-deg turn using the width of the lake, which made the turn easy for me.

About halfway through it, I saw something I did not want to see! There was only one other boat using the lake, and we were now approaching its wake! I bent my knees to let them absorb the jolt from each wave. I made it over the first two waves, but the tip of my ski tilted downward and dug into the third wave; *it was all over!* I was going a little faster than the boat, maybe 70 mph, when I hit the water! While arms and legs were flailing all over the place, my entire body was *skipped across the water* like a hurled stone! John asked, "Do you want to try it again?" I asked for the ladder and climbed into his boat. I was not sure if my skin would peel off my body or remain!

There was a new girl at the beach. She was the same age as Midge, and Midge encouraged me to date her. She was shorter than me, cute, and seemed shy. Her name was Paulette. About midway through the summer, I asked her out, and she said, "Yes." She introduced me to her mother and stepfather, and they wanted her home by midnight, which was fine with me. We went to the drive-in because the second movie was *The Longest Day*, about the D-Day landings. During the first feature, almost all our conversation was about Midge, since she was the one thing we had in common, and we silently watched the intense second movie. I got her home about 11:45, she opened the door, told her folks she was home, and we were going to talk. Sometime later, her mother told her she had to come in. She walked me to the car and for the first time ever, I kissed a girl on our first date!

On the way home, I looked at my watch and it was after 12:30! My shift started late the next morning, so I figured I would *again* be harassed. When I arrived, Midge pulled me to the side and said, "What did you do last night? Paulette's been grounded for a week!" I was surprised and asked, "Why!?" She said it had to do with how late I got her in! I told her what happened, and we figured they were not happy we sat on the porch so long. This bothered me! When I saw her again, I apologized, and we did set up a second date. When I picked her up, her stepfather was working outside and I tried to apologize, but he would have nothing of it and just made a grunting sound; he *never* talked to me again! We went to the movie and she was *inside* by 11:45 p.m.!

On one date her mother asked if we could babysit. Paulette had a younger sister about nine, and her mother wanted to spend the evening with her husband, who bartended in Barrington. As I drove all four of us to the train station where her mother caught the train, the car radio played an ad for a bridal shop, and Paulette mentioned about how at her wedding she wanted this or that, almost as if the wedding was soon. *This* caught me completely off guard because just going into my sophomore year meant I had a long time before I wanted anything to do with *my* wedding! At the end of our b*abysitting* date, I left their house about 11:45 p.m. just in case a neighbor might be keeping tabs on us! We had weekly dates, and toward the end of the summer, she semi-pressured me to introduce her to my folks, which did not happen.

The season was over, and it was time to store everything. Dave and I borrowed a single scuba tank from Carl to do the rafts. When I wore the tank, I swam under a raft and came up under it. There was plenty of air space, but I spit out my mouthpiece before surfacing, and my tank got caught in the anchor chain! I struggled fiercely and was able to just barely get my lips above the water to get air. An inch lower, I would have been a goner! I was afraid to untangling myself for fear if I did not get completely free, I might not to be able to get air again. Dave was on the raft, so with my lips pushed as far forward as possible, I said, "Dave, help me. I'm caught," and hoped he heard me. A few seconds later, he pulled me under, untangled the chain and pushed me up under the raft so I could get air. Dave was my guardian angel and *saved* me. Two things bothered me: First, I panicked! Second, I did not find my own solution! Doing something simple like loosening the front harness strap would have been all I needed, but I blew it! Nightmares of this still haunt me. A week later, I was off to school.

Chapter 26

Sophomore Year, Fall Semester, 1963

DAD HAD TO VISIT THE ELWOOD PLANT, SO HE took me back to Purdue. My room was the first one on the southern first-floor hallway in East. We unloaded my things and went to lunch. When we came back, we met my new roommate, Donald Field. Don was a freshman, and as we unpacked, we started to get to know each other. I set up my electronics, then showed him how to operate everything so he could use it when I was gone, and he thanked me.

Tom Hintz had a single room down the hall, and his freshman brother, Ken, was on an upper floor. Mike Hatch was on the second floor directly above my room, and Rick Rozelle and Tom Bartels were on the northern end of the second floor. Bart's roommate was Dave Smith, a big, 240-pound guy. I became better acquainted with junior Tom Otto, who also transferred from West. We had another junior on our hallway, Dave Snyder, who I would befriend. I do not remember our hall counselor's name, so I must have been a *good little boy* and had no visits from him!

I helped with the orientation sessions but worked behind the scenes. Two weeks later, East had their freshmen/upperclassmen flag football game. As usual, the freshmen kicked off to the upperclassmen, and we eventually scored. I was a defensive end! Yep, at five feet, seven and a half inches tall and 130 pounds, I *dominated* the right side of their offense! They had a good quarterback and moved the ball every play. When they got to our twenty-five-yard line, I felt they were coming my direction, so when the ball was snapped, I took three steps straight into their back field. Their quarterback threw the ball to their slot back who was behind me, but it was thrown low, so I was able to tip and catch it, and took off running. I heard footsteps behind me, so I ran as fast as I could without looking back. When I scored, I turned to find it was my own teammate, Mike Hatch. We celebrated!

For the first time, I got to take electrical engineering courses, an EE circuits class and lab! Also, my schedule had electricity and optics physics, and my third calculus and Air Force ROTC classes. Purdue required us to take a minimum of six- and twelve-credit-hour sequences in two schools other than engineering; I planned a twelve-credit-hour sequence in psychology/sociology, so I took elementary psychology, which brought me to seventeen credit-hours. Later, I would do a six-hour sequence in speech because Dad told me when working, he always had to write and talk, so I figured, *half a loaf is better than none!*

For the EE circuit class, the head of the EE Department, Dr. William Hayt, did his lectures by TV. His instruction was like Dr. Spalding's: theory, then sample homework problems. My problem was the EE lab because of the graduate student who oversaw us. Half in our class were Navy guys, who were selected from their technician ranks to upgrade to an engineer. Our instructor told us, "Only the Navy students will get the As or Bs." I was teamed with a Navy student, so experimental setups, measurements, and final calculations were the same, and on *every* lab report, he got an A and I got a C! There were times when I actually did the entire lab, with my partner watching, and again he got an A and I got a C! My partner even went to the instructor pointing out this error, but it did not change his mind. This guy was *horrible* and *unfair!*

East sophomores had football seats about three-fourths of the way to the top on the northeast curve of the stadium, which gave us a good view of what was happening on the field. We lost our opening game but squeaked by Notre Dame. The rest of the season seemed to go: win one, lose one, win two, lose two, and so forth. Finally, we beat IU in the "Bucket" game and ended 5–4 (4–3—fourth place in Big Ten). It was always a successful season when we beat both Notre Dame and IU! We were champions of the State of Indiana!

Life this semester was pretty common. Politically, it improved! I won my first election and now represented East in Cary's Joint Council. *Amazing!* As promised, I wrote Paulette weekly. Some of her letters indicated happenings at school and with friends, but others were emotional ones about us. The latter ones were the ones that bothered me most. Almost every weekend, Susie came to see Hintz, and like last year, Hatch and I joined them for weekend meals. Susie's birthday was coming up the weekend before our Thanksgiving break, and she wanted to host a party in Indianapolis, so Hatch and I agreed to join them. Susie wanted to set us up with her friends, but I hesitated. She knew about Paulette and said, "It would not be that *kind* of date," so I agreed.

I liked my schedule because Friday's classes ended early for me. My last class was physics from 1:30–2:20 p.m. On the Friday before Thanksgiving as I walked back to East, I saw Hatch leaning out his window. He yelled, "Rick, did you hear? The President has been shot!" I replied, "What's the joke?" When I got to my room, Don had my radio on, and I instantly knew Hatch's statement was true! I immediately went to Hatch's room where he was listening to Walter Cronkite, who was doing a quick recap. A few minutes later he read a bulletin from a government official, which stated, "President Kennedy was shot and died about 2:00 p.m.!" *Wow!!!* A President had been *assassinated* in the United States! Unbelievable! It will be a moment I will remember the rest of my life! By dinner time, President Kennedy's body was on the way back to Washington, DC, and Lyndon B. Johnson was sworn in as our thirty-sixth President! All you could hear while eating was the clinking of silverware against plates; it was eerily quiet. The next morning after our Saturday classes, Tom, Ken, Mike, and I headed for Indianapolis.

Mr. and Mrs. Hintz welcomed and showed us where we would sleep. After lunch, Hintz helped Susie, and Ken took us downtown. It did not take us long to negotiate the streets to get to The Circle. In the center of Indy was the Soldiers and Sailors Monument, an obelisk just under 300 feet tall. Ken drove around the circle and took an off street. He pointed to a couple of the buildings, and said, "Isn't it amazing how tall they are? Have you ever seen anything like this before?" I replied, "Ken, I'm from Chicago, and these do not compare to theirs!" With a deflated, "Oh," we continued and drove by the Indianapolis Motor Speedway on the way back to his house.

That evening, Susie introduced us to *our dates* and we chatted and danced. Susie did not turn on her TV because there was only one thing on that night! We did talk about President Kennedy, and it put a damper on the evening; we were quite subdued. About 11:00 p.m., we went back to the Hintz's and went to bed. The next morning while watching authorities transferring the suspected killer, Lee Harvey Oswald, we saw someone jump out of the crowd and shoot him! *Wow!* We just witnessed a *live assassination attempt* as Jack Ruby gunned down Oswald! It was *successful* since Oswald died ninety minutes later at the *same* hospital where President Kennedy died. We sat there with our mouths open! What a series of unbelievable events took place in the US in less than forty-eight hours!

On Sunday, President Kennedy's flag-covered coffin was in the rotunda of the Capitol Building. Monday was declared a National Day of Mourning, and Purdue cancelled all classes. His coffin was on a caisson, which was pulled by black horses to the National

Cathedral, and onto Arlington National Cemetery, where he was laid to rest. The most striking picture of this whole event was when the Kennedy family watched the President's coffin pass them. Mrs. Kennedy was holding her daughter's hand, and on her other side was little three-year old John F. Kennedy, Jr., saluting his daddy as he passed! It was actually his third birthday! Everyone who watched this funeral will vividly remember that scene!

On Wednesday night before Thanksgiving, I picked up Paulette, and we headed to the high school's basketball game; however, we decided not to go to it, so we headed for the Tastee Freeze. After we got our snacks, we had some alone time. During our conversation, I started to feel uncomfortable. I had problems getting into what she was saying; our two worlds were not matching well. I got her home at our usual time, kissed, and said, "Goodnight!" As I drove home my mind was in a quandary. I liked Paulette, but I felt uneasy when she again pressured me to meet my folks. Also, when she talked about *our* future, I had problems seeing us in a long-term relationship, plus I felt too immature to get serious. Finally, her stepfather never forgave me; I always had great relationships with the parents of the girls I dated, but this was different, and it truly *bothered* me. I thought about calling her again, but in the end, I thought it best to end our dating.

Rog and Sybil were getting married the next weekend, so I had to find a wedding present for them. Mom suggested everyday silverware, so I bought a setting for eight. I also checked out and bought a few new tubes for my TV set. I figured I would not use it much in the next couple of years, so if Rog and Sybil could use it for a while, so much better.

Once back at school in the solitude of my room, I was not proud about it, but I penned a "Dear Jane" letter to Paulette. I was sorry I would hurt her. It was not her fault; it was more about timing, my immaturity, trying to live in two separate worlds, and my relationship with her stepfather, all of which assaulted me. I truly hoped her future life would be a wonderful and fulfilling one! I kept it until Wednesday because I wanted to read it over, make sure it said what I wanted it to say, and to even decide if I really wanted to send it. I put the letter into the mail!

Friday morning, Hintz drove me to the Purdue Airport, and I caught a flight to Chicago O'Hare. I never flew before, so I was nervous. The plane was a tail-dragging DC-3! I could see the pilots and all the instruments, including the 4,382 buttons on the control panels! They started the engines, and the plane shook! We taxied, got onto the runway, revved the engines to full power, and off we went. Once airborne, we banked, and I could see Purdue's campus; *what a sight!* Forty-five minutes later, I could see O'Hare airport beneath us. At our terminal, I found my bag and happily met Mom, Dad, and Grandma! The drive to Iowa was uneventful, we checked into our motel, and went to the wedding rehearsal where Rog introduced us to Sybil's folks and two siblings. Rog's roommate and past roommate were his best man and second groomsman, and I was the third one. The rehearsal and rehearsal dinner went well.

That night when Rog and I shared the motel room, he filled out paperwork from our draft board; they were interested in drafting him. He marked he was *married*, signed and dated it the next day, his wedding day, and gave me the envelope to mail! After going to bed, we talked a long time about our upbringing and many of the things, some stupid, some *very* stupid, we did over the years. It was well after midnight when we finally stopped and went to sleep. The wedding went off perfectly, so what he told the draft

board was now true! After the reception, they departed. I got back
to East Sunday about 11:00 p.m. and was tired!

Mid-week when I went to my mailbox, I received an envelope
with a return address I instantly recognized. I gulped as I opened it
and started reading. Paulette was not screaming as she wrote, but
I could tell tears were probably involved. She did not understand
why, was not happy about my decision, and toward the end was
noticeably perturbed at me. I believe I did not respond.

Christmas break was welcomed, but for the first time since I
came into this world, my brother was no longer with us! The whole
day was subdued for us, even though we had Christmas dinner
with Grandma Hunziker and Uncle Burne's family. Our house
was much quieter, and I spent much of it in my room.

The most fun I had this break was playing football! We received
a foot of fluffy snow, and one day, about twenty of us gathered at
Dave's house and had the best game of football I ever participated
in. When we ran, our feet slipped and slid, but if we tried to cut
or stop, we probably ended up on our keester! Tackles were not
hard because no one could run fast, and with our winter coats on,
we had padding! After each play, we just laughed because of how
someone fell, slid, or ended up in a pile of snow. It was a great time
and way to spend with close friends. Sadly, I would never see many
of them again or at least not for many, many years. It was pure joy
for those of the Class of 1962!

Chapter 27

Sophomore Year, Spring Semester, 1964

S EMESTER BREAK WAS A DULL WEEK AT CRYSTAL Lake. Ken Hintz indicated he was not happy with his roommate, and Don wanted to move in with a friend, so on Sunday evening, I helped Don and Ken make their moves. While in class, Ken made major changes to our room, including my stereo set-up, without ever asking me! This initially put a strain in our relationship, but we did settle into a reasonable rooming rapport.

Classes somewhat followed the same pattern. I had calculus, Air Force ROTC, Circuits II and EE lab, an electronics class, and social psychology for seventeen credit-hours. My problem class was again the EE lab! Why? I had the *same* graduate student! My partner and I worked well together but we usually both got Cs and Ds on our lab reports. Everything this semester went fairly well except for the EE lab, but at least I got credit for successfully completing it!

On February 9, 1964, a special event happened: Ed Sullivan hosted the Beatles! The lower lounge in East was packed, and the TV audience was huge. It was reported they were paid $100,000 for this three-song appearance. Look, I am for everyone making a buck, but this got to me because the President of the US was only making a $100,000 for the *whole* year! I penned a letter to the *Chicago Tribune*, which expressed my frustration that financially things were getting way out of whack! After composing it and working on my English, I let Hintz proofread it. As he was making suggestions, Hatch and Ken arrived. After being told what I was doing, they added tidbits to it, like including real Latin beetle names and adding a statement like, "Does anyone want to join our group, The Weavils of Purdue (*cylas formicarius elegantulus*)?"[21]

All four signed it, but I was still the first author. On Thursday, it was printed! When Dad got to work that morning, someone put a copy of the *Tribune* on his desk with my name circled! His first thought was, "What has he done now?" However, when he read it, he took the paper home to make sure Mom saw it! About three days later, I received a letter from a young female guitarist which basically said she wanted to join *The Weavils of Purdue!* She signed her letter, and her return address was on the envelope. We quickly generated an application which asked for lots of *data* and a picture. Several days later, I got her application, and she also had a friend send a request for one, which we immediately sent to her. OK, now we had two applications, but what do we do with them? After much debate, we decided to end it, and I sent them rejection letters. We never heard back from either again!

Ross sent me a tape and said his dad retired from Pure Oil, sold their house, and moved to Maine. I was surprised and asked what he was going to do this summer. He said he was not sure where

---

21 *Chicago Tribune,* "A Line o' Type or Two," "Beatle Reaction—Campus Division," Chicago Illinois, February 13, 1964.

he would be, but part of it would be at a summer camp due to his Navy ROTC scholarship. As it turned out, the previous Christmas break's snowy football game was the last time I saw him for twenty-three years, at our class' twenty-fifth reunion! *Ugh!*

This spring many of my upperclassmen friends were wearing new Reamer pots and carrying their wood reamers. There were eleven new pledges and the ones I knew were Bart, Clevitz, Dave Smith, and Tom Otto. What a *great* group of new Reamers!

Right before spring break, Cary held its elections for the next year. Since I had served on Cary's Joint Council the past year, I put my name in for Treasurer of East. When I submitted it, I knew no one else had applied; I just hoped it would stay that way until nominations closed. I got more votes than *no*, so I became the keeper of East's moneybox which had about $57! Being an officer, I was on Cary East's Executive Committee and had to give reports at all official East meetings. Also, Cary had a new president, Dave Smith! He and Bart moved into the President's Executive Suite. It was well deserved!

Spring break gave me some *quiet time* at home. One afternoon I ran into Charlene. We talked for a few minutes, and as we departed, I asked, "Would you like to go out to a movie or something this weekend?" She replied, "I cannot; I already have dates!" Shot down big time! I remembered how tough it was for Mary Anne and me to reconnect, so I promised myself to permanently cross Charlene off my list of potential dates and move on. Reichert returned me to Purdue, thus ending my door-to-door service since he would graduate.

The first week in May was a big deal at Purdue; it was called Gala Week, basically a spring homecoming. The main campus-wide event was a Go Kart race to mimic Memorial Day's Indianapolis 500 race. The guys working on East's kart kept coming to me for money because they needed tools or parts to get it ready. Before it was over, I depleted our treasury; however, I had receipts for everything. We did not meet the minimum qualification time, so our kart sat idle in the attic on race day! *Darn!*

Chapter 28

Summer 1964

M R. BOB SEAVER, MY EIGHT-GRADE "HIT 'EM low at the knees!" football coach, was our new boss. Dave and I mentioned we had been paid the same rate each summer and wondered if we could maybe get a bonus! Our idea was if a guard made a *save*, they got $5. He wondered how we determined if it was a *save* or not. We suggested the other guards could determine it. Then he asked the ultimate question, "What if the victim died?" Dave quickly answered, "$2.50!" A bonus system was *never* enacted!

We basically had our same guard crew from the previous year. Opening day was warm, so everyone worked! Bob's first weekend went well, and I averaged ten hours each day. Starting on Tuesday, like last year, I was pretty much the only guard available again. Midge was already out, so she watched the main gate. Since I had my WSI and participated in Grafton's swimming sessions the past two years, Bob also asked me to help set them up, which I happily did.

Paulette was helping Midge and Elve in our concession stand, and we had not seen each other since Thanksgiving. Like my initial feelings toward Charlene after she broke up with me, Paulette harbored similar feelings towards me. I tried to be friendly, but she basically did not acknowledge I existed. I understood this, but was hoping we could eventually become friends; however, that was not the case. Every time I came into the building, she would not acknowledge my "Hi" and just turned away. This bothered me tremendously, so I tried to stay out of her way all summer.

Dad wanted to go to Crane Lake, so in mid-June he, Bill, and I headed north. We now had favorite fishing spots, and the next couple of days were successful fishing ones. Mid-week another family joined us. They had a nice runabout and two male pre-teens. One late afternoon when we came back, they were trying their hand at skiing, but the boys could not get up. I taught many how to water ski, so I watched closely and then made a couple of simple suggestions. The father was quite put off and basically told me to go way. I told Dad what happened, and he said, "It's their loss!"

The next day was hot and fishing was horrible, so we decided to ski. When we arrived, our neighbors were still trying to get the boys up on their skis. This trip, besides Dad's *surfboard* and my regular slalom ski, we brought my trick skis. Dad and I each slalomed around the bay, cutting across our boat's wake and jumping it many times, and *never* falling. I used the trick skis and did a bunch of 360 turnarounds, skied backwards for one full loop, dropped a ski, and skied backwards on one ski for a second loop. When we got done, the neighbors were still struggling with the boys. This time when I offered advice, the father very gladly accepted it. Within ten minutes, I had both their boys up on skis! *Really!* Their smiles were from ear-to-ear!

Like last July, I taught swimming lessons in the morning and afternoon. Our old Grafton crew of teachers were back, and two new ones were added, one of which was Bob's wife, Sue. One afternoon, Alice and I were sharing the deeper pier. On the west side, Alice was working with her swimmers' class, while I was on the east side working with my intermediates' class. Suddenly, I heard something hit the pier and a splash behind me. I looked down, saw Alice's clipboard on the pier, saw her swimming hard to the west, and then I saw why! There was a motionless little girl floating face down! I yelled at our students to get on the pier and stay there until we came back and dove in after Alice.

She was one stroke ahead of me when we reached her, jointly lifted her out of the water and carried her to the shallow pier. Her lips and skin around her mouth were an icky pale and purplish color. We cleared her mouth, but she was not breathing. I yelled for the resuscitator, but no one heard me, so I dove off the pier, jumped the seawall, grabbed the case's handle, jumped down from the seawall and hit the water running. The water tripped me, and at that time Alice looked up and saw me fall with the case going under; I will never forget her horrified expression! I threw the case onto the pier and put the system together while telling Alice it would work! With one hand, I held the mask tightly over the girl's mouth and nose and pressed on her stomach with my other hand to make sure oxygen was not going into it.

We watched as it did its job pumping air into her lungs and sucking it back out. The gauge showed the tank was only 20 percent full, so I turned toward shore to yell for more in case we needed it. Alice and I wondered how long she had been floating, but we had no idea. I remembered a statistic: *Eighty percent of drowning victims do not recover after four minutes under water!* Also, if she did recover, would she have mental problems due to lack of oxygen? We both stared at her as the resuscitator continued to work. About two minutes later, the gauge was down to 15 percent, and I was about to call for the other tank when the resuscitator started clicking, and Alice asked, "What's happening?"

I lifted the mask off her face and held it closely so she got a steady stream of oxygen since she was breathing lightly. Then something happened no instructor or book every told me: her mouth filled with a white liquid! We realized she was vomiting, quickly rolled her over onto her stomach and helped her drain her mouth. I should have been prepared for this; I had vomited after my inner tube problem in Wisconsin! What happened next was miraculous—*she cried!* We kept her for another minute, giving her oxygen to make sure she continued to breathe on her own, and then Alice carried her into the concession stand. I washed the resuscitator and pier off, repacked it, carried it to the main gate, quickly went back to our students, and told both classes to sit quietly.

Whistles blew, and the guards let everyone back into the water. I did not even realize the guards had gotten everyone out of the water. I do not know what transpired in the concession stand between the mother, girl, and others, but what I do know is that hour she was supposed to be in the class of the other new teacher! The question had to be asked, "Why was she by herself and away from her teacher?" This is *the* reason why I split up my beginner's classes because it is too hard to keep track of twenty-five-plus kids at a beach!

There was also another problem we faced. When Alice and I lifted her out of the water, I slipped into a hole. After our lessons, I went back to where she was and walked around. Suddenly, I stepped into a hole about eighteen inches deep and five feet across. A new spring had opened. The next day, we placed an old tire, filled with concrete, holding a "Danger" sign in this spring!

Ask any guard what is one of the worst parts about the job, and many will say, "I feel like I am a babysitter!" Parents came by the beach early, dropped off one or two munchkins with a dollar for food and drinks, and came back in the evening to pick them up. *This* little five-year-old was one of those kids! For the next three days, her mom brought her, watched her during the lesson, and then took her home. Four days later, her mom came by the beach early, dropped her off with a dollar for food, and came back in the evening to pick her up! *Unbelievable!!!* One good thing came out of this: she now had no problem putting her face under water! The question remained: Why was she not with her teacher?

The next day before classes, I asked Alice, "Did you sleep last night!?" She said "No!" I thought it was just me, but this had the same effect on both of us! It scared the heck out of me, but I was content with what I did! When I realized what Alice was doing, I could have let her handle it, but I did not and *got* involved. The other thing I was surprised about was my focus, especially about the resuscitator. Initially, I concentrated only on grabbing its handle! Second, when bringing it to the pier, in my mind I went through the procedure of how to put it together several times. I do not remember seeing or talking to anyone when either going from or back to the pier, except for Alice's expression! Later, Bob commented on how fast and efficient I was, and concluded, "You were the second one to ever walk on water, but the first guy wasn't carrying a twenty-five-pound resuscitator!" That made me smile. If Alice had not seen her and acted when she did, I would have never seen that young innocent face again! Alice was her guardian angel and literally *saved* her!

My "love life" life was basically nonexistent that summer. Mid-July, Elve wanted to date Chuck but did not want to go out alone. They begged Midge and me to join them. After telling Midge, "We're like brother and sister; if we go out that could change our relationship and put our friendship in jeopardy," we doubled with the *love birds*. The following day when I got to work, Midge was shying away. I stopped her and said, "See! This is why I didn't want to do this. You have different feelings now; we're no longer brother and sister!" She apologized and we did reestablish our previous relationship, possibly to her chagrin.

In early August, I had to close several times, and another girl, Kirstin, a friend of Paulette, kept hanging out as I locked up, so after a few nights talking, we agreed on a date. We did miniature golf and went to the drive in. We talked a lot during the first movie, got snacks, and settled in for the main one. We did kiss a few times during the second movie, a first for a first date! The next day while guarding, I was poked; it was Kirstin. She said she had a good time, talked a little, and said, "Goodbye!" The next day she was flying to Sweden to spend the rest of the summer with a cousin; I knew about it and had no problems with it. However, I did learn one thing from my date with her. She smoked a few cigarettes while at the drive in, and the *taste of smoke* in her kisses left a negative impression on me. I never forgot it, and I did not want to date a smoker!

Chapter 29

Junior Year, Fall Semester, 1964

WHEN I CAME BACK TO SCHOOL, I HAD A ROOM-
mate from Wisconsin, Don Post. We got along very well.
Being a freshman, he had to go through *orientation* but had no
problems with it. Hintz and Snyder still lived down the hall from
me, Ken moved back upstairs with a new roommate, but noticeably absent was Mike Hatch, which left a big void.

   This semester I was back up to eighteen credit hours. I had signals and systems, electronics II, EE Lab, numerical logic, abnormal
psychology, and basic mechanics. It turned out all gave me heart-
burn, except the EE lab; I had a different instructor, and it went
well! In abnormal psychology, Bart's old roommate, Ron Wenzel,
sat behind me.
   Basic mechanics was held in Smith Hall and down the hall
from our lecture room was a display box. In it were three things:
A picture of Mr. Smith, who donated the money for the building,
and a plaque and picture dedicated to the man who built it, my
grandfather, Dr. Otto F. Hunziker, Sr.! Every time I came into the
building, I winked at Grandpa and said a silent, "Hi!" None of my
buddies noticed this until one day when getting ice cream cones.
One said, "Hey Rick! Here's a guy with your last name, and he

even spells it the same." I replied, "Really," walked to the display, and acted like I was reading the plaque. After a moment, I turned away and said, "Oh, that's just Grandpa!" They did not believe me, so over Thanksgiving I brought back a few of his books to prove he *really* was my grandfather!

Our football team was picked to be last, mainly because we had an unknown, sophomore quarterback named Bob Griese. We split our first two games, and the third was Dad's Day, and Mom and Dad visited. As we talked, I brought up something I was not sure they would support. Two nights earlier, I was invited to a Reamer Smoker. Everyone stood, gave their name, course of study, and hometown. Kermit Ross, the president, welcomed us, and gave us a quick overview. He told us Sunday they would conduct interviews for the Purdue Reamer Club. They had a sign-up sheet, and I signed up, but before I went to the interview, I wanted to make sure it was all right with my folks since they were *Greeks!* They thought it was great and encouraged me.

When I interviewed, there were about thirty actives present, all wearing their black and gold pots. I was asked how I found out about the Reamers. I told the story about our family going to the 1956 PU/NW football game when I saw the Boilermaker Special for the first time, but could not figure how it ran without railroad tracks! They all laughed and I was asked several other questions. Kermit said *Tap Out* was the next week.

Tuesday morning at 5:00 a.m., I was nudged awake by Tom Otto, wearing his Reamer pot. He told me to get dressed and meet him in the upper lounge in ten minutes. As I got up, Post said, "Hey, you made it!" I said, "I guess so, but there is a lot more to come!" I quickly dressed, used the bathroom, and was in the upper lounge in *five* minutes! Tom put a blindfold on me, led me to the courtyard where I joined others being *tapped* in Cary. We ended up in a large dining room in the Union and were treated to a wonderful breakfast.

Kermit told us to be at a certain room at 7:00 p.m. that night where we would have our first meeting with our pledge trainer, Paul Grisafi. They gave us a black-and-gold pot and wooden reamer to carry. We had a group picture taken for the Purdue newspaper, *The Exponent*. Nineteen of us were *tapped*, but I did not recognize anyone! When I walked into abnormal psychology wearing my new Reamer pot, Wenzel just sighed and said, "You fool! What have you done? Don't you remember what happened to Bart's grades that semester!?" I shrugged my shoulders and smiled! He sat there, just shaking his head *no*.

When we met with Grisafi, there were only seventeen pledges. He went over the rules, passed out song and information sheets, and told us to elect a Pledge Captain. Paul Westerman, who was a Senior 9, was elected our captain and we spent time getting to know each other. On Thursday, the entire pledge class met from 12:20–12:30 p.m. at Lions. The purpose was to increase school spirit; after all, the Reamer Club was known as, "The Spirit of Purdue!" We sang songs, did cheers, and so on. Sometimes, the Special was there with the pledges. If you are a female student, beware! Sometimes the Lions roared through the P/A system on the Special! Many a female student's face turned bright red as the lions roared when they walked past!

Every Monday night the Reamers held a business meeting. Like any organization, they had reports from each officer. When all formal business was completed, the pledges were brought in as a group for a *line-up*. The purpose was to get the pledge class to act in *unity*! *All* learned to sing and loudly accomplish cheers while the actives *coached* us! Next, each pledge was brought in by himself for *additional honing*. I was the first one for the individual *line-up* because of a test the next day, but I made a deal with my *brothers*. The actives *coached* me to become a *leader*! When my time was up, I left the Union and threw pebbles at the pledges' room window. They opened it, and I explained what happened so the others were not blindsided. As I went back to Cary, I said to myself, "I can do this!"

As I mentioned earlier, the Reamers raised funds for the operation and upkeep of the Special. We blew up and sold helium-filled balloons and worked parking lots for all home football games. Other times we worked at local parks tearing down old buildings, clearing land for a new structures, and so on. Some activities involved the whole club; others were just for the pledges. Most Purdue students had no idea Reamers did these! The first project our pledge class did was to sort and stuff *pink slips* into envelopes to be sent to parents of students in jeopardy of failing a course. This day we were playing at Michigan, one of *the* top teams in the country, and we listened to our team beat them while we worked! Also, we yelled out if we came across a slip for one of our *brothers*; there were quite a few, including *three* for me!

One of the coolest things about being a Reamer, or a Reamer pledge, was the people we got to meet. We made a plywood 8X12 inch R. Our pledge brothers signed the back, but on the front, we collected the actives' and top Purdue University officials' signatures! I do mean the *top*! As an example, the whole pledge class had an hour-long audience with Purdue's President, Dr. Frederick L. Hovde, and we could ask any question! Not many students get to do that! When it came to getting the signatures of other officials, we had our own one-on-one visits; this included: Dean of Men, O. D. Roberts; Registrar, Nelson Parkhurst; Athletic Director, Guy "Red" Mackey; The Voice of Purdue, Johnnie DeCamp; Team Trainer, William "Pinky" Newell; Reamer Faculty Sponsor, A. K. Meerzo, plus others. What an experience!

In late October, one of my EE friends introduced me to their hometown freshman, Ro Ann. I called and asked if she wanted to go on a Coke date. These dates were usually time limited because it was done between classes. For several weeks, we met twice a week and had drinks at the Union's Sweet Shoppe. I asked her to Cary's Winter Formal, which was right after Thanksgiving, and she said, "OK!" As we continued these coke dates, she seemed perturbed I was not spending more time with her. I explain that my Reamer pledging took a lot of time, and I just did not have more time to give; however, the Friday night before Thanksgiving break, East was having a hay ride, so we agreed to go on it.

At the hayride, I introduced her to Hintz and Susie, and it turned out Susie was staying at her residence hall that weekend. During the hayride, she did not seem to be into it, so we just quietly talked. When I leaned in to kiss her good night, she gently put her fingertips on my lips, and said, "No." *Wow!* That never happened before! Sunday, I ate with Hintz and Susie. They asked how my date went, and I told them about it, including the *non-kiss!* They looked at each other and said, "We have something to tell you! On Saturday night as we were saying good night, we noticed a girl, who we believed was Ro Ann, kissing a guy very passionately!" *Pow!* So that is what happened! That night I called her and suggested we cancel our date for the Formal, which she readily agreed to, and I wished her well. She was the only Boilermaker I dated more than once!

When Thanksgiving break came, I had no success finding a ride! I lugged my suitcase to Lafayette's train station, bought my first James Bond thriller, caught a train to Chicago, and transferred to the Chicago & Northwestern Station to catch one home. It took ten hours to get home instead of the normal three-plus-hour drive! I vigorously tried talking Dad into letting me buy a car, but he was firmly set on me waiting until I turned twenty-one! The trip back to school allowed me to finish my book!

Reamer pledging did not skip a beat, and the first Sunday back we had a joint active/pledge workday cleaning a park. After the work, we had an active/pledge two-handed touch football game. Of course, the pledges kicked off to the actives, and they lateraled the ball to big Dave Smith who ran it up the middle. Many of our players, including me, two-handed touched him, but he kept running, and they counted it as a touchdown! When we got the ball, I tried to do a rolling body block on an active, but as I hit him below the waist, he brought his legs forward and put his knees into my ribs. It hurt badly, but I got up quickly, so no one knew I was hurt.

I played defensive back, and one play they threw a flank pass to Dave Smith, but our defender slipped in the snow, and Dave was off to the races. I had an angle on him, hit him at the knees, like Mr. Seaver taught me to do, and Dave hit the ground. The actives gasped as the smallest pledge had just taken out the biggest active! On fourth down of the actives last series, they threw a high pass to Clevitz since short me would be guarding him. We were together as we both went up for the ball; he got both hands on it, but I also had my right hand on it to push it away. We came crashing down, but the way I hit while putting pressure on the ball caused my right shoulder to separate! I yelled and when he fell on top me, it rotated back into position, but it sure hurt. Clevitz held onto it for another TD!

Because of my shoulder situation, the Reamers awarded me their coveted *Purple R Award* for *being injured in the line of duty!* The next morning, I did not get out of bed and *worried* Post talked me into going to the infirmary. It was not my shoulder, but my side where the active kneed me that hurt and was swollen. I skipped classes and struggled to the infirmary. The doctor took her hand and made it like one of Mr. Tingleff's *spears* and pushed it into my bad side, which hurt badly! She said, "You probably have bruised or cracked ribs and maybe internal bleeding. Go back to bed and rest!" *Really!* It took all I had to get downstairs to eat dinner and go to the Reamer lineup.

The next weekend was the infamous all-night pledge work detail and initiation. After the work was completed and the sun started to rise, the final act of initiation occurred. *Ouch!* So, with that, the only thing left was the Initiation Dinner at the Congress Inn on Sunday night, December 13.

When our electronics lecture met on Wednesday after my injuries, everyone was sitting in every other seat in EE129. I asked what was going on, and someone said, "Don't you remember, Monday they told us we have a major test today!?" Gulp! I had not done any homework problems the past three weeks, so I knew I had nothing to offer. I wrote down a few formulas, but I had *no idea* how to solve the problems! The next day I got my result, *eight!* The average was *seventy eight!* Personally, I thought my *eight* was generous! After class I asked the instructor if I had a chance to pass; he looked at my scores and said, "If you win a Nobel Prize in electronics the last weeks of this semester, I'll pass you!" I knew what I would do. I was hurting in *all* my other classes, except my EE lab. I blew off this class and would use my time trying to salvage the others, if that were even possible!

For Christmas I was able to get a partial ride home from fellow Reamer Roy Rysden, who lived in Chicago. He dropped me off at the Chicago & Northwestern Station, where I caught a train home. I needed rest and used my time to catch up on my classwork and spend *quality time* making progress. When this break was over, Rysden picked me up in Chicago.

I did go to the final electronics test and memorized the problems since I knew I would be repeating it. My abnormal psychology grade was not good, but it was not one I could improve. Being the psycho guy I was, I spent more time on my signals and systems, logic, and mechanics classes; I was hurting badly in all three! The mechanics class was the most critical; fortunately, its final, I kid you not, had only *one* question: "Write the formula for the flapping wings on a fly, which is walking up a moving windshield wiper on a car going around the Lobe Fountain, as seen from the moon!" It was a relatively easy question as long as I started with the smallest (the fly's wings) and moved out from there. The other two courses showed improvement too.

Before the end of the semester, the Reamers held elections for the next semester. We had seven "official" offices: president, VP/pledge trainer, treasurer, recording secretary, correspondence secretary, historian, and Special chairman, and one "unofficial" office, dirty, I will explain this one later. Dave Fry was our new president.

My grades were not good! As expected, I failed my electronics class, but I did get my B in my EE lab. All other grades were Ds; that was fourteen credit-hours of Ds! I pulled three of them *out of the fire*, so my Christmas effort paid off, and I did not have to repeat the complete semester! I was relieved those courses were now behind me because I no longer cared for EE courses. I had no idea what to switch to, so if I could do better the next three semesters, I would graduate and could do whatever I wanted to with an engineering degree, although not a *brainy* one!

Chapter 30

Junior Year, Spring Semester, 1965

TOM HINTZ GRADUATED; I APPLIED FOR HIS ROOM and I got it. Let me emphasize, Post and I got along *great*, and he was very supportive during my long hours of Reamer pledging. I could not have asked for more from him! I wanted more privacy, and now I had it, but to get it I lost a *great* friend. *Ugh!*

Tom Hintz and Susie got married; Ken was the best man, and Reichert and I were groomsmen. I thought it interesting a guy from Indianapolis picked two groomsmen from the *same* small town in Illinois! During the rehearsal, the priest talked about Communion. He understood not all the attendants were Catholic, so he said, "If during Communion I should forget you're not Catholic and I come in front of you with the Sacraments, just slightly shake your head 'No;' do *not* open your mouth to say, 'No,' because it will already be in!" The next day the wedding went as planned, including not getting Communion, and the reception was fun! They rented a very small house next door to Harry's Chocolate Shop, which was convenient for visits.

I was now taking one of the most feared courses in the entire engineering curriculum, modern physics; we called it *Buck Rogers's Physics* after the fictional space-traveling character! It started with Einstein's theory of relativity and went downhill and deeper after that! Some students took it three times before they passed it! It also had a two-hour lab that met on Saturday morning. *Ugh!* My partner was East's Dean Hatfield, and we did well on most experiments. I was happy with my solid C!

Motor and field theories were interesting and easy because they were straightforward. Our EE lab combined motors and fields experiments, and we had two graduate-student instructors, Moore and Yake. Because the motors were huge and their voltages and currents were dangerous, we had to be carefully checked. During one experiment, Moore checked our DC motor circuit and told me to connect us to the central power panel. This power station had multiple levels of high-power AC and DC service, and each experimental station had ports near it, so I connected the two. Moore checked another power station connection, and we thought he checked ours too. He came back and told me to apply power. When I threw the switch, a loud *bang* occurred at the same time as a big *flash* appeared in the power station and took it out! Moore went to the power station, called me over and asked, "Is the voltage supposed to be *wiggling* or *steady*?" I answered, "Steady," so he pointed at the power panel and said, "Then why did you plug into the *wiggling* voltage!" Sure enough, I plugged into AC and not DC! *Oops!*

During one of the field labs, we had a tank filled with water, and on opposite sides were metal plates, which provided a uniform electrical field. We placed metal cubes, spheres, and so forth, into the water and measured the fields for changes. We showed Yake our measurements. He said, "They look good, but to get a quick idea, all you had to do was take your index and little fingers, keep them several inches apart, dip them into the water and you'll feel a little tingle. The greater the tingle, the stronger the electrical field." He looked at me and said, "Why don't you try it, Mr. Hunziker?" I looked him in the eye and replied, "I'm a lifeguard; when it lightnings, we get people *out* of the water!" He laughed and walked away. After he left, I did try it, and it was only a small tingle!

In February, the Reamers did their smoker, interviews, and selection; nine new pledges including Conrad and Cartin donned new Reamer pots! It seemed weird for me to hold things over their heads, especially since they were four years older; however, I saw no reason to be overbearing on *any* new pledges. At a home basketball game, the actives and pledges were sitting together. A cheerleader came up and picked Cartin and me to come down to the court and do a cheer with them. Other than Dave Smith, Cartin was probably the next strongest one, and I was now the smallest Reamer. I do not remember the cheer, but when it ended, I was sitting on Cartin's shoulder!

The end of February, the Computer School sponsored a dance, but the dates had to be matched by computer. Dave Snyder and I filled out their personality questionnaire and applied. The evening of the dance, we dressed up and went to the Union Ballroom. The girl I met was shorter than me, of slight build, and nice looking. Obviously, we had questions for each other, but her answers were always short and very to the point. Also, I believe she was even shyer than me! Snyder came over, introduced his date to us, and I introduced us to them. Snyder's date was a blonde *knock-out*! As the evening wound down, I felt uncomfortable with my date, so I did not kiss her nor ask her out again. The next day when I saw Snyder, he said his date was engaged and she and her fiancé were seeing if they would be matched by the computer. So much for computer dating!

At spring break, Rysden dropped me off in Chicago. I had saved money for a car, so Dad and I checked out local dealers; the best deal appeared to be a 1961 Plymouth Valiant. It was in great condition, only had 18,000 miles, was an upscale version, had snow tires, and sported a three-speed manual on-the-floor transmission, but we went home to *think about it*. After Dad got home Monday night, we went back, and he handled the negotiation, so when we agreed on a price, he asked them to include floor mats and seat belts for the two front seats. They agreed and said I could pick it up late the next day. On Tuesday I *had* a car, called Rysden, and told him I did not need a ride.

On Sunday night, April 11, Post knocked on my door. When I answered, he asked, "Don't you live in Crystal Lake?" I answered, "Yes," then he said, "I just heard on the radio Crystal Lake was blown away by a tornado!" I grabbed a bunch of quarters and dialed home many times, but always got a busy signal. It was now after 10 p.m. and I had a 7:30 a.m. class, so I went back to bed, but worried. The next morning after my first class, I tried home again, but always got busy signals. I called Dad's office in Chicago, and Maxine, his secretary, answered. I said, "Maxine, this is Rick, is Dad there?" She replied, "No ..." and paused! My heart sank! Then she continued, "He's at the Clearing plant. He called and said he would be back in the office this afternoon. Want me to have him call you?" I explained the situation and said I would call him tonight. If he went to work, then everything at home was OK. *Whew!*

That night we connected, and they were all right, but that was not the case for all of Crystal Lake. The tornado came within a mile of our house, did damage near South Elementary, destroyed a barn south of the Crystal Lake Plaza on US Rt 14, then destroyed some stores in the Plaza as well as several homes and businesses northeast of it. Six people were killed, including a classmate I had in freshman shop and usually stood next to during attendance in gym classes. His name was John Holter! His folks were also killed!

Our tornado was one of many infamous Palm Sunday tornadoes. Six states were hit on April 11–12; forty-seven tornadoes killed 260-plus and injured 1,500; Indiana was hit the worst, losing over 135! One of Indiana's badly hit towns was Russiaville. The Reamers wanted to help, so the following Saturday morning, our caravan went to the town of Mulberry, which is southeast of Purdue and was where the Russiaville tornado first started. Homes, barns, and silos were completely destroyed. Dave Fry picked a farm because they needed their fields cleared of debris to plow. Their house was a jumbled stack of lumber, and their two preteen kids were looking through the rubble to see if they could find anything of use. They found a pair of dice and were tickled to find something they could use! *Boy, that put things in perspective!* We scoured and cleaned their fields until sunset. The Reamers were always doing something for different charities because we wanted to give back to our community. This is one of the prize attributes I learned being a Reamer!

After our pledges were activated, the Reamers held their election for the next semester's officers. Bart was elected president and I was elected treasurer. My co-signer for checks was Mr. Parkhurst, Purdue's registrar. Whenever I needed his signature(s), he happily obliged; we became well acquainted, and I looked forward to each visit. Since I wanted to drive the university-owned Special, I paid Indiana personal property tax on my car, registered it, and obtained an Indiana driver's license.

One day while getting check signatures, I asked Mr. Parkhurst, "Since I paid taxes to Indiana and am a registered driver here too, why do I have to pay out-of-state tuition?"

He smiled and said, "Because you don't qualify as a resident! First, you must be a resident for a year before attending Purdue, and second, you cannot have a Purdue residence hall as your *official* home of record!" Darn, but I thought it was worth the try! Then he shocked me, "By the way, do you really think you can afford a car!?" Oh boy, here we go again, so I replied, "Look, my dad said I had to wait until I was twenty-one before I could buy a car, so I am not going to start this all over again with you!" He laughed and said, "OK, I think you're good to go!" I just cannot emphasize how neat and fortunate I was to have an opportunity like this to get to know the people who made the decisions at Purdue. Being a Reamer made this possible!

During spring football, one of our players died! Coach Jack Mollenkopf requested a meeting with a representative from each on-campus organization. Dave Fry asked me to represent the Reamers. Coach Mollenkopf wanted to raise money and do other things for this family. During the meeting, he looked at me since I was wearing my Reamer pot and said, "The Reamers could use their *train* to make announcements throughout the campus." I kind of gasped since we *never* called the Special a *train!* That was a *big no-no* for us! I replied, "We do not call the Special a *train*, and yes, we would be glad to use *the Special* to spread the news!" He just stared at me for a minute, and then went on. The Special did make announcements around campus on this player's behalf.

One Saturday I was riding the Special. Purdue happened to be playing Illinois in baseball, so I stayed and watched part of the game. When it was Illinois' turn to bat, I recognized the third-base coach, it was Paul Koch from CLCHS! After their bats were over, he came over to the fence for a second, and we talked. At the end of the next inning, we spoke again, and I left. It was good to see he was able to fulfill one of his dreams: to play baseball at the college level!

Since the next year I was going to be a senior, I wanted to get a jump on it. I went to a clothing store and bought a pair of senior cords. Next, I purchased a large set of colored, ball-pointed paint tubes used to draw on and paint the cords. Finally, about three weeks before school was out, I quit shaving, so when I went home, I had a full beard and mustache! I did all right for grades, though nothing to brag about, but they did get me closer to graduation! I packed *my* car and headed home!

Chapter 31

Summer 1965

W HEN I GOT HOME, DAD LOOKED AT MY BEARD
and said, "I'm not sure I can *live* with that!" I reminded
him *why* I was growing it. Over the next couple of days, he kept
repeating the same comment. Finally, I suggested a compromise,
"I will shave the mustache if you let me look like Abe Lincoln!" He
grudgingly agreed!

Grafton did not open for three weeks, so I drove to Florida
to see Rog and Sybil for ten days and got to Jacksonville right
before Memorial Day weekend. They had a cat, Nutmeg, who just
stared at me while we visited. The first night I was about to fall
asleep when Nutmeg jumped onto my chest and started to growl.
He sat there a while, and then he left. The next morning, I told
them what happened, and they both laughed. They said he was
not *growling* but *purring!* Since I had never been around a cat, this
was new to me! On Memorial Day, Sybil cooked a meal I never
forgot—southern fried chicken! *Oh my gosh*, it was good, and I ate
three pieces! On Tuesday, Rog had to go to Texas, so Sybil and I
saw some movies.

I also started painting my senior cords; the first two pictures
were the big EEs and the Greek letters Gamma Delta Iota (GDI—
Gall Darn Independent) down the front of my legs. On my back
pockets, I had the letters P and U and between them was the *business end* of a skunk with its tail raised! This was just the start of
this project since I later calculated I spent over 200 hours creating

them! One night we watched astronaut Ed White become the first American to walk in space. At the end of the week, the Gemini 4 astronauts docked in Mayport aboard the USS Wasp aircraft carrier. The deck was lined with sailors, and the Gemini 4 capsule was displayed with our two *spacemen* standing next to it. What a thrill to be part of American history! We quietly spent the weekend at the beach and in their home, and on Monday, I headed north.

Grafton continued to be closed, but Mr. Battles, who broke a foot, hired me to be his chauffer. He was a manufacturer's representative for freezer companies and had to visit clients. The next day I got behind the wheel of his Buick Electra 225, and we headed for the Palmer House in Chicago. I dropped him at the front door, and while he visited, I leisurely circled the block until he came out. The next day we visited businesses in northern suburbs, so I dropped him off and parked where I could watch for him. I had a book, so now he paid me to read! On Friday, he worked in his home office, and I mowed grass. The next week on our visits, he used these opportunities to semi-mentor me about sales, and I visited with him and his clients! Cool!

In mid-June, Grafton opened, and it was nice getting back to our routine. A week later, Charlene was interested in getting a puppy, not just any puppy, but a specific breed. She talked to a woman in Joliet, but her parents did not want her driving by herself. She asked if I would drive her, and I said, "Sure." I still liked her and thought maybe this time together might help. We followed the dog owner's directions; Charlene picked one out, lifted it, the dog licked her in the face, and they bonded instantly. The owner then said, "I'm glad the puppy is going to a cute couple like you guys!" Charlene, without waiting even a millisecond, answers,

"Oh, we're not a couple!" The owner quizzically looked at me, I shrugged my shoulders, smiled, and said, "We work together as lifeguards at a beach." I think she saw something in *my* eyes other than just *friendship!* As we got into my car with the puppy, the owner said, "Good luck," but I do not believe it was about raising a puppy! On the way home, she was so into playing with the puppy, we barely talked, but she thanked me when I got her home. Had she given me a *hint*, I would have removed her from my *No Date List* and would have dated her again! That hint was *not* there!

Like past years, sometimes the guards sat together in chairs on top of the seawall and talked. We had our area of interest to watch and we paid attention what was happening in them. Topics of discussion varied. One time there were dark storm clouds with slits so beams of sunlight showed through all the way to the ground. Dave said, "To me, those beams look like the fingers of God!" Hmmm, I wondered about that! Another time after a very hot day, we talked about the heat and bright sun, then Charlene insightfully said, "You know, when we get old, our skin is going to be very wrinkly and full of cancers!" We knew skin cancers were a problem, but back then no one had lotions with SPFs. If girls used anything, it was baby oil with iodine, an orange-colored solution. Most of us used zinc oxide, a thick, white cream which was semi-waterproof. I mostly used it on my nose, but some of the fairer-skinned guards put it on their shoulders. No one really knew how well it worked, but we used it anyway. The summer before I peeled thirty-three layers of skin off my nose, so I just hoped I had a nose in my old age!

This summer I was the only male instructor at both beaches, so I ended up with all the lifesaving classes. I enjoyed working with the older students, so I liked this arrangement. I did add one thing to each lifesaving class; to warn them should they be doing resuscitation, be aware at some point the victim will probably vomit; this resulted in many "Eews!" One student in the first three-week session at the main beach had lifeguarded since Memorial Day weekend, well before taking the lessons! I kidded her, "What happens if you fail?" She said, "I would take the class again the next session, hoping I would have a different instructor!" *Ouch!* The last four days of the sessions were grueling when I had the students do their *saving* exercises. Twice I had double classes, each class had about twenty-five students, and I required eight *saving* drills be done on me; I had to *drown* about 400 times in four days! When a testing day ended, I was *waterlogged!*

One night I received a phone call from Betty Goss, who got my number from Mr. Willis. She indicated she had three grandchildren who needed private swimming lessons, and she had a pool, so she gave me her address. She lived just south of the Plaza and had a beautiful, large pool. I complimented her on it, and she said, "My husband, Rae, built it for our grandchildren. We used to have a barn next to it, but in April a tornado hit the barn while he was inside, and he was killed!" *Wow!* This hit me like a *ton of bricks!* Rae Goss was one of the six who was killed on Palm Sunday along with my classmate and his folks! I mentioned them, and she said she heard about them too. I got into the water and started lessons right then. Since they were *water rats*, they advanced quickly and in only six sessions, they could easily swim several laps. Grandma was happy!

After the first session at the main beach was concluded, I decided to check on the student who had been guarding before passing her lifesaving class. When I got to McHenry's beach, I immediately saw things I did not like. The Fox River, the same one in Brookfield, was about a third of a mile wide, muddy, and had a 2-mph current! There were two girls overlooking the river beach; one was my ex-student, Linda. She introduced me to her co-worker, and we talked about the lay of the beach, the muddy water, and the current. I was impressed they were *comfortable* with their situation. The beach closed at 5:00 p.m., so since Linda was no longer my student, I asked her if she would like to go out, and she said, "Yes!"

The night of our first date, her parents were obviously wondering about my beard, so I explained why I had it. We went miniature golfing and to a movie, and when I took her home, I did give her a goodnight kiss. The big elephant in the room was our age difference, *four* years, the most I ever had. We went out almost weekly in August and early September. One time I even brought her to dinner at our house, and the Battles were over for pre-meal cocktails. At dinner, Mom served *peas*! The next day Mr. Battles said, "Linda seemed nice, but awfully young!" On another date, we went to Barrington to see *The Yellow Rolls-Royce*, which was about a car's three lives and it was rated "R." When I bought our tickets, the women in the booth asked to see my ID since I had to be eighteen. As I got my ID out, I asked her, "Would you like to go for a beer after the show!?" She turned a little red, but still checked my ID!

In August, Mom got a call that Grandma Hunziker was found dead. She immediately called Dad, and we met him in LaGrange. We learned no one had seen her for a couple of days, so someone alerted the superintendent, who entered and found her. Dad called his three sisters and brother, and the funeral was a few days later. During the service, Uncle Burne kept looking at me. When we got to visit, he asked, "Why the beard!?" When I explained everything to him, he turned to and chastised his younger brother for making me shave off my mustache! I always liked Uncle Burne!

We cleaned out the condo, and Dad was also stuck as the executor of her estate. It took him two years to gather everything, pay the taxes, and distribute the money five ways. He never took a penny for his work, but he was not happy when Cook County took a large chunk of it! He once told me, "If I am having a heart attack in Cook County, put me in a car and get me out of the county because I do not want to die there!"

After Labor Day Weekend, like three times before, we pulled all the equipment out of the water and locked everything up. Dave and I guarded for four years, and, fortunately, never had a drowning. Much of that credit also had to go to Alice Hoeft's decisive response when seeing that little girl face-down in the water. Having lost no one was momentous; it felt like we did our part protecting those who came to Grafton to enjoy time with family and friends. I think both Dave and I felt uneasy as we realized our lifeguarding days were now over. As I drove away, I had tears in my eyes as the beach faded in my rearview mirror. I would not trade those past four summers for any other! What I did not know was so many of the people I worked with would never, ever appear again in my life. I had contact with only three!

Chapter 32

Senior Year, Fall Semester, 1965

I PACKED *MY* CAR AND HEADED TO PURDUE. LAST spring, we got word Cary Northwest and West would reopen. There were some who moved back to West, including Bart and Clevitz, and some newer ones like Bob White, and Bill Chidley. The upper classmen met and voted Chidley, who was Clevitz's roommate, our president. The number of upperclassmen moving back was limited, so West was mostly a freshmen hall. I applied for Hintz's old first-floor single room, but my room assignment stated Cary West, Room 212, so for the first time, I had to climb more stairs! Our corridor had a few sophomores, two seniors, and the rest were freshmen. Our counselor, Jan Cooney, was the other senior and was taking mechanical engineering. I had to pass his room to use the washroom, eat, or leave West, and his door was always open, so we spent loads of time together. My guardian angel moved me one flight higher because lifelong friends like Jan Cooney, do not occur often!

One marvelous thing was each day's dinner. Having good, long-time friends probably produced more laughter at our table than any other because we knew how to push each other's buttons. Occasionally, another guy joined us. The president of the 1,500-men Cary Hall could eat in any unit; this way he had contact with *all* residents. His name was Jack Jackson, and he replaced Dave Smith. Bart, Clevitz, White, and Chidley all lived near him last year and liked him, and he spent more than his fair share of time in West because of them. He had a good sense of humor and was willing to joke around. We slowly got to know each other better and enjoyed bantering back and forth. He even mentioned, "I remember you at last spring's meeting with Coach Mollenkopf! You're the guy who told off Mollenkopf about calling the Boilermaker Special a train!" Jackson would play a *major* role in my life!

Because of the large number of graduating seniors last spring, the Reamer Club was relatively small this fall, with only twenty-one actives. This hurt us because many had to do double duty to meet and accomplish scheduled events. In addition, since most of us were seniors, personal appearances were not the best. Like me, almost all had beards! The good news was we became a very close-knit group and worked well together!

This semester I was going to have my heaviest load ever—twenty credit-hours! Of course, I was retaking electronics II because I did not get my EE Nobel Prize! The other EE courses were circuit models, EE lab, and engineering administration. None of them thrilled me! I had two speech courses: advanced public speaking and business interview. The latter one I thought might help me during my job interview cycle. Finally, I had Social Problems, which was in the Life Science building. Two things were neat about having a class in this building: First, Susie Hintz worked there. After class I stopped by to see how they were doing. Second, this building was next to Smith Hall! Occasionally, I went there, winked at Grandpa, and got an ice cream cone!

Our football team was expected to be good this year, and a tenth game was added to our schedule. The Reamers were awarded the first two rows, between the 45 and 50 yard lines, right behind the opponent's benches, and we made sure they heard us! After annihilating our first opponent, the next weekend was Senior Cord Day, and we played the *Number One* team in the nation: Notre Dame. Riding the Special, we donned our senior cords and Reamer pots, joining up with the Purdue All American Marching Band and all the other seniors to enter Ross-Ade Stadium! The Special was parked inside the fence near our players' dressing room. We formed our corridor, and it was a thrill to stand on the field, cheer our varsity team, and be close enough to recognize player's faces as they passed. *Hail Purdue!* The game was a barn burner, but behind Griese's passing of 19 for 22 for over 280 yards, we prevailed!

After the game while standing near the Special, a guy asked if he could take my picture, so I let him. I entered the senior cord contest that night, but all the judges appeared to be *Greeks*, so my GDI down the front leg instantly sunk me. Back at West, I shaved off my beard! My face was quite tan after lifeguarding, but under the beard, the skin was *pure* white! When the NCAA football polls came out on Monday, guess who was rated *Number One* in the nation? Yep, the gold and black Boilermakers of Purdue! When going to classes in the late afternoon, I heard the marching band practicing to the cadence, "We're Number One!" It was cool!

The next weekend was an away game, and Dad and I listened to it as we heard our team lose their *top* ranking when they tied! I was home because Linda and I were going out that night. When her mother let me in, she commented on how different I looked. When Linda came into the room, she put her hand up to her mouth and gasped a little! I made a joke about it, and then we left. We went to a movie and got something to eat afterward. Like with Paulette when we saw each other after being separated, there seemed to be a lack of connection. Conversation was forced, and we just had problems finding common ground. I did kiss her good-night when beardless! Late in the week, I got a letter and our time together was over. I do not remember if our age difference, or if she was scared about what I *really* looked like was the reason, but it was over! I hope she had a wonderful and fulfilling life!

We won again, but had to play *at* Michigan for the third straight year! The Reamers left at hours, 1:00 a.m. on weekends, to take the Special. I drove my car and transported another five to the game, including Conrad and Cartin. One of the other guys joining us was Jackson. When it was time to go into the stadium, I had to sneak in my cow bell! Late in the game, Michigan led by a point. We made one last drive, and with fifteen seconds left, Bob Griese kicked a field goal, and we went wild! I vigorously rang my cow bell as hard as I could, but then it went silent! I looked at it; the strap broke and the bell flew off! I looked behind me and Jackson was holding his chest trying to breathe after the bell punched him! (Note: If you ask him, he will say it hit the guy next to him, but I believe I am right!) We found the bell and, for-tunately, neither Jackson, nor anyone else, was carted out of the stadium on a stretcher!

The next week was Homecoming. Friday night's pep rally was huge because we were tied for first place in the Big Ten, and the winner of this game would probably be in the Rose Bowl! At the rally, I ran into Jackson and his girlfriend, Arleen Henderlong, who went to Ball State University (BSU). She was cute and ener-getic, and the three of us talked before going our own ways. For the Reamer actives and pledges, it was *all hands on deck!* We started blowing up balloons at 5:30 a.m. and had about 7,000 available to sell, and parking lot sales went great! Since we were sitting so low, it made seeing parts of the field difficult; jumbotrons were not invented yet!

Late in the fourth quarter, we were ahead, but MSU was driving. On a fourth down they threw a pass for a what would be the win, but it was incomplete. We started yelling, but one of the referees had thrown a yellow flag, and they got the play over. This time they were successful, scored, and won! *Ugh!*

The next week, we lost, but won the following two games. What was interesting about the latter game was the Purdue Football Program. When I sat down, Dave Fry tapped me on the shoulder and said, "Congratulations!" I asked why, and he opened the program to page 48, which had a full-page picture of me in my senior cords, Reamer pot, and beard. I had lost the senior cord contests, but the guy who took my picture after the Notre Dame game, recognized my *superior* artistic work on my cords! *Vindication!!!*

The last football game was at IU. I piloted the Special, and a crew of four Reamers joined me. We left campus early, but as we got onto the highway, we noticed a new noise; it kept getting louder and louder. We thought it was a wheel bearing going, so when we got to Crawfordsville, we stopped at a service station, and I asked, "Do you think you have a wheel bearing for my train!?" The Reamers *groaned* about me using the word *train*. The attendant looked at me dumbfoundedly, and then I added, "It's got a bus chassis!" With that he lit up and said, "Sure!" Since I was the treasurer, I signed for the bill and we left. They allowed us to park it inside the northwest corner of the stadium. We could stand near the Special and still watch the game, especially when it was being played near our end. We kept *The Bucket!* No bowl, but we beat Notre Dame when they were Number One and added another P to the Old Oaken Bucket for the third straight year! Indiana State Champions again!

One night after Thanksgiving, I got a call from Susie Hintz; she was in a panic. She tried Ken first, but he was not in. She asked if I could come over and help catch a mouse. Tom was out of town, and this mouse was eating their dry food and leaving *presents* in their kitchen. On the way over, I bought a package of three traps. When I got there, she showed me where the problem was, and I set all three traps nearby. We talked for a few minutes, and I went back to West. The next night I was telling the guys at dinner about this, and they all laughed. On Monday night at our regular Reamer meeting, everything went fine. After all the main reports were given, it was time for *The Dirty Report,* I told you I would cover this subject! Bart and White made sure they had all the facts wrong as they reported on my *sordid affair* with a mouse named Susie while her husband was out of town! The *Office of Dirty* does not necessarily have to deal with *true* facts, but just make sure the story was *dirty* and *funny!* (College humor!)

Just before Christmas, Bart came to my room and gave me a Christmas present. I protested, but he said it was not a big deal and requested I wait until Christmas to open it. While opening presents with Mom and Dad, I picked up Bart's present, undid the wrapping, and opened the box. Sitting there was a brand-new *rat trap!* On the underside was written, "For Hun-Zee-Pooh. From Bart and Whitey." So now I had to explain everything to Mom and Dad; hence, the reason to wait until Christmas. With friends like these, I do not need enemies!

The Reamers activated our four pledges, so our numbers swelled to twenty-five! When it came to graduating seniors, only two were leaving, Bart and one of my pledge brothers. Another pledge brother, Tom Martin, was elected president, and I was elected historian, and I took copious quantities of pictures for the Reamers during my last semester.

Semester break was the busiest I ever had. It started by bringing Bart home to Crystal Lake. It was the first time my parents met Bart; Dad had a lot of conversations with him. Sunday evening the Chicago Black Hawks hockey team was playing, Bart and I drove to Dundee, picked up Clevitz and his younger brother, and headed for Chicago. The game was close and the crowd was noisy. On one bad call (my opinion), someone threw an octopus onto the ice! Hockey fans were *crazy* and it was a spectacular evening!

On Tuesday I drove Bart back to Purdue because Wednesday was his commissioning ceremony. White and I met Bart and his parents at the Stewart Student Center. After a bunch of speeches, they were sworn in and pinned on their gold 2nd Lieutenant bars. Bart looked great as an Army officer, but one thing he said always stuck with me: "The neatest and proudest parts of my Army uniform are the two US pins!" In the hallway, I ran into the first guy I ever met at Purdue, Jim Shutt! He was also commissioned, but in the Air Force, and he was with his wife, Eloise. White and I went back to West with Bart to helped pack the last remaining things into their car, and I got to talk to his dad. Finally, Bart, White, and I said our goodbyes, and they drove off, leaving White and me behind. I was not worried about Bart because he had orders to Germany, instead of Vietnam. God Speed old buddy! I do have to add, later his Germany orders were rescinded, and he was sent to Vietnam, but he returned unharmed! Thank you, guardian angel!

Wednesday night Jackson arrived because he and I were going to David Lipscomb College in Nashville to see his middle brother, Rich, play basketball. We got there Thursday afternoon, met with Rich, ate, and that evening we stayed overnight at one of Rich's friend's home. The next morning while Jack showered, I rolled over and the bed *crashed* to the floor! The *thump* was loud, and the father came into the room while I was laying there trying to figure out what happened. He accused me of *jumping* on the bed and did not believe me when I said I just rolled over! He asked us to leave! We met Rich and told him our situation. He said he could get us a room for the weekend nights.

Friday afternoon we went to the Grand Old Opry. During weekdays, the quality of the people on stage was not great! One trio was quite bad; however, we decided we wanted everyone to suffer longer, so after what was to be their last song, Jack and I started yelling, screaming, and loudly applauding. Our enthusiasm was so great, they brought them back for two encores! When they really left the stage, we left, and most people around us were happy to see us go! That night we went to a girls' intermural basketball game. This was the old style where the girls in the back court could not cross to the front court, and vice versa. Midway through the first half, one team replaced a girl with another. As the game resumed, someone yelled for the new girl, Judy. We started cheering for Judy like we did for the trio at the Opry! She got so shook up they had to take her out before halftime because she had almost fouled out! Rich got us a room, and that night we destroyed *zero* beds!

Saturday afternoon they showed the movie, *Shenandoah*, in their auditorium; Rich and his girlfriend were sitting right behind Jack and me. It took place during the Civil War, and the opening scene had a waving Confederate Flag passing across the screen. Everyone in the theater cheered and screamed! About fifteen minutes later, there was a similar scene, but this time it was the US flag, so I cheered! Rich said in a quiet voice, "It's sure going to be fun watching the hangin' after the movie!" Two hours later, we got word the visiting team could not cross the mountains due to a snowstorm, so as it turned out, this trip was a bust from the standpoint of watching Rich play.

The next morning, we left after breakfast and saw signs for Mammoth Cave. Neither of us had been there, so we took a one-hour tour. There were six on tour: a honeymoon couple, two tall elderly ladies, and us. Once in the cave, the guide showed us *total* darkness by turning out all the lights for a minute! Later, he then showed us various forms of stalactites, stalagmites, dripping water, and so forth. All through this, Jack and I were joking, cutting up, and laughing, which was starting to irritate the elderly women. At one point, the guide shined his light onto the ceiling where a bunch of blind cave spiders resided. One of the elderly women asks, "What do they eat?" From behind her, I answered in a deep voice, "People!" She turned, looked down at me, and replied, "Little people I hope!" *Pow!* Everyone laughed, probably me the hardest!

Chapter 33

Senior Year, Spring Semester, 1966

M Y LAST SEMESTER WAS FULL WITH SEVENTEEN credit-hours. The EE courses were transformer design, instrumentation, and my only computer design class. We also had an EE seminar featuring cutting-edge technologists showing their latest accomplishments. Remember, 1966 was still early in the solid-state revolution. One scientist talked about having a chip containing 100 resisters; now they contain a whole sophisticated computer! An engineer demonstrated a low-powered Ruby laser; now the military are deploying laser weapons! It was interesting seeing the new technologies on the horizon!

I had two non-EE classes. The first elective we called *Marriage Analysis!* We started with a male and female baby and took them through each development stage through senior adult years. Jackson and I occupied two, side-by-side, front seats, which made it tough on our instructor. One time we were talking about pre-marital sex. The point came up if a girl was found pregnant, and if there were two individuals who admitted to having relations with her, none could be sued for support. Obviously, this was before DNA! A few minutes later, we were discussing whether a male would more likely use protection with a girl he cared for, or with a prostitute. Jackson was trying to get his point across, saying, "I don't understand that point because I have a problem..." When he paused, I quickly and loudly interjected, "What, finding two witnesses?" The room erupted in loud laughter! He just narrowed his eyes, looked intently at me, and said, "I'm going to *get* you!" He never *zinged* me like that in class!

My last class was another elective about humor in American literature. The reading was fun, but the amount was overwhelming! Our instructor was super great! For one of our assignments, we had to deliver a funny speech. After one of the speeches, there was a big argument in class about how to enunciate a certain word. Many native Hoosiers speak a *different* English language than the rest us. The word in question was *creek*! Most enunciate it with the *EEs* being a long E! However, there are many Hoosiers who will say "*crick*" with a short "i." After ten minutes of debate, our instructor whistled to stop the bantering, then he added, "Where I come from, we call them *bayous!*" The whole class busted out laughing. Being the next speaker, I worked in a reference to a bayou and got a big hand!

One story we studied was Uncle Remus's *Br'er Rabbit*! When our instructor read from this, the whole class was deathly quiet and listened intently. I do not know if you ever read this powerful, southern, black American dialect from the 1800s, but to read it and get anything out of it, I had to read it out loud so I could *hear* myself! The bad part of this class was we had many themes to write, some of which were in class, so mine were horrible, and they took my grade down; however, I will always remember *Br'er Rabbit*!

In late February, I started interviewing seriously. My on-campus General Electric interview led to a trip to Ft. Wayne where I toured their facility. Everything went well, probably because they did not ask about *grades!* Over spring break, I had interviews scheduled with Continental Can in Chicago, General Motors in Milwaukee, Allen-Bradley Company in Milwaukee, and Hewlett-Packard in Palo Alto, California.

The weekend before spring break, West was having their annual Monte Carlo night. Midweek, Jackson told me, "Hey, I have a date for you! Arleen is coming this weekend, and she is bringing her roommate!" He kept after me to meet her, so the next day, I said, "OK." He then dropped *the* bomb, "We have to pick them up on Friday night, but they have a ride back Sunday afternoon!" I gasp, "You mean this blind date is for the *whole weekend!*?" What did I just get myself into! After Friday's dinner, I drove us over to BSU, and we met them. She was shorter than me (Good!), cute (Good!) and when Arleen introduced us, she smiled and said encouraging words (Good! That's 3 for 3!). Her name was Susan Dohner. When I opened the front passenger door, she slid in and moved towards the center of the seat (Good! That's 4 for 4!). While driving to Purdue, conversation was easy, and when asked a question, she gave real answers, not just a word or two (Good! That's 5 for 5!).

Sue said she was studying to be a business and English teacher. I needed English help! (Good! That's 6 for 6!) When we got to Lafayette, we stopped for food. The table conversation was humorous. Jackson, being Baptist, made a statement to Sue, who was also Baptist, "You know we're going to a Monte Carlo party tomorrow night, which means gambling, *and* it is one of the *three* big sins, along with sex and drinking!" Sue made her first goof of the weekend, she replied, "Well, I plan on trying all *three* this year!" With that, Jackson and I did a high five! (Great! That's 7 for 7!) She then realized what she said and turned bright red; the laughter was long and hard! Since it was getting late and I had class in the morning, we took them to their residence hall, and I kissed her good night (Good! That's 8 for 8!). When I got back to my room, I thought maybe Jack did well setting me up with her; after all, she was eight for eight! That's a good start!

After my Saturday class, we picked them up and spent a leisurely day together. Dinner was in West's dining room, and at 7:00 p.m., we hit the roulette wheels and card tables. Jack drove us for food about 10 p.m., and then, much to my chagrin, he drove to the field near the football stadium and parked! He and Arleen had been dating for about three years, so they were used to this, but Sue and I had just met! We did do kissing. (Good! That's 9 for 9!)

I was a very self-conscious since I had never double dated doing anything like this before. As women's hours approached, we took them back to their hall, and I kissed her goodnight. One thing I noticed when we kissed, she did not taste like cigarettes! (Good! That's 10 for 10!)

Jack took me directly to Lions where I joined the other Reamers for our overnight charity project. About 7:00 a.m., I got back to West, showered, and took a short nap before we went to church. Losing a night of sleep did not bode well for church! Sue gently poked me to keep me awake! (Bad! That's 10 for 11!) We had lunch and a couple of hours later they caught their ride back to Muncie. As they drove off, Jack turned to me and asked, "Are you going to invite her to the Spring Formal!?" My mind was mush, but I had already thought about it. In the car as they drive off, Arleen asked Sue, "Are you going to the Spring Formal!?" The next two weekends were the bookends for spring break; the Saturday after those weekends was Cary's Spring Formal. The next day, I bought a cute and funny card, wrote a short note, and mailed it to Sue. By Thursday I had a similar card in return. (Good! That's 11 for 12!) I got another card and asked her to the Spring Formal but gave her my home address, hoping I had a positive answer when I returned from California!

Spring break was busy! I followed Jack to his folks' house in northwest Indiana. I met his mom, dad, and twelve-year-old brother, Chuck. What a great and friendly family; I felt like I belonged the second I walked into their home. I invited Jack home for the first weekend of our break, Easter weekend, so he followed me. At dinner, Jack told my folks about how much *kissy face* I did the previous weekend with Sue; I hoped he would stop and move on! On Easter, I took him to the Methodist Church; back home Mom asked how it was, and he said, "It was a little strange and the church's name was St. John something." She just laughed. That night on TV, they aired *The Ten Commandments*, and Jack quoted scripture throughout, which impressed us.

On Monday morning Jack headed for Indiana, I headed for Chicago, and Dad headed for a plant. The Continental Can gentleman who interviewed me was quite cordial and friendly. The position they wanted to fill was assistant plant manager. They thought I might be a good fit because I learned quite a bit about the business from Dad, which was true, but I was not comfortable about being *a plant manager*. As a result, I left a little earlier than planned, but first I said "Hello" to Maxine.

On Tuesday, I had an interview at General Motors south of Milwaukee. They had military contracts, which bothered me. I was not anti-military, but I had a friend who worked for a large company when their military contract was cancelled and hundreds of engineers were let go. I was interested in stability; Dad took his job with Continental Can and never worked elsewhere. General Motors' work was interesting, but when I expressed my concern about their government contracts; it resulted in no job offer.

On Wednesday, I visited the Allen-Bradley (A-B) Company in Milwaukee. This was a large manufacturing firm making electronic components and motor controls. The engineer doing my tour had been with them only six months, so next winter I could be doing this. They had a twelve-month training program before being assigned to a division or a sales office. I liked their structure and the fact they offered *stability*. Their personnel seemed dedicated to A-B, like Dad was to Continental Can, so I hoped for an offer.

From A-B, I drove to O'Hare, caught a flight to San Francisco, landed about 10:00 p.m. and I took a taxi to my Palo Alto hotel. I got to bed about midnight their time, about 2:00 a.m. *body* time. I could not sleep; my weird mind would not turn off today's visit or stop anticipating my visit at Hewlett-Packard (HP)! I watched the clock go around and even turned a radio on, hoping music would help! Finally, at 7:00 a.m., I got up and had breakfast. A car from HP took three of us through the lush countryside to the plant. I had two interviews with technical personnel who told me about their instrumentation equipment and wanted to know my interests.

At lunch, I rejoined the other two interviewees and other HP engineers; we had a round table discussion. By this time, my body started to melt down, and I had major problems staying alert! I had one more interview after lunch, which was extremely difficult. Afterward, they called a taxi for me, but I was the only one leaving, so I figured this did not bode well for me. I had a little time before my flight, so I bought a postcard, wrote a short note, and sent it to Sue. It had a picture of the prison island, Alcatraz, and at the top in red letters it said, "Having a wonderful time! Wish you were here!"

We landed about midnight, so by the time I got home, it was approaching 2:00 a.m., and I was exhausted! When I quietly opened the front door, there was a letter addressed to me. My heartbeats increased as I opened it and started reading. Sue wrote a nice letter, telling me about classes, and in the last paragraph, she said she would be glad to go with me to Cary's Spring Formal! (Good! That's 12 for 13!) I slept well that night!

Over the weekend, Dad and I had lots of talks about jobs, traits one should have like integrity, how to handle people, and so on. One thing he told me, which completely caught me by surprise, was, "The major thing you have going for yourself is common sense! You have more common sense than most young people I know!" *Wow!* That blew my mind! He also suggested that I should rate each offer for potential stability, advancement opportunities, location, education opportunities, and so forth. I started a list of things important to me, and when I got back to school, I had over thirty items and determined their *importance rating*. This list was tweaked daily. Finally, Dad offered to pay for my schooling to get an MBA; however, I would have to pay for housing. That put a twist on things as I went back for my last eight weeks at Purdue!

I talked to Cooney about what it would take to become a counselor. He told me what I had to do and said he would be glad to give me a letter of recommendation. He also indicated in May, the

Graduate Record Examination would be given, and I had to take it to get into the MBA program. This also was a lot to ponder too.

My mailbox had a letter from Sangamo Electric, Springfield, Illinois. I interviewed with them on campus before spring break, and on Monday when I called them, they asked if I could visit this Thursday. I said, "Yes," and they said a plane would pick me up. Thursday, three of us boarded their plane at the Purdue Airport. How cool was this! When we arrived, they put us in a classroom and gave us tests, which did not thrill me. These were aptitude tests. After my problems with them in high school, I was a little apprehensive, but it was better than writing a theme! We toured their facilities where they manufactured power meters for use in homes and factories. They also had a facility in North Carolina where they did military contracts for sonars and radars. Their training plan included six months in Springfield and then transfer to North Carolina. Interesting! Everything went well, and we were flown back to Purdue.

Friday night Arleen and Sue got a ride to Purdue. When we first met again, we kissed! (Good! That's 13 for 14!) They stayed with Arleen's friend at a sorority, and after my morning class, Jack and I picked them up and spent a leisurely afternoon before they left to get *beautiful*. When we picked them up, *oh my gosh*, Sue was *gorgeous*! (Good! That's 14 for 15!) She had on a black crepe dress with shoulder straps. After dinner at Cary, Jack drove us to the dance at the Union. The music was great, they had lots of slow songs, and the floor was always full of couples closely entwined. Since my feet were three feet above the floor all night, I was able to stay off Sue's toes! It was truly great holding her close as we swayed through the room, and I thoroughly enjoyed having her in my arms. It was *unbelievable!* (Good! That's 15 for 16)

Jack dropped us off and we got into my car. We were alone for the first time, and we did a lot of talking about family, education, dreams, and so forth. (Good! That's 16 for 17!) I learned I was less than a month older than her even though we were a year apart in college; she worked the year after high school. (Good! That's 17 for 18!) We talked about Jack and Arleen, and we learned Jack played both ends against the middle! While he was telling me that Arleen was bringing Sue to Purdue, he told Arleen I wanted her to bring Sue! Oh well, I guess it worked out! After one long kiss and hug, I was thinking, "I love you!" but then realized I was not thinking it, but I said it out loud! Her answer—*silence! Deafening silence! Death Valley silence!* (Bad! Still 17 for 19!) I never said this to any girl and was in shock I said it, but in my heart, I knew I also meant it! After my *expression of love*, we both backed down though we kissed. (Good! That's 18 for 20!) I did not sleep well because I was worried about what would happen the next morning, but Sue was her same self, which relieved me. (Good! That's 19 for 21!) I was afraid she was going to run, and I would never see her again, but no, she stayed with me until their ride took them back to Muncie. *Whew!* (Good! That's 20 for 22!)

I got three job offers: GE, A-B and Sangamo Electric. Then there was Dad's proposal to get an MBA. I went through my job-rating matrix and found no matter how I did the numbers, the GE job in Ft. Wayne always came in last. So, I eliminated them via a phone call. My final decision between the other two companies and the MBA would wait.

For the rest of the semester, Jack and I saw our girlfriends every weekend. We alternated places, and sometimes when we went to BSU, we only saw them for a few hours and drove right back. The weekend after the dance, we arrived on Saturday afternoon, and Jack and Arleen suggested we go to their room during visitor's hours. Sue was hesitant, but we went. It was much nicer than what I was used to because it was a brand new facility. They each had separate desks, and on Sue's was a picture of a military person, which I assumed was her brother. We went out to eat, and then to a small park near campus. Sue and I got out of Jack's car so they could have some privacy, and we sat on swings and talked for a long time. We even talked about religion. She mentioned she had never been baptized, so that put us on equal footing. (Good! That's 21 for 23!)

Everything was all right between us, so when we took them back to their hall and said, "Goodbye," I kissed her and resaid, "I love you!" She smiled back, and Jack and I drove away. I told Jack what I had said to her; he was surprised, but supportive. He asked if I saw the picture of the military guy on her desk. I said, "Yes," then he said, "That was her *boyfriend!*" That completely *floored* me! He told me they had been on and off for a while, but now he was stationed in Paris, France. He also said he did not know how serious she was about him. (*Ugh!* That's 21 for 24! She loses a point!) Also, he told me he got a job offer from GE in Ft. Wayne! I told him, "You have got to be kidding me! I just turned down an offer from them!" We discussed the possibility of working together, so on Monday I called GE but was told, "Sorry, that offer is no longer available!" What an interesting turn on *two* fronts!

I needed to make decisions! First, I was not up to taking a battery of tests which others spent months preparing for; therefore, I dropped the idea of pursuing an MBA. Second, I had to decide between A-B and Sangamo Electric. In my gut, I liked Sangamo, but I was worried about when I had to move to North Carolina, which meant fewer trips to see Sue, assuming we were still dating. While Sangamo's offer was higher, my matrix always tipped the selection in A-B's favor because there were many opportunities to continue schooling in Milwaukee, but not in Springfield. After much consternation, I picked A-B in Milwaukee. Before saying "No" to Sangamo, I called A-B to give them my positive answer and made sure everything was set! Now having a job, I called Sangamo, and they said they could *increase* their offer a little. When they said that, I wondered if I had done the right thing! I will never know!

During this semester, Cooney and I talked often. One subject was job offers, and when I told him I picked A-B, he said he had a good mechanical engineering friend, Jerome Engerski, who was also going to work there. He said he was married, and we should get together before graduation, but it never happened. There were too many nights we stayed up to 1:00, 1:30, or even 2:00 a.m. talking! Oh, for a little more sleep! But the *fellowship!*

One weekend we took the girls to the movie, *Those Magnificent Men in Their Flying Machines.* While a very funny movie, the closing scene had the Eiffel Tower falling! As we walked out, both Jack and Arleen were talking about how even the Eiffel Tower, *in Paris, France*, fell; hinting to Sue she needed to *collapse* that connection with Paris. They knew what I was still telling Sue each weekend, and they were rooting for me!

Two interesting events happened the last month at Purdue. First, I came back from class and a guy was working on my room's door. At the top of the door, he was installing a 1 x 3-inch brass plate; it had my name and "EE 1966." This was a tradition in Cary; *how cool!* Second, Cary held their annual Seniors' Recognition Banquet. Each unit submitted candidates for numerous awards, and one was selected as the winner. I was nominated by West and won the Spitzer Literary Award. Did you get that!? I *won* a *literary* award! Why? I was the only one published! Remember the Beatles letter to the *Chicago Tribune* where I was the first author? You might ask, "Who is Spitzer?" He was the guy who donated the land where Cary Hall was built, and Dad told me Spitzer used to pal around with Grandpa Hunziker! *Pretty cool, eh!?*

Classes were going all right. My instrumentation class was a challenge. I did well on the labs, but my tests scores were mostly Ds. On the final, I got 98! Since I did so well, I talked to the instructor about my grade. He looked at my previous tests scores, so he thought I should get a D, so I said, "Obviously, I know how to do measurements since my lab work showed it, and on your final, I got the *highest* grade in the class by ten points! I think that also proves I understand this technology!" He hesitated, then asked, "Do you have a job?" I told him I was to start at A-B the week after graduation. He was quiet again, then concluded my grade was a C. *Great!*

The bottom line is: I am still "Mr. Average!" If C is average, then that is me! Since I did not have a grade-point average of exactly 4.00 (Purdue was on a six-point system) but had *change to spare*, I guess I could consider myself *above* average! Remember when we were told to, "Look left, look right, and one of us would not graduate?" Well, we were also told, "Only 20 percent of the engineering students graduate without an additional semester or summer session!" If that is the case, I am in the *top 20 percent!* That *is my story*, and I am *sticking* to it!

The day before graduation, I followed Sue's instructions to her home. "Take US 35 east out of Kokomo and go to State Route

37, then go north toward Marion. When you get to the junk yard, turn left because that is 16th Street where we live." "Wait!" I ask. "I turn at a *junk yard*?!" She said, "Yes, that is 16th Street and take it until you cross the railroad tracks. We are the fourth house on the left." "I turn at the *junk yard*, go until I cross the railroad tracks, and you're the fourth house on the left," I repeated! I am thinking, "What have I gotten myself into!?" The good news was her instructions were accurate (Good! That's 22 for 25!). The fourth home on the left was a three-bedroom ranch with two driveways. There was construction near in the rear of the first driveway, so I parked in the second one.

As I got out, a woman about Mom's age and size introduced herself as Sue's Mom, Trussie, and said, "You must be Rick!" I said I was, she invited me in, and called for Susie. We instantly bonded! Her dad, Milburne, came in from the construction area and while shaking my hand said, "I was hoping to be sitting on the front porch with a shotgun on my lap, but I guess I missed my opportunity to scare you off!" With greetings like this, what can go wrong!? He showed me the foundation for a new, 1,300-square-foot detached garage! I thought, *Oh, to have a garage this big!* Sue grabbed my hand and took me to the house next door and introduced me to her dad's mother, Grandma Grace, and her mother, Great-Grandma Harrold. A few minutes later, a car drove up, and she introduced me to her brother, Cary, who was about to graduate from high school. I had now met the entire Dohner clan *left at the junk yard!* That night we had a wonderful meal, and it was topped off with a dessert I never had before, Cherries Delight. It had a graham cracker base, a whipped cream mixed with cream cheese center, which was topped with cherries in a sweet red sauce. *It was good!* And she sold me on her cooking! (Good! That's 23 for 26!)

The next day was graduation day, but before heading out, Sue gave me a present. A few weeks earlier she asked if I wanted anything for graduation, and I said, "Yes, I would like a picture of you!" She got dressed up on the hottest day of the spring and had a professional portrait made! When I opened and saw it, *I was blown away!* It was *so* sweet of her to do this! (Good! That's 24 for 27!) At Purdue I introduced her to Mom and Dad, met up with the Jackson clan, and headed to the Hall of Music. Jack and I got in our procession lines and entered the hall. Once seated and after several soon-to-be-forgotten speeches, we walked to center stage, received our diplomas, and returned to our seats. We met our folks outside, but before we left, I grabbed Jack and asked him to whisper in Sue's ear, "I hope you're not disappointed in Rick's home!" At Cary Hall we took pictures and the Jacksons invited all of us to their home for a bite to eat. On the way, I said, "I hope you like what Mom and Dad recently did to our house. We live in a converted barn, and they really tried hard to fix it up!" We stayed about three hours at Jacksons, but Mom and Dad took off about an hour earlier.

When we were on the Illinois Tollway, I said, "By the way I have to tell you something. I need you to be aware of this before you spend time with my folks. I have an illegitimate sister and she is mentally deranged living in the mental hospital. I have no idea if the subject will come up, but if it does, *just sit quietly*. One time when Rog and Sybil were home, she came up in our conversation, Sybil said something, Dad got mad, hit her and gave her a black eye, so *please don't say anything!*" I figured I had to get back at her for *turn left at the junk yard*, which was true! It was late and dark when we got home, and I could see Sue out of the corner of my eye, looking at our tri-level, and she finally said, "Where is the barn?" and lightly hit me (Good! That's 25 for 28!). When we got in, I showed her where everything was and kissed her good night.

The next morning, we slowly gathered around the kitchen table. Mom and Sue migrated to the patio and had fun talking; she made good headway with Mom. (Good! That's 26 for 29!) That afternoon we went to the Gate 13 beach where I took her out in the boat and showed her the two beaches where I used to work. Dad grilled steaks, and Mom prepared the side dishes.

At the dining room table, everything looked good, but then I saw we were having *peas*! I turned to Mom and said, "Really, Mom!" while pointing at them. Sue had no idea what was happening, so I told her the story about *peas!* She laughed. (Good! That's 27 for 30!) Sue realized my story about a *crazy* sister was a hoax, so she proceeded to tell them and, while looking at Dad, said "And he said you even gave Sybil a black eye!" Dad did not miss a second before he replied, "But it didn't stay black long!" This caught Sue off guard, and there was a *lengthy* pause before the four of us started laughing! (Good! That's 28 for 31!) The rest of the time at home was quiet, and Sue started to feel very comfortable.

The last night we went to a movie, stopped at the Tastec Freeze, and I parked my car in front of our house. We kissed and I told her, "I love you!" for the tenth or twelfth time since the Spring Formal. She pulled back, looked me in my eyes, and said, "I love you, too!" *Wow!* The kiss following her statement was long! She told me she sent a letter to Paris and ended it! She also said, "Before I said, 'I love you' to you, I wanted time to make sure I really meant it!" *Wow!* (Good! That's 29 for 32! Point! Set! Match! Game Over! A .906 batting average!) I had *won* her heart! The next day, Tuesday, I took her back to Marion. She brought me into town a different way, so I did not turn *left* at the *junk yard*; I turned *right*! We unloaded her things, had a quick lunch, made a date for ten days from now, had a long kiss or two, and I took off to drive home.

My report day at A-B was on Thursday, and I already made reservations to stay in midtown Milwaukee. I wanted to get there early Wednesday so I could see the *lay of the land* near A-B. I got up relatively early, packed my car with the minimum I needed, but with my graduation present from Sue, said, "Goodbye" to Mom, entered my chariot, and headed northeast toward my new home, Milwaukee. As I drove the country back roads and saw farms, ponds, and beautiful trees, my weird mind went wild with questions:

Did Sue really mean it when she told me she loved me? How were we going to do this long-range relationship? Could we survive the separations? Would we still have time with Jack and Arleen? If not, how would that affect our relationship? Should we get engaged? When should we get engaged? Married? Would we have kids? How many? Would I be able to provide her a nice home?

Should I have taken the Graduate Record Exam just to see how well, or bad, I did? Should I have taken Sangamo Electric's offer? Could a C student really make a decent wage and do the work properly? When should I start an advanced degree? What should it be in? Would Sue want to work after getting her teaching degree? Where would we live? Would she be able to find a job wherever my job took us?

None of these questions were answered while driving to my first job!

Epilogue

I STARTED TYPING *HEARTLAND RAISING* IN 2012, occasionally worked on it for just under three years and got into my high school junior year! The book sat dormant until mid-March 2020, when Covid-19 struck. Since I had nothing to do, I finished the initial draft (245,000 total words!) in about seventy-five days. Eventually, I was told by publishers I needed to cut it down to 100,000 words, so I had to delete three out of every five pages! My intent was always to end *Heartland Raising* going to my first job.

Because of the nature of my Air Force work, I planned on writing a second book covering my *working years*. However, since this project took *sssooo* long, the fact several co-workers said they did not want their names mentioned, and I would be required to get Air Force approval, I figured I may never get a *working years* book written, approved, and published. I know I cannot describe programs, but I wanted to talk about the people, even if I had to use false names, and about crazy things which happened, such as almost taking down a power grid (sounds like an EE lab!), literally coming within *one inch* of falling out of a helicopter at 10,000 feet, doing a scuba dive eighty-three miles from communist territory when our boat sank, and so forth. Incidentally, the first two involved the same program, one of about sixty I managed! Because of all the above and the low probability of accomplishing a *working years* book, I want to conclude with a summary of my career as well as inform you about many friends I mentioned earlier. I will try and do this in semi-chronological order.

I cannot report on anyone mentioned in the sections about Elmwood Park or Brookfield; however, my Crystal Lake and Purdue friends will be scattered throughout my epilogue.

Three weeks after graduating from Purdue, I swam out to a raft at Grafton. The beach was crowded, and I did not recognize any guards and was about to leave when Charlene joined me. She wanted an update. I told her about my job and that I found a girl I loved; she said she was happy for me and she was dating a great guy, too. She then said, "The beach just isn't the same without you and Dave!" A few minutes later we swam to shore, waved to each other, and said, "See you around!" I never saw or talked to her again!

I worked at Allen-Bradley until the end of March 1967. During this time, Jerome Engerski, Cooney's friend, and I became good friends and always ate lunch together. In early-October, Sue and I got engaged, but by late-October I decided to leave A-B. Instead of being drafted, I signed up for the Air Force. Sue and I got married in February 1967. Roger was my best man, Jan Cooney and Tom Hintz were my groomsmen, and Sue's brother, Cary, ushered. Jackson was at Marine boot camp, but his wife, Arleen, was Sue's matron of honor! Susie Hintz helped all the bridesmaids, and Jerome and Judy Engerski were in attendance. My future father-in-law told the pastor, Rev. Charles Wagoner, "Please tie a *tight* knot!" Last, I will add one more noted accomplishment after our honeymoon: Sue's first-date prophesy about participating in the three major carnal indulgences was fulfilled in only eleven months! (Good! That's 30 for 33!)

Mid-April I reported to Officer Training School (OTS) at Lackland Air Force Base (AFB), San Antonio, Texas, and graduated on June 30. I was assigned to the Electronic Warfare (EW) Division of the Air Force Avionics Laboratory (AFAL) at Wright-Patterson AFB, Dayton, Ohio. First Lt. Terry Yake, my graduate student lab instructor, was assigned to the same division. He and his wife, Maggie, would go with us to Purdue football games and came to our New Year's Eve parties.

I must tell one *working* story. My supervisor instantly realized I could not write! *A surprise!* He sent me to a technical writing course where I learned to write *Governmentese!* My lightbulb finally came on, and I made an unbelievable transformation! I know you just read hundreds of pages I wrote, so you do not feel I am any good at writing, right? But, I was good at *Governmentese* writing! Really!

We rented an apartment and became good friends with our neighbors, Jerry and Pat Carter; in fact, their son, Jeff, babysat for us after our first son was born. A year later, we built our first home. We had two sets of wonderful neighbors, Tom and Linda Stevens and Les and Gail Eastling.

The *biggest* and *most important event* in our lives unfolded and changed us altogether! Both the Stevens and Eastlings went to a Baptist church. They invited us, and we often joined them. In September 1968, we learned Sue was pregnant! We were delighted, but we also felt something was missing in our lives; we wanted to bring our children up in a godly home. We went to bed on a Saturday night and talked again. We both got up, knelt on our side of the bed, and asked Jesus Christ to come into our hearts and guide us as a family. At the end of Sunday's service, we met with the pastor, Bro. John Kurtz, and told him what we did. He asked us questions to confirm our commitments, had prayer, and then introduced us to our new church family. The next Sunday, Sue and I were baptized.

Those Saturday night prayers changed our lives! This did not come out of the blue; there were hints for me through all my life: Sunday School in Brookfield; comments Mary Anne made about Jesus's blood curing the lepers; Dave's description of the shafts of light looking like "The fingers of God," Jackson always making sure we went to church, and Sue's guidance because she had been brought up in a strong, godly home. The churches we attended became major parts of our lives; I taught weekly Bible classes in four of the six, served as a deacon in three, chaired a fund-raiser for a new sanctuary in one, plus many other endeavors. Jesus Christ changed our lives forever! It was about this time Jackson was shipped off to Vietnam as a Marine helicopter pilot. I took him on as my first major prayer concern. I had this feeling if I missed one day praying for him, he would be killed in action; therefore, for thirteen months, I made sure I prayed for him *daily*, and he came home safe and healthy![22]

You too can experience what Sue and I did. The following words and scripture (New International Version Bible) are what I used to lead my sons and others to Christ. Romans 3:23 states, "For all have sinned and fall short of the glory of God." We have all sinned (i.e., told a lie, exhibited road rage, etc.) and have come short of the sinless Jesus Christ—"the glory of God!" As a result of our sin, we have earned "wages," which result in eternal death as stated in Romans 6:23, "For the wages of sin is death, but the gift of God is eternal life in Christ Jesus our Lord." However, Christ bore our sins on a cross and died for them as we see in Romans 5:8, "But God demonstrates his own love for us in this: While we were still sinners, Christ died for us." He became our sacrifice and took our punishment! He offers us salvation as a "gift" we can choose to accept or reject—our choice! Romans 10:9–10, 13 states "That if you confess with your mouth, 'Jesus is Lord,' and believe in your heart that God raised him from the dead, you shall be saved. For it is with your heart that you believe and are justified, and it is with your mouth that you confess and are saved … (for) Everyone who calls on the name of the Lord will be saved." Since Jesus was resurrected from the dead, we have hope for eternal life. You can experience the same joy with Jesus Christ that we do by praying the following prayer with your heart and mouth:

---

[22] Laine Boyd, *Way Beyond the Blue*, Marquee Publishing, 2018. p. 73. (Note: Marine Colonel Jackie Jackson has recently published his memoirs of his years of service to our Country. It is humorous, gripping, interesting, and compelling read about his life, service, beautiful and wonderful wife and family, but, foremost, his love and faith in his Creator, the Lord Almighty.)

Lord Jesus, I confess I have sinned against you and others. Please forgive me of all my sins. I believe that you came, lived a sinless life, died on a cross for *my* sins, were buried, and resurrected on the third day. Please come into my heart and live within me as my Lord and Savior. I commit to follow you in my life. Thank you for giving me eternal life. Amen.

Now that you have done this, you should go to the church of your choice, talk to the pastor, follow Christ in scriptural baptism, and get involved! God Bless you!

I spent four-years at W-PAFB, but from mid-January to mid-June 1969, I was on a special training program for young research and development officers to work in an operational environment. I was sent to the 4750th Test Squadron, Tyndall AFB, Panama City, Florida. They were under the Aerospace Defense Command and flew F-101s, F-102s, F-106s, and T-33s. I got to fly in F-106s and T-33s; the best time of my entire career! While there, we experienced the birth of our first son, Eric, who initially cost us $0.875/per pound, which was cheaper than hamburger; however, the upkeep would be more! Unfortunately, while there, we lost Grandma Alexander, and I knew I lost more than a grandma, but a good friend, even if she could not take good pictures! I made captain on June 30, 1970, and that summer I got to brief the US Deputy Secretary of Defense, Mr. David Packard, along with twenty-plus generals.

In July 1971, I was transferred to the Arming and Fusing Division of the Air Force Weapons Laboratory, Kirtland AFB, Albuquerque, New Mexico. Tom and Susie Hintz moved about then and we, unfortunately, lost contact! In 1972, we took a vacation, stopped in Colorado Springs, and visited Tom Bartels and his wife, Karen; a few months later they stayed with us. Of equal importance to the birth of Eric, in March 1973 was the birth of our second son, Kirk, who initially cost us $0.85/pound; therefore, there was no inflation for four years! He also had upkeep costs! The timing of Kirk's birth coincided with my decision to leave the military. I applied for a US government civil service rating and called my old W-PAFB supervisor to use him as a reference. He was now a branch chief and said he had two slots open. I always enjoyed the work and found it interesting, but I did not want to live in Dayton; however, on October 2, 1973, I signed in as a GS-12 civilian back into my old EW Division!

Mom and Dad wintered in Florida, and in March 1976, she got the flu, her sodium electrolytic dropped, and she became brain dead! Two weeks later, at fifty-nine, she passed away. The woman who got me through my tough growing up years was now gone and I missed her terribly! Mr. Battles made the arrangements for her two services. Rog and Sybil attended the Florida memorial, and Sue and I attended the Crystal Lake service. Seeing Dad standing at home by himself as we drove away was heart wrenching. He sold our home that summer and moved into his travel trailer in Florida. In October 1976, I was promoted to a GS-13, and in May 1977, Dad married Martha Zeller, who was a wonderful and fun addition to our family.

Our neighborhood had significant annual turnover, so in 1977, we built a home in Vandalia for a stabler environment for our sons. We lived there the next twenty-two years; both boys graduated from their high school, and Sue taught business and English there for almost twenty years. We had great neighbors like Larry and Marilyn Lehman and Dale and Joy Bazill. We played double-deck pinochle for eighteen years with the Lehmans, Bazills, and another couple, Bob and Trudy Barton; we still get together with the Lehmans. In 1979, Sue developed her first melanoma, a very serious one on her neck. My weird mind kept wondering how I was going to raise five- and nine-year-old kids on my own! Thankfully, our guardian angel came through again. Sue had major surgery, but we had to wait two years to confirm she was free of it!

One evening in 1983 while Roger, Sybil, Sue, and I visited Dad and Martha in Florida, their phone rang; it was Mr. Archambault. After the call it was brought up that I used to date Mary Anne, so, while sitting next to my wife, I stupidly say, "Yeah, she was the prettiest girl I ever dated!" The *moans and grown* from around the table were deafening! (Bad for Rick! 0 for 1 and losing badly!) When they arrived, Mrs. Archambault showed me photos of all their children and grandchildren and told me about each. Mary Anne was married to a tall doctor, so I smiled to myself, knowing she could now wear high-heel shoes! They lived near Chicago but had a condo in Florida.

In March 1984, my base supervisor, his wife, Sue, and I formed a business partnership, and started and ran a franchised travel agency. We ran the paperwork through W-PAFB's legal office and got their approvals. The timing was not the best since the airline industry was going through major deregulation changes, and we had very limited time daily to visit and enlist corporate clients, so we sold it right before Christmas 1985.

Because of technical successes, the generation of many new programs, and the fact I secured outside funding to substantially reduce AFAL's funding to accomplish my technical programs, I was awarded a Technical GS-14 promotion in 1986.

In 1987, we were *kid less* for spring break. One of Sue's co-workers, Nancy Kerschner, invited us to join her and her husband, Don, on a cruise. Twelve of us went on a one-week cruise to the Caribbean. Cruising became our *thing!* For Christmas 1991, we took a one-week family cruise from Jamaica to the Panama Canal. It was great and would be one of the last times all four of us opened presents together on Christmas morning. We have taken twenty-seven cruises, ten of them with Don and Nancy. Our longest cruise was forty-three days from Vancouver to Australia and New Zealand. We were scheduled to go on a twenty-eight-day cruise from Vancouver to Alaska, Japan, and South Korea in September/October 2020, but Covid-19 canceled it. People ask me, "Why cruising?" My answer is simple, "While I sleep, our *hotel* takes us to a new place, and I do not have to pack and unpack every day!" Over the years, Don and Nancy, while being good friends, have cost us a *lot* of money!

We lived in Albuquerque at the time of my tenth CLCHS reunion. CLCHS's committee lost our address for the twentieth one, but we attended the twenty-fifty, thirtieth, and fiftieth reunions. In 1987, our Norwegian student, Jo, was able to attend. That night our dinner table had Jo, Polly Rosenthal, Ross and Michele, Ken and Pat, and us. It was great having most of the *Lakewood Four* back together. That night I heard Tom Peterson came home after serving in South Korea, got married, started a family, but lost his life trying to save his daughter when their house caught on fire. Also, Randy Schulze had a job with a research laboratory, but he died in the 1970s. For the thirtieth reunion, we had a joint CLCHS/C-GHS one! I spent time with Tim Frisch, Mark Baer, and others who had been pulled away from us. That night we broke bread with Bob and Chris (Hurley) Frenz, Ken and Pat, and Sam and Carol Cardella. Long-time friends are great!

In 1988, Dad was diagnosed with prostate cancer, and for four years he did well; however, by February 1993, it crippled him! I believe his goal was to see Rog's oldest daughter, Heather, get married in mid-July. He was at the wedding, but a month later, two weeks before his seventy-eighth birthday, Dad died. Rog and Martha were with him, but I was on a plane on its descent into the Tampa Airport when I felt a disturbance; later I found out it was about that time he passed. I had lost the *giant* in my life, and I miss him!

Shortly after Dad's passing, Mrs. Battles also passed away. After Mr. Battles retired in the early seventies, they moved to Florida. He developed prostate cancer and passed in the late eighties. They were great friends to Mom, Dad, and Martha, and were always there for them. I cannot complain about Mr. Battles's treatment of me during the years I worked for him. He even asked if I would be interested in taking over his manufacturing representative business; however, with the draft hanging over me, it would have been years before I could have done it, so he looked elsewhere. This couple were integral to Mom, Dad, Martha, and my lives, and were sorely missed!

In January 1995, my supervisor retired, and I took over our group. A reorganization occurred in April 1996; *groups* no longer existed, and my group was combined with another to become the Electro-Optical Warfare Branch, of which I became its first chief. Our division chief retired in early January 1997, and right before Christmas, I was named the new acting division chief of the Electro-Optical Technology Division. In two years and one day, I went from an engineer to a group leader to a branch chief to a division chief! I was promoted to the equivalent of a GS-15 and served out the rest of my career in this position. As division chief, I had eighty-five technical personnel evenly split between bachelor's degrees, master's degrees, and PhDs, but their leader was a guy in the lower third! I retired from this position on September 3, 1999, after thirty-two-plus years with the Air Force (active duty and civilian).

My career was an amazing ride! From a technical standpoint, it was super interesting. I got to work on cutting-edge technologies and concepts, and in most cases led the way by conducting first-ever lab, field, or flight tests in my areas of expertise. When I was quickly moved up the ranks in the mid-1990s, I was still conducting multiple critical field and flight tests that proved concepts' viabilities. Even as a division chief, I was finishing a field and a flight test! I was fortunate to develop and deploy technologies, which entered the AF operational inventory; this was extremely gratifying! The director of the Sensors Directorate presented me with the Air Force Outstanding Civilian Career Service Award Medal at my retirement ceremony. The Association of Old Crows, an International Electronic Warfare Technical Professional Society, included me in their third class of inductees into their Electronic Warfare Hall of Fame in 2003. I *really do* appreciate the work others went through to get these approved and presented to me. It certainly is wonderful to feel appreciated; *however*, to me, it was not the awards that were important; it was the people who I worked for, alongside, or supervised during this journey, who were important! When I came back to W-PAFB as a consultant, I received what I believe was my *greatest award* or *compliment*. Almost every person I talked to begged me to come back and retake my division chief's job! What I had been doing must have struck a chord, and I was very humbled when they expressed these heartfelt *thank yous* to me!

We started building our retirement dream house in January 1999, and in September 1999 it was finished, so we immediately moved to Bradenton, Florida. Sue and I started a company, Hunziker Associates, Inc, (HAI), and I consulted for the next eighteen years.

When Purdue played in the Outback Bowl in Tampa on January 1, 2000, the Bartels stayed with us and helped to ring in the millennium! Bart told me about a conversation I had with his father just before they took him home after his commissioning. He said I told his dad, "Purdue will not be the same without Bart!" While I do not remember saying this, that statement was *very true!* Bart was more than a friend and fellow Reamer; he was a mentor and person I admired.

The year 2001 was not the best for us. Of course, the main tragedy was the horrible terrorist attacks on the US on September 11th!!! President George W. Bush provided an interesting story in his book, *Decision Points*. His folks had left the White House earlier that morning to fly home. They finally connected by phone that evening and the President asked his mother where they were. "'We're in a motel in Brookfield, Wisconsin,' she replied. 'What in the world are you doing there?' 'Son,' she retorted, 'you grounded our plane!'"[23] I guess Brookfield is famous for others besides Eddy Mathews and me!

Like father, like son, I was diagnosed with prostate cancer right after 9/11; the day before Thanksgiving I had a radical prostatectomy, and the cancer was *all* removed. A few years later, I was having my annual physical by our new female primary care physician. While she was poking around on my abdomen, she noticed my scar from this surgery and asked, "Is this where you had your hysterectomy?" Five minutes later, I quit laughing!

For about fourteen years, Jerome and Judy Engerski kept a Sarasota Purdue Alumni Club alive by hosting a spring dinner. We went in 2000 and 2002, but when very few showed up at the latter one, Jerome resigned, so five of us agreed to establish a full-fledged club. Dr. Roger Stover was our president, I became the

<hr/>

[23] George W. Bush, *Decision Points*, Crown Publishers, 2010. p. 136.

VP, and we started having almost monthly events. After two years, I took over and ran the Club for the next five years. During my presidency, we developed a logo, started scholarships, and initiated food pantry help for our counties. I stayed on the board, served as secretary for four years and as the scholarship chairman until I resigned from the board in March 2018.

We missed CLCHS's fortieth reunion because a niece was getting married. I heard Jim Harwood was at there, so I was disappointed to have missed him. The last time I had seen him was about the time Mom passed away in the mid-1970s. We sadly got word Ken Kies passed away in 2003!

The years 2005 and 2006 were not good, especially for Sue. Her dad's congestive heart failure got worse, so she flew home to see him in February 2005; then in April he passed away. Sitting in the back at his funeral was Bro. Charles Wagoner, thirty-eight years after he married Sue and me! I whispered, "Just like a Baptist, sitting in the back row! Thanks for following Milburne's request to tie a tight knot for Sue and me!" He smiled in return! We spent time with her mom and even tried to talk her into coming to Florida the next winter, but she declined. It was *very tough* to have to leave her!

We always spent Thanksgivings at Sue's folks and with her brother's family too. On Wednesday morning the week before Thanksgiving 2006, Trussie's neighbor called. He found her lying on the bathroom floor, called 911, and was told by the medics that it looked like she had a stroke. When we got there Thursday morning, the prognosis was as dire as it was for my mom thirty years earlier. The next morning, she was removed from life support and passed peacefully. That Friday morning, the world lost the kindest and most wonderful women I ever knew, and I had the amazing privilege of having her as *my* mother-in-law. I think every time we visited, she made me Cherry Delight! She was always helping someone from her or Milburne's workplace, church, or neighborhood. Every year she made a tin full of cookies for each of her and his workers, and several churches' staffs. At her funeral, Rev. Ben Gray said, "I always cleaned the tin and gave it back to her so I could get more cookies the next year!" Trussie took care of Great-Grandma Harrold, her mother Grandma Persinger, Grandma Grace, and Milburne, so Cary, Carolyn, Sue, and I always felt the Lord called her home because she had no others to care for. I always said, "If Baptists had saints, then Trussie would be one—St. Trussie of Marion, Indiana!"

In late-winter 2009, Sue and I took a cruise called the "Norwegian Coastal Express" from Bergen to Kirkenes and back. When we arrived at Bergen, I called Jo, and she asked why we came to Norway. I said, "Because of you!" After a long pause, I added, "If you remember, I asked you many questions about your country and as a result, I always wanted to see Norway!" We talked for about twenty-five minutes, and she wanted me to call again when we got back to Bergen. We did call her the second time and discussed all the places we visited and things we did. We communicated a couple of times via email, but about a year later, my email to her got bounced!

We lost Jim Shutt in 2010. When Sue went to BSU, the first girl she met was a freshman who lived directly across the hall from her, named Eloise. Unfortunately, Eloise left school after her freshman year to marry—Jim Shutt! So, the first person I met at Purdue and the first person Sue met at Ball State married each other! It is a "small" world! Unfortunately, shortly after Jim passed away, we lost contact with Eloise. What a shame!

In the summer of 2012, I took Sue on "The Great Hunziker History Tour." The tour started with the CLCHS Class of '62's fiftieth reunion, visiting old homesteads and ended with a Mid-1960s Reamer reunion (*Note*: The Reamer Reunion will be covered later.). Before our fiftieth reunion, we heard from Denise Harwood that Jim had a severe stroke four years earlier, so they were not planning to attend. They lived in Barrington, so on Saturday we visited their home and went out to lunch. Ross and I were pleasantly surprised to see how well Jim was doing, but we figured it was still tough for them. That night our dinner table consisted of Bob and Chris (Hurley) Frenz, Ross and Michele, Bill and Bob Fanter, and us. It was the first time I saw the Fanters since our football game in the snow behind Dave Thompson's house!

The morning after, we got into our old home on Broadway, drove past South Elementary, and stopped at the junior high school behind it. I did not know it was named for Janet Lundahl's dad. *Cool!* As we passed South again, people were there. The woman, Lisa Gatt, was the current principal. She let us look around; I showed Sue the gym, lunchroom, and my fifth- and sixth-grade classrooms. On the way out, I noticed a plaque; it grabbed me because I recognized sixty percent of names on it. When the principal came out, I explained who all the people were on the plaque, and she mentioned my principal, Mr. Husmann, now had a school named after him, "Husmann Elementary." *Cool!*

We visited where our Elmwood Park home had been; it is now part of a church parking lot! While near Chicago, we visited both of my grandparents' homes, told my story, literally got inside both and had tours. In Grandma Alexander's house, I had a picture taken of us standing exactly where Mom and Dad stood when they got married! *Cool!* In Grandma and Grandpa Hunziker's home, we toured all three floors, and they gave me a letter Uncle Karl received in Switzerland in 1928 from his fiancé; they found it taped to the bottom of a dresser drawer!

At Brookfield, I talked our way into our old house because I had pictures of it the first summer we lived there. Down at the Fox River, I stood on the railroad bridge where Rog and I threw the bottle with a message into the water! *What a high!* We even went to Pine Ridge and had dinner there. I stood in awe where Dad taught me to fly-fish! *Goose bumps!*

In December 2012, I found a wedding register for the Crystal Lake area and looked up the names of the girls I dated. Three were listed, so I checked the internet for information about their husbands in hope of seeing tidbits on them. Unfortunately, I lost my notes, so what I write below is from memory, Mary Kleeman and her husband lived in Utah or Colorado. In Linda Petrillo's case, her husband's name took me an old obituary; it was detailed and long. She went to Michigan State University as a music student, met her husband, married, and had several kids. They got divorced in the mid-1980s, so the narrative on her stopped.

In early January 2013, I looked up Mary Anne's husband's name on the internet, and it shocked me; it was an obituary! He passed away in August 2012, only five months earlier! Sue helped me compose a letter we enclosed in a sympathy card. In our letter, we told her about my book, how my research gave us her husband's name, which led us to his obituary, and we were now expressing our sympathy. We also included a short paragraph about our life since college. A little while later, I got an email from her about the heartbreaking loss of her husband, what he did, her family, and that in the mid-1980s they moved to Florida. We emailed several times and once came close to visiting her as we drove near where she lived, but she was heading for a trip herself. In one of her emails, she attached a picture of the Class of 1964's twenty-fifth reunion, and I saw she was still as pretty as ever. Interestingly, sitting almost in front of her is Charlene! We both sold our homes, moved about the same time, and our emails changed. For the last five years, we have not communicated.

About eight years ago, my picture was in the *Purdue Alumnus Magazine*. In a picture on the same page was Terry Yake! We communicated, but unfortunately, he had advanced pancreatic cancer; he passed away in 2013. We sent a sympathy card and note to Maggie. I mentioned to her about my "getting people out of the water when it was lightning" comment to him in my field's lab, and she wrote back and said she had heard that story many times, but from his perspective! *Cool!*

In 2015 we sold our on-water Florida home and bought a small condo close by. Kirk and Jen lived northeast of Indianapolis, and the house across the street from them went up for sale, so I asked them, "Could we play *Everybody Loves Raymond* and live across the street from you?" There was a lengthy pause after which Kirk replied, "Well—Mom can, but not you, Dad!" *Ugh!* Now you know where I stand in *my* family! We built a ranch home a half mile away and use it as a summer home.

Bonnie Albertz went to school, married a wonderful young man, John, and moved to Indianapolis. In 1968, her folks sold their home in Crystal Lake and moved to Western Springs. Unfortunately, Mr. Albertz had a stroke, but he did progress fairly well. Sue and I visited them a couple of times, but they eventually moved to Indianapolis in 1975 so Bonnie and John could help. Bill passed away in 1979, and several times when we visited Kirk in the Indy area in the 2000s, we visited Mrs. Albertz. The last time we visited her was in December 2012, when she was 103 years *young*! She kiddingly said, "I think the Lord forgot I am still here!" She told us how she cried for three years after Mom died because they were so close; the best of friends! She handed me two old pictures and said, "These are pictures your mother bought for her mother back in the 1920s, and your grandmother kept them. When she died, your Mom gave them to me, but I think they should go back to your family!" *Wow! How cool!* I kept one and gave Rog and Sybil the other one. Unfortunately, she passed away mid-January.

While I mentioned many times about her living room light always being on when I brought Mary Anne home from dates, knowing Mrs. Albertz, I am sure she was *not* spying on us; I was just too shy and scared to kiss her! Bill and Winnie Albertz were *truly* loving friends to the *entire* Hunziker clan. Now every time we are in the Indy area, we go out to dinner with Bonnie and John. One thing I recently learned from her was they always went up to the Boulder Junction area to fish, so Mr. Albertz knew where he was going when he took Rog and me fishing that summer! She also said, they still go there with their family, so this is their *Pine Ridge* adventure! *Neat!*

The fall of 2018, we took a twenty-eight-day European cruise. While on the ship, Sue ruined her Achilles tendon and really limped badly. We met with our podiatrist, and she went through rest, and physical and injection therapy. Finally, in June 2019, she had surgery to *lengthen* her tendon and many more months of rest. In the meantime, I went to our dermatologist in May 2019, and she biopsied a *pimple* under my right lip. It came back positive as squamous cell carcinoma. In July I had four rounds of MOHS surgery before he finally got it all; he took one-third of my lower lip and three-fourths of an inch of the skin below it. He told me, "This was a life-threatening situation, and I recommend radiation therapy!" *Wow!* That caught me off guard! He stitched me up, but if you saw me now, you would not know I had this surgery! I had twenty-five radiation treatments on both my lip and the lymph node area located under it. Had I listened more to Charlene, I probably would have put zinc oxide on and around my lips, too. So far, my nose is still attached!

While Ross and I regularly knock each other via the internet, we did get together. We traveled up the East Coast and stopped and stayed with them in North Carolina several times; it was always a delight! Recently, he sent me an email he got from Paul Koch, which talked about Paul playing golf in Florida! Paul said he always played once a year with Dave Thompson and Bill and Bob Fanter. Somehow in 2020, we all connected, found others online, and now send messages to a small group of 1962 Tigers: Steve Mudgett, who lives in South Korea, Powers McGuire, Bob Frenz, Ross, Bill and Bob, Paul, and Dave. This was the first time I heard from or about Dave since we put away the Grafton equipment after the 1965 Labor Day weekend! We discuss intelligent things like bleach suppositories to rid ourselves of Covid-19 (WARNING: *A joke!* Do *not* do this!), or about stupid things we did in yester-years! During one of our "strings" of email, Ross asked Powers how he got his name Muley; he replied, "Muley—I am told I went on strike one day on a walk with my fam—wouldn't be budged."[24] You have now heard it from the ~~horse's~~ (Oops!) mule's mouth. I guess my brother had it wrong; however, I like the movie theater version better! Through this group, I also got reestablished with Jo!

My closest friends in college seemed to communicate better and longer. In 2010 and 2012, the Reamers had major mid-1960s reunions. There were about thirty-five Reamers, plus spouses, at each. The highlight was having a tent banquet at John Pickett's house in Lafayette. Our proverbial song leader, Bill Smith, led us in all the old serenading and pep songs. Conrad and Cartin were there in 2010! Recently, I got included onto the pledge class right before mine's email list, so now bedsides just Bart, I hear what is happening from others. Unfortunately, we lost Dave Fry in 2016 and Dave Smith in 2020. The Jacksons and Cooneys have always been close. We constantly email, and in the case of the Cooneys,

---

[24] Kid McQuire, *Email to Ross Annable, et al.*, April 29, 2020.

we go out to eat at least once when we stay in Indy. Every few years we, fortunately, spend time with the Jacksons. It is amazing how with certain friends, like the Jacksons, Cooneys, Bartels, and Annables, it seems like we continue right where we left off before, and without missing a heartbeat!

My sons' summary: Eric graduated from Purdue in Management in 1991; he had much better grades than me! He fell in love with a wonderful girl, Kellie Smith from Huber Heights, Ohio, and they married in April 1995. They have three lovely young adult daughters, Megan (23), Emily (19) and Lauren (16). Eric is a VP and head of claims for a fairly large insurance company and lives in Cincinnati. Kirk graduated from Bowling Green State University in telecommunications in 1995. He fell in love with a wonderful girl, Jennifer Knepp from La Port, Indiana, and they married in March 2000. They have three lovely young adult children: Dakota (18), Kiley (16), and Cooper, (13). Kirk has over twenty-two years on the frontline as a firefighter, delivered four babies, and lives northeast of Indianapolis.

Sue and I often talk about our daughters-in law and figured we could have never found more precious young women for our sons to marry! All ten are active in the Lord's work. When we look at what the Lord has given to us, He has blessed us immensely! Many times, we ask ourselves, "Why us!?" With five granddaughters, we try not to show favoritism, so when talking to any of them, I always encouraged them by saying, "You are in the top five of my favorite granddaughters!" However, I do have a favorite grandson, Cooper! It is easy to have a favorite when you only have one! Last, I do have to mention that Cooper is the Hunzikers' namesake for our branch. For the last four generations, it has been the *youngest* sibling (Dad, me, Kirk, and Cooper) who carried on the Hunziker name! *Weird!*

Closing Comments

I WALK FOUR MILES PER DAY TO SOMEWHAT STAY IN shape. I just calculated since 1988 when I started jogging and later walking, I have almost gone around the world one and a half times, assuming I could walk on water; luckily, I do not have to carry a twenty-five-pound resuscitator! The walking, along with my fifteen minutes of physical therapy before I get out of bed, help my bad back. Four orthopedic surgeons have described it as *a mess*, so I guess that must be an *approved* medical term! During my walks, I listen to a radio; it and our car radios are always tuned to an "oldies" or "classic" station. Many of those songs conjure up memorable thoughts of a special event, place, but mainly it brings back memories of *people* I enjoyed or associated with! My cool-down time is my main private/quiet/prayer/Bible study time with the Lord; other times also exist too. I give thanks for all He has done for us as well as praying for family, friends, neighbors, sick, those who lost loved ones, and so on. My list is long, and I try to lift each to the Lord daily. Lord, please bless each one!

My final thoughts are of and always will be of my Lord, grandparents, Mom, Dad, aunts, uncles, brother and his family, wife, sons, daughters-in-law, grandchildren, mother-in-law, father-in-law, and brother-in law and his family! It has been a pure joy to have had all of them in my life and to have spent many memorable times with each. I guess for the latter half of the above list, I must think back fifty-four-plus years when Jack Jackson *forced me* on a blind date, and I met that wonderful, cute young woman who said, "Yes" when I asked her if she would marry me! And, oh yes, after fifty-three-plus years of marriage, Sue and I still *like* Jack!

As I hunt, murmur, and peck these last words to my readers, it is Memorial Day, May 25, 2020. There are certainly many I wish to thank for their service to our country, especially to those who gave the ultimate sacrifice. Our country is currently just starting to open after a two-and-a-half-month shutdown due to the Covid-19 pandemic. What will happen after this, is anyone's guess. Before I leave you, I do wish to tell *one last story*. It is a story of *hope*, and it could apply to the Covid-19 pandemic!

Sue and I knew an elderly woman who, in the summer of 1918, became pregnant. This was the time of the horrible Spanish flu pandemic which killed between 20–50 million and infected over a half billion people worldwide. This woman was one of those infected, but survived even with her pregnancy. In February 1919, she started hard labor about two months before her due date. Her husband got the doctor to come to their house, and he delivered a baby weighing only a few pounds. The doctor told them to put the baby in the corner because it would die. The father would not give up. He kept the baby on a pillow and used an eyedropper for feeding; however, the doctor was right, the baby died—eighty-seven years later! The baby was St. Trussie of Marion, Indiana. So, you see, *there is hope*!

God Bless; be safe and healthy.
Rick Hunziker

Hunziker
Photography Section

THE HUNZIKER CLAN

1928 Switzerland: (L-R) Floor: Otto F., Jr. (Ricks' Dad); Sitting: Emma
(Grandpa's sister), Grandpa Otto F., Sr., Grandma Florence, Maria and
Karl R. (Grandpa's sister-in-law and brother), Edith (Karl R.'s daughter);
Standing: Thelma (Rick's aunt), Isabelle (Rick's aunt), Walter Burne (Rick's
uncle), Florence (Rick's aunt), Karl O. (Rick's uncle), Alice (Karl R.'s
daughter).
(Photographer Unknown)

MOM AND DAD

1937: Mary F. Alexander AND Otto F. Hunziker, Jr., at Purdue University.
(Photograph by Bill Alexander with Otto's camera)

ELMWOOD PARK, ILLINOIS

1945: Mary Hunziker, (L–R) Roger and Rick. (Photographer Unknown)

1947: Rick with broken arm. 1948: Rick and Roger.
(Photographs by Otto Hunziker)

BROOKFIELD, WISCONSIN

Summer 1950: Rick helping to prepare and grow the front lawn! *Right!*
(Photograph by Otto Hunziker)

1951: Rick rows Big Siss!
(Photograph by Otto Hunziker)

1954: Playful Pronto!
(Photograph by Otto Hunziker)

CRYSTAL LAKE, ILLINOIS

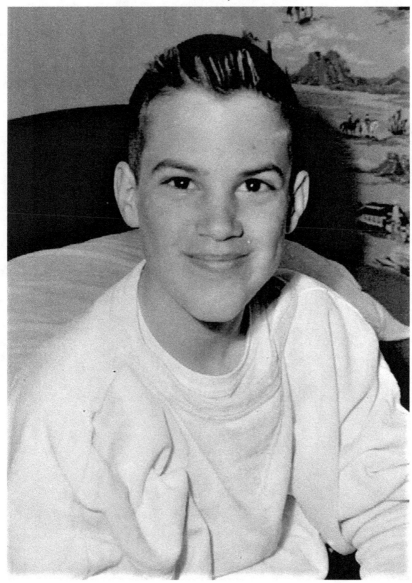

1956: Next-door neighbor, Jim Harwood.
(Photograph by Rick Hunziker)

Summer 1959: Ken Kies and Mom blow up Rick's ten-foot weather balloon!
(Photograph by Rick Hunziker)

1959: Our home, 1410 Broadway, Crystal Lake (Insert), and in 2012.
(Photographs by Rick Hunziker)

1959: Grandma Hazel Alexander.
(Photograph by Rick Hunziker)

Dec. 1960: Hunziker Christmas Open House. (L–R): Mrs. Archambault, Mrs. Albertz, and Mrs. Battles. (Photograph by Rick Hunziker)

Aug. 1961: Chippewa Flowage float trip makes Rick the winner with a 30"
Northern Pike. (Photograph by Otto Hunziker)

Fall 1961: Senior's "WILDCAT-ER-KILLER" float. Class of 62 first class to carry a float! Pat Dewey guides the carriers. Rick is second set of legs with white shorts in tiger's head. Two freshmen walking in front on right side are (L-R) Tommy Archambault and John Reichert. (Photograph by Mary Hunziker)

Fall 1961: Sadie Hawkins Dance. Mary Anne Archambault
picks Rick up for the dance. Note the corsage she made for Rick.
(Picture by *amateur* photographer Grandma Alexander)

Summer 1962: Rick starts lifeguarding at
Grafton Beach. (Photograph by Otto Hunziker)

Fall 1962: Picture and Plaque Memorial dedicated to Grandpa, Dr. Otto F. Hunziker, Sr., in Smith Hall on March 1962. (Photograph by Rick Hunziker)

Fall 1962: Jo Elsrud wears Purdue sweatshirt Rick sent her.
(Photograph by Elling Elsrud; Photo reproduced with permission)

Summer 1963: Rick skis backward on *one* ski.
(Photograph by Otto Hunziker)

Summer 1963: (L–R) Gene Bacon, Ross Annable, and Rick.
Guess who lifeguards and who works in a bank?
(Photograph by Mrs. W. G. Annable; Photo reproduced with permission)

June 1964: Bill Albertz fishing Crane Lake, MN.
(Photograph by Rick Hunziker)

1964 Grafton Guard Crew: (L–R) Bill Speechley, Rick Hunziker, Charlene Fay, Sandy Zimmerman, Chuck Porter, and Dave Thompson. (Photograph by *Crystal Lake Herald*; Photo reproduced with permission from Shaw Media Local News Network)

March 1965: Rick buys his first car, a 1961 Plymouth Valiant.
(Photograph by Otto Hunziker)

Fall 1965: Road Trip! Purdue beats University of Michigan, 17–15! (L-R) Front: Greene, White, Ankney, Burkhart, Bartels, Benson, Lidy; Sitting in BMS: Conrad, Fry, Jackson; Standing in BMS: Collins, Martin, Cartin (white sweater). (Photograph by Rick Hunziker)·

Fall 1965: Rick gets his picture taken after the win over No. 1 Notre Dame and photo is published on page 48 in Purdue's Football Program for Purdue vs. Minnesota on November 13, 1965. (Photograph by Jim Deverman, Pekin, IL; Photo reproduced with permission of the Purdue Athletic Department)

November 1965: Rick, along with four other Reamers, drove the Special
to Indiana University for the Old Oaken Bucket game, which Purdue
won 26–21!
(Photograph by a Reamer brother with Rick's camera)

April 1966: Rick and Sue Dohner's second
date—Rick's "I love you" date!
(Photograph by Jack Jackson with Rick Hunziker's camera)

June 1966: Sue Dohner's graduation gift to Rick! *Wow!*
(Photographer Unknown)

June 1966: Purdue Graduation Day. (L–R) Rick, Sue Dohner,
Arleen Henderlong, and Jack Jackson.
(Photograph by Otto Hunziker)

Summer 1966: (Front) Chet Battles, (Back) Mom and Florence Battles in our MFG boat. (Photograph by Otto Hunziker)

February 25, 1967: Wedding Day. (L–R) Back: Judi Arnott, Sheila Persinger, Arleen Jackson, Bride Sue (Dohner) Hunziker, Groom Rick Hunziker, Roger Hunziker, Jan Cooney, Tom Hintz, and Cary Dohner; Front: Harold Hodge and Debbie Sparks.
(Photograph by Otto Hunziker)

New Year's Eve Party—Dec 31, 1968: (L–R) Sitting on floor: Tom Stevens and Terry Yake; Sitting on Chairs: Pat's mother, Pat Carter, Jerry Carter, Linda Stevens, Gail Eastling, Sue, Les Eastling, Jeff Carter, and Maggie Yake. (Photograph by Rick Hunziker)

Christmas 1991: (L–R) Front Row: Martha (Zeller) Hunziker and Otto Hunziker; Middle Row: Kirk, Eric, Sybil, and Sue; Back Row: Roger, Birgit, Heather, and Rick.
(Photograph by Rick Hunziker via camera timer)

Thanksgiving 1993: (L–R) Sitting: Milburne Dohner, Carrie Beth Dohner, Grandma Grace Dohner; Standing: Trussie Dohner, Cary Dohner, Caryn Dohner, Eric, Kellie Smith, Kirk, Sue, Carolyn Dohner, and Rick. (Photograph by Rick Hunziker via camera timer)

2016 HUNZIKER CLAN

2016: (L–R) Front: Cooper (9), Kiley (12), Dakota (14), Lauren (12), Emily
(16), and Megan (18). Back: Sue, Jen, Kirk, Kellie, Eric, and Rick.
(Photograph by Rick Hunziker via camera timer)

Sue and Rick going into the future together!
(Photograph by Kirk Hunziker)

Acknowledgments

MY BIGGEST DEBT IS TO MY WIFE, SUSAN E. (Dohner) Hunziker, for her love, invaluable encouragement, suggestions, perseverance, overall support and especially her patience as she read, re-read, re-re-read, and so on, to make sense of my initial and follow-up drafts (*over 20!*) of this book. I cannot thank her enough as she uncomplainingly allowed me to spend my time on this endeavor. Without her super love and support, this would not have happened. She has been my awesome and lovely soulmate for the last fifty-three-plus years, and I still pinch myself sometimes to believe she attached her life and love to me! *Wow!*

I would be remiss if I did not thank my late Mom and Dad, Mary F. (Alexander) Hunziker and Otto F. Hunziker, Jr., for their patience, perseverance, and wisdom they showed me from the time I was born until they passed away. They were my parents, protectors, guardians, coaches, instructors, tutors, mentors, and friends! Without them, my life would have changed drastically. My brother, Roger, was *there* for me more times than I probably ever knew, and I wish to acknowledge his protection and in our latter years, his friendship and love, which became the strongest I could ever expect to have enjoyed. His wife, Sybil, helped me to understand potential problems and signs of dyslexia and encouraged me to document these stories, so she also had them for her daughters and grandchildren.

I want to thank my Aunt Peggy (Alexander) Abbott for her written and verbal inputs about her parents; she allowed me to present them in a loving light. Unfortunately, because of space limitations, I was not able to print all she provided. My sons, Eric and Kirk, their wives, Kellie and Jennifer, respectively, and our six grandchildren all provided encouragement. I wish to specifically acknowledge Kiley because she was eager to know and understand her heritage, and for her proofreading skills, especially *worrying* that my mother was mean by *shooting daggers!* Kirk needs to be thanked for photographical editing and for providing the book's photographs in their required format. I want to thank my late mother- and father-in law, Trussie I. (Persinger) Dohner and Milburne E. Dohner, for being wonderful and loving examples of who and what a Christian should be, do, and speak. Sue's brother, Cary, and his wife, Carolyn, encouraged me to write about my times and relationships with Sue's parents.

There were many who were not directly related to me who provided encouragement, insight, support, details, and/or information such as Ross Annable, Paul Koch, Bob Frenz, Mary Anne Archambault, Jack and Arleen Jackson, Tom Bartels, Jan Cooney, Bonnie Albertz and her husband John, Dave Thompson, Powers (Muley) McQuire, Steve Mudgett, and Jo Elsrud. Thank you all for standing by me in this endeavor.

I wish to thank Michael A. Wilkins of Broyles Kight & Ricafort, PC and Outlook Christian Church for his insight, comments, concerns, and legal advice in the preparation on this manuscript; they were all invaluable.

Finally, I wish to thank my editor and publisher Xulon Press for their editing skills, publishing consulting, production management, and sales and marketing support. Without this support, my project would have not occurred and been professionally accomplished.

CPSIA information can be obtained
at www.ICGtesting.com
Printed in the USA
FSHW020852180421

9 781662 814150